POLITICAL PROMISES

BOOKS BY NELSON W. POLSBY

Community Power and Political Theory (1963)

Politics and Social Life: An Introduction to Political Behavior (Edited, with Robert A. Dentler and Paul A. Smith) (1963)

New Perspectives on the House of Representatives (Edited, with Robert L. Peabody) (1963, 1969)

Congress and the Presidency (1964, 1971)

Presidential Elections (with Aaron Wildavsky) (1964, 1968, 1971)

Congress: An Introduction (1968)

American Governmental Institutions (Edited, with Aaron Wildavsky) (1968)

The Citizen's Choice: Humphrey or Nixon (1968)

Congressional Behavior (Edited) (1971)

Reapportionment in the 1970's (Edited) (1971)

The Modern Presidency (Edited) (1973)

Political Promises (1974)

POLITICAL PROMISES

Essays and Commentary
on
American Politics

Nelson W. Polsby

New York

Oxford University Press

1974

ع

For Linda O. Polsby

Acknowledgments

The number of people who have helped me understand American politics a little better and who are thus in some way responsible for one or more of these essays is legion—and there are too many of them to list here. I remember each and every one of these friends, however, with fondness and gratitude. Many of them write about American politics themselves, invariably with skill and sensitivity.

I would like to say a special word of thanks to my brothers and sisters in law, Allen and Gail Polsby and Daniel and Maureen Polsby, who have sheltered me in Washington with unfailing good cheer no matter how frequently or inconveniently I descended upon them. Along with my brothers, my oldest and closest Washington friends, Micah Naftalin and David Cohen, have through the years been singularly generous in providing me with an on-going grasp of national events and much wise counsel. I am grateful also to my colleague Aaron Wildavsky, who collaborated with me in writing one or two of the essays reprinted here, and who is a steady source of ideas and stimulation.

Linda O. Polsby has shared with me all of the days in which these essays were written. If I have been able to keep things in perspective, it is in no small way due to her, and to Lisa and Emily Polsby.

Permission to reprint my work was graciously granted by the following original copyright holders:

The American Association for the Advancement of Science for: "Congress Looks at Social Science," *Science*, Vol. 157, 28 July 1967, pp. 413–414. Copyright 1967 by the American Association for the Advancement of Science.

The American Political Science Association for: Review of "Mr. Republican," *American Political Science Review*, Vol. 67, September 1973, pp. 1024–1025; and Review of "Kennedy Justice," *American Political Science Review*, Vol. 66, March 1972, pp. 212–214.

Harpers Magazine for: "Truth and/or Fairness in the News," *Harpers*, March 1972, pp. 88–91.

The *Daily Californian* for "Election Night Television," November 4, 1968.

Time, Inc. for: "Does Congress Know Enough To Legislate for the Nation?" in Editors of Time, Inc., *The Role of Congress: A Study of the Legislative Branch* (privately printed by Time, Inc.).

The *Minnesota Law Review* for: "Two Views of Campus Turmoil," Vol. 55, June 1971, pp. 1275–1285.

The *Los Angeles Times* for: "Topical Comment: Any Vice President Is in Dilemma," August 28, 1968; "Topical Comment: Inside Congress: Seniority System Isn't All Bad," September 26, 1968; and "Topical Comment: Choosing Presidents: The Electoral College Isn't All Bad," November 5, 1969.

Public Administration Review for "A Note on the President's Modest Proposal," Vol. 26 September 1966, pp. 156–159.

Rand McNally and Company for "Two Strategies of Influence in the House of Representatives" from R. L. Peabody and N. W. Polsby, (editors) *New Perspectives on the House of Representatives*, 2nd edition, copyright 1963, 1969 by Rand McNally and Company. Reprinted by permission of Rand McNally College Publishing Company.

The *Washington Post* for: "The Trial of President Nixon," June 3, 1973; "Misreading the Primaries," April 19, 1972; "The Politics of Hair," June 3, 1972; Review of Paul H. Douglas, *In the Fullness of Time*, May 3, 1972.

The *Wall Street Journal* for: "Is Nixon the Favorite?" February 23, 1972; "Polls, Primaries and Populist Ideology," May 25, 1972; "Is McGovern

Another Goldwater?" June 5, 1972; "Measuring Character in Our Candidates," September 24, 1973. Reprinted with permission of the Wall Street Journal, Copyright 1972(3) Dow Jones & Company, Inc. All rights reserved.

The Western Political Quarterly for: "Political Science and the Press," Vol. 22, March 1969, pp. 47–60. Reprinted by Permission of the University of Utah, copyright holder.

The *Reporter Magazine* for: "A Voice from the Floor," November 22, 1962, pp. 52–55; and "Representing the House," May 6, 1965, pp. 40–45. Copyright 1962, 1965 by The Reporter Magazine Company.

The American Scholar for "Our Quadrennial Drama," Vol. 39, Winter 1969–70, pp. 160–165.

The Clarendon Press, Oxford, for: "Towards an Explanation of McCarthyism," *Political Studies*, Vol. 8, October 1960, pp. 250–271.

Transaction, Inc. for: "Turn On, Drop Out, Fail" Vol. 6, April 1969, pp. 56–58; "Such, Such Were the Masters," Vol. 8, May 1971, pp. 58–61; "McCarthy: A Celebration of Political Repression," Vol. 6, July–August 1969, pp. 58–60.

N.W.P.

Berkeley, California
June 1974

"There is no political science, I can assure you . . ."

—Richard M. Nixon

Contents

Introduction
Pray Take Away This Pudding

For years I entertained the delusion that too few of my opinions were available to the world at large. Sooner or later, I found ways to arrange for this delusion to entertain me in return. This explains the origin of almost all the essays collected herein. Most of them bubbled up out of God knows where as the result of some stimulus—usually a political book or a current event—irritating one or more nerve endings. Many such nerve endings are in human beings to be found in the locus of political belief, the viscera. What distinguishes a political essayist from the man in the street, or from the justly celebrated Clarance Day, Sr., is, of course, the fact that his viscera are directly connected to his writing hand, and so when something mashes his emotional buttons, with one or two detours that I will describe momentarily, out come political essays.

Now for the common theme that these essays explore. I am reminded of the anecdote that Harold Macmillan tells about Winston Churchill. Churchill is sitting in the dining room at The Savoy Hotel, and the waiter sets before him "a rather equivocal and shapeless pudding." Churchill motions to the waiter: "Pray take away this pudding," he says. "It has no theme." This story is generally cited as authority for the proposition that good books should be like good English puddings, and have a theme. Is it not enough for the author to warrant that his work in no other respect resembles traditional English cooking, and that it is neither leathery, nor watery, or overdone, or tasteless? Apparently not.

Well then. The theme of this book is provided mostly by its subject matter, which is contemporary American national politics. For a little more than ten years, I have earned a living teaching about this subject (among others) to college students, both graduate and undergraduate. The title I carry while going about this work is "Professor of Political Science." Perhaps that requires a further word of introduction. People generally know what a man does when he calls himself an "economist" or a "historian," but they flinch at the pretentiousness of the title of my calling—a survival from the optimism of certain nineteenth-century political philosophers who inspired the founding fathers of the academic discipline of political science around the turn of the century.

One amusing consequence of the unwieldy and overblown name of my profession is that political scientists who achieve some sort of public notice are frequently identified as something—anything—else. It is a fact, however, that a political scientist named Woodrow Wilson once held the Presidency of the United States. Indeed only a few years before that he had been President of the American Political Science Association. How many people remember that Ralph Bunche's doctorate was in political science, and that he served as chairman of the Department at Howard University before going to work for the U.N.? Political scientists, I daresay, are the only ones who remember, or care. We have even contributed our share to the best and the brightest of the last few Administrations: Henry Kissinger, McGeorge Bundy, John Roche, Daniel Patrick Moynihan, political scientists, ex-political scientists, or crypto political scientists all. Some of the people who have denounced the public works of these men most vigorously and effectively have also been political scientists—Hans Morgenthau comes to mind for example. Obviously, I do not come from the same part of the academic iceberg (that is, the above-water part) as these eminences. All the same, at one time or another, we have met classes, read blue-books, and taught students under the same banner.

One of the settled obligations of college professors, at least in the high-toned sorts of places in which I have been privileged to teach, is that they undertake on a regular basis to maintain and update their knowledge of their subject matter. For a political scientist who teaches in the area of American national politics, this generally means doing a prodigious amount of newspaper reading, and making periodic trips to what J. Edgar Hoover used to call "the seat of government," for the purpose of observing the activities and hearing the conversations of the national politicians who work there, and the people who watch them.

In the last dozen years I have done these chores diligently—even eagerly. To me the workings of the American government are fascinating. And, as to most other close and competent observers, they are also surprising and in some respects mysterious. This lends a joyful element of risk to ventures at interpretation that scholars, no less than other observers, make of contemporary events. If this is so, then a puzzled reader may well inquire if there is anything advantageous in the perspective of the political scientist, as compared with a reporter or a columnist, or for that matter a politician.

In many important respects the answer is no, there is not. When a political scientist writes timely copy for the newspapers or popular magazines he gives away a significant advantage that his work might otherwise display, namely the omniscience of the person who knows how everything came out. However, a few differences do remain. The journalist is paid to run around and witness events, or at least process the press releases that are the spoor of contemporary political events. But he is not paid to think, or at least to think much, about what he has seen. It is a singular tribute to the caliber of the Washington press corps that so many journalists do nevertheless think and write with acuity and perception about American politics. But even in the best of circumstances, they are always pressed for time.

Political scientists do not need to be pressed in the same way. Although their first-hand access to the flow of events is commonly far less impressive than that of journalists, they are able to think a little bit about current events before putting pen to paper. Moreover their thoughts ought, at least in some cases, to reflect the results of the education they have had. This consists mostly of a grounding in the main theories that purport to explain how societies and social organizations work. And it may also consist of a passing acquaintance with the findings of research which may bear on the factual premises of political decisions.

It is a peculiar fact that these theories and these findings are not terribly well known, and their mastery is certainly not a ticket of admission to general discourse about current politics—as, for instance, mastery of the rudiments of economic theory is increasingly necessary for people who want to be taken seriously when they write about money.

I find this particularly odd when I read periodicals devoted, for example, to book reviewing for general audiences and see the high intellectual standards, the seriousness which editorial policies so frequently demand for the reception of works of philosophy, for literary criticism, even for cook books. Indeed not even the English translation of the Russian word *pochuya* is permitted to go without copious annotation and correction. Meanwhile the discussion of political questions, surely serious questions even by the elevated standards of literary persons, is not uncommonly conducted without much intellectual discipline and in a tone that can best be described as shrill.

No doubt what is intended by the loud and abusive tone of much fashionable political conversation in this country is to convey the outrage of writers of high and self-conscious moral sensibility. There is evidently a community of such persons who admire one another, and themselves, with sufficient ardor and articulateness to create a major market for political books.

A political scientist may, as much as the next person, feel indignant about the course of politics. When you prick us, do we not bleed? So it is with mixed feelings that I give fair warning that this book does not aspire to be fashionable in that sense at all. It aspires to express annoyance, to be sure, where appropriate, but in a moderate tone. It accepts as given a substantial share—

some would say an appalling share—of the world's injustice, ugliness, and brutality. And it does so out of an abiding pessimism, born of my own belief that most of what exists in the way of political beliefs and political machinery in the world is, at least in my lifetime, here to stay. And so we must come to terms with this machinery, these attitudes and institutions. Consequently, this book looks upon political institutions first and foremost as objects of study and—with all their shortcomings—as probably indispensable for the pursuit by anybody of a decent and peaceful life. This includes most of the American institutions that have come under fire in recent years—and in many cases for good reason: schools, universities, corporations, courts, bureaucracies, political parties, newspapers, even the Congress of the United States.

I suppose the simple affirmation of such empirical premises—that without such institutions in some form more people would be worse off than they presently are, and that most changes and all different status quos entail costs and disadvantages—the affirmation of such sentiments brands a writer as unfashionable, as "liberal" (a fashionable term of opprobrium), or maybe as "conservative." I will have to take my chances with this, because I do not believe that my indignation is so fascinating a commodity that it adds much to political discourse, at least not without also throwing in an attempt to understand how a few political institutions work. For whether we like them or not, political institutions are daily at work in America; moreover they are being worked by people who understand them. I believe that this sort of understanding—the sort that raises the possibility of making institutions more responsive—is the right of ordinary citizens in a democracy.

One purpose of public discourse about politics is to help people understand what is happening to them in their lives and to aid them in finding their own ways of dealing with these events. Hopes, imaginings, anticipations, and ideals, these are the exclusive property of humankind on this planet, and more and more of these in our increasingly interconnected world are attached to events and institutions whose origins are far away from our doorsteps, but whose consequences reach right into our homes.

Not all of these events and institutions, nor even a lot of them, can long engage the serious attention of a single writer of finite talent. What I have gathered here are the fruits of speculation and study about only a sampling of America's political institutions and problems in our time: the Presidency of Richard Nixon, Congress, a Presidential election and its effect on the American party system, the Press, political extremism, some perspectives on social stratification and political behavior.

Rather than claiming a monopoly position with respect to serious political conversation, I have argued that political scientists can consequently claim that they bring something a little different to the general din—a small dose of conventional wisdom, perhaps, sometimes useful and illuminating, sometimes not. We certainly cannot claim special access to common sense, or to historical anecdotes, nor are we unanimous in our feelings or preferences about good public policy. On these matters, as is true also of other commentators, we vary widely.

Like journalists, active politicians ought to have a mastery of the operational details of politics that far exceeds the grasp of relative outsiders such as political scientists. On the whole, however, politicians—at least American politicians—are not much given to public rumination. It is at a minimum irrelevant to the proper advance of their careers, and has occasionally been known to be harmful. Being an American politician or public official is frequently so demanding an occupation that even if the inclination to analysis and reflection is present, the pressures of time prevent its gratification. And, of course, many politicians lack not only the motive and the opportunity, but also the requisite insight.

In general, when a politician engages in public discourse, he does so as a political act, either to announce or to cement an alliance, to focus or to exploit an issue. The goals in short of those who write to further a political position and those who write at least in part to advance general political knowledge are somewhat different, even though their audiences may be the same, and the level of their discourse roughly comparable. I recognize, by the way, that this distinction is not always wholly tenable; all writers about politics write in part to persuade. Understanding of a general kind can easily arise from perusal of a self-serving politician's tract, and conversely an above-it-all academic may be perfectly capable of subtracting from the sum total of human knowledge while pushing his preferred nostrums. So I can suggest only that while nostrums are what political scientists may offer, they are not what we have uniquely to offer.

Now that we have established that these essays are about national politics and written by the hand of an irritable but essentially moderate political scientist, what else can be said about them? They are, with only a couple of exceptions, addressed primarily to general audiences and not to scholars. The distinction here is surely not in the intelligence level of the two populations, but in their preoccupations, and in what may be presumed about prior acquaintance with certain ideas and catchwords. For the most part, these essays are written in plain talk, and do not presume a professional preoccupation with their subjects. They do, obviously, presume a considerable interest in American politics. This, however, is the obligation and in some cases the pleasure of any citizen.

POLITICAL PROMISES

I

Watergate

It seems to me appropriate to begin this collection with a sermon about a subject that for a political scientist has to be Topic A. As these words are written, at Christmas 1973, Watergate is still pending business. Impeachment of the President is being taken up by the House. Watergate-related trials are in progress in various courts, and grand jury investigations are continuing. A Special Prosecutor, Leon Jaworski of Texas, is at work, as is a special committee of the U.S. Senate. A great deal more is bound to come out before this issue has run its course, and so the essay printed below must be considered as tentative in character.

What it seeks to do is explain how the Nixon administration got into the difficulties it has thus far suffered over Watergate, without attempting to explain except indirectly whatever further difficulties may be in store. My interpretation of Watergate relies heavily upon a distinction that political scientists frequently make but which is not commonly used in general discourse about American politics, namely, the distinction between a consensus view that develops in the subculture of Washington elites and the tenor of public opinion generally.

President Nixon's publicity men have frequently argued that

the President's extreme unpopularity with the public at large over the Watergate revelations is no worse than that suffered by Harry Truman over the firing of General MacArthur, and therefore could be expected in time to blow over. The key difference, of course, is in the sharply contrasting postures of Washington political elites on the two occasions. When the elites are with the President, he can ride out an unfavorable public opinion rating. When they are against him, general unpopularity comes as still another bale of straw on the camel's back.

Consider the events surrounding the dismissal of Special Prosecutor Archibald Cox by President Nixon in comparison with what happened when Truman fired MacArthur. When Nixon fired Cox, Attorney General Richardson and Deputy Attorney General Ruckelshaus resigned also. The F.B.I. was temporarily instructed to seal off the offices of the departing officials, and to block their access even to personal material stored there. This at a time when ex-Vice-President Agnew, by then a convicted felon, was still riding around town in a government limousine. For a short while, in the words of a right-wing commentator, official Washington became acutely conscious that they must have seemed to outsiders like "downtown Santiago."

When General MacArthur was fired, his immediate superiors in the Truman administration evidently breathed a sigh of relief. Far from quitting, Secretaries Marshall and Acheson and Undersecretary of Defense Lovett seem to have fully approved of the move. Republicans, especially in Congress, it is true, took up the hue and cry in MacArthur's behalf. MacArthur returned home to a hero's welcome, and Truman's popularity in the Gallup polls slipped badly. Senator Richard Russell convened an investigation of the Senate Armed Services Committee, however, with the flimsily concealed purpose of letting the air out of the MacArthur bubble, which he effectively did.

Can we assign an equally benign purpose, from Mr. Nixon's point of view, to the Senate Watergate committee? Not even all the Republican members of the Committee were at any time favorably impressed with Mr. Nixon's conduct of Watergate-related matters.

In short, the elites were with Truman, and against Nixon. Truman was able to convince members of his own cabinet, substantial numbers of Congressmen, and observers in the press corps that regardless of the risks for his own short-run popularity he had good and sufficient reasons for doing what he did. And so he willingly suffered a non-recurring loss of political capital in the country at large by dumping MacArthur.

Mr. Nixon's record has in comparison been a tale of misfortune. Cabinet and subcabinet officials and even members of his official White House staff have left, visibly dissatisfied with his response to Watergate. Far from a one-shot liability, Watergate has been for him a running sore, utterly sapping his capacity to deal with most other Presidential business.

Thus, in looking at Watergate, it seems desirable to look beyond the particular precipitating events, beyond even their lessons for the future conduct of public office, and see if we can understand the causes and effects of Watergate in the light of the way the Nixon administration as a whole has situated itself in the American Constitutional order. This is the aim of the essay that follows.

ALIENATION AND
ACCOUNTABILITY IN THE
NIXON ADMINISTRATION

There is little doubt that Watergate is here to stay, in the fundamental sense that observers, analysts, moralists, and historians will be ruminating for years and years to come on the causes and effects of this extraordinary, bizarre injury to the American body politic. It is certainly too soon for a full assessment of the damage that has been done, or for a very convincing argument about how to prevent another such shattering series of events. History never repeats itself with sufficient precision to make very appealing the strategy of locking the particular barn door through which the most recent horse has bolted. Perspective is needed in order for us to see whether in the end it is the faulty architecture of the barn, or an attractive nuisance in the neighborhood, or merely a rusty padlock that needs to be fixed.

At close range, before time has begun to temper judgments and mellow viewpoints, it is possible to indulge in a few speculations about the causes of Watergate. A parallel with the Dreyfus case immediately suggests itself. Musing on the conduct of that celebrated outrage, Mark Twain said: "To my mind, this is irregular. It is un-English; it is un-American. It is French." Many observers of Watergate find themselves making the same comment. The English, as we all know, have scandals about sex. The American tradition—hallowed by Yazoo, Crédit Mobilier, Teapot Dome, and countless lesser occasions (including the recent unpleasantness surrounding ex-Vice-President Agnew)—is to have scandals about money. It is characteristic of the French civic culture, by contrast, for political belief to curdle into fanaticism, for ideology to justify political irregularity, and consequently ideology is what French political scandals are about.

Yet as the Watergate story has unfolded before our eyes we

6

have seen Americans justify all manner of extraordinary—and ir-regular—political activity in the name of political commitment. It is un-American . . .

Behind all this there is still another level at which the Galliciza-tion of American politics can be observed, and this is the essen-tially plebiscitary theory of Presidential accountability that the Nixon administration has apparently embraced. While this theory has strong roots in American history, its major modern exponents have not been Americans at all, but rather continental European adherents to the Rousseauean notion of direct democracy—most notably in recent times General de Gaulle.

This theory holds that public officials are primarily accountable to mass electorates rather than to one another, and that the results of the last election are in principle capable of conferring powers on political leaders that can override the prerogatives, the prefer-ences, and even the legitimacy of competing elites. Thus I refer to this theory as a mandate theory of accountability.

In its most attractive form, the mandate theory goes by the name of strict majoritarianism; in a slightly different guise, popu-lism. Its beginning as a significant force in American politics dates from the rise of mass political parties and from the Presidency of Andrew Jackson. Of course it is not necessary for there actually to be popular majorities in the electorate in favor of any particular policy for a President to assert that he is operating under a man-date theory of accountability; all that is required for him to make this claim is that he be a duly elected and sworn incumbent of of-fice.

An alternate view holds that in America periodic elections are an essential part of the Constitutional design to secure the ac-countability of officials, but are the smaller part nonetheless. More significant has been the creation of an interdependent set of governing institutions, each with its own incumbents and prerogatives, constraints and opportunities. From the very beginning, this theory holds, it has been fundamental to our polit-ical system to rely upon a plurality of elites as the central device for compelling the accountability of public officials. This struc-tural theory of accountability is, of course, espoused by the authors of *The Federalist*, where it was advocated as the principal means for preventing tyranny. Another adherent of this theory, Thomas Jefferson, as President brought it a logical step forward through his energetic efforts to create out of the "separate battalions" of the Washington community an elite subculture capable of responding to Presidential leadership, but retaining significant autonomy and legitimacy in its component parts.

If I am right in my surmise that our Constitutional order provides for an extensive network of interdependencies among various public officials, it is hazardous even for a President of the United States newly elected by a landslide to proclaim his exclusive devotion to the mandate theory. For others have their mandates as well, and strict pursuit of a patented mandate in our political system means that political leaders, instead of working toward a reconciliation of political aims and an accommodation of policies, may find themselves at loggerheads, unable to conduct their business effectively, suspicious of one another's legitimacy, and ready to invoke ultimate sanctions.

Nothing I have said so far hints of the possibility of wrongdoing among the President's most intimate staff, or by members of the cabinet. That possibility aside, it appears that a significant part of this administration's troubles since the Watergate revelations began is rooted in a loss of confidence among other Washington elites that Mr. Nixon seems to have suffered well before everything came undone as the result of his adoption of the mandate theory of accountability. This explains—if anything can—the satisfaction that nearly everyone in Washington expressed over the dismantling of the high command of the Nixon administration in the summer of 1973. Assistants to the President—even cabinet officers—have fallen from grace before, but never, it appears, to such sustained bipartisan applause from McLean to Chevy Chase, from Georgetown to Hollin Hills. Perhaps it will be worth our while to look again at certain characteristics of the pre-Watergate Nixon Presidency.

It was a strong Presidency, but one uncommonly devoted to enhancing its power by attempting to cripple, discredit, or weaken competing power centers in national politics. In certain respects, this aggressive posture toward competing power centers has been dictated by considerations of policy; in other respects it has been the consequence of President Nixon's administrative style; and in other ways, it appears to be the product of a genuine spirit of alienation between Mr. Nixon's values and those of his closest associates on the one hand, and the values and attitudes that dominate the thinking of leaders of most other Washington elite groups on the other.

For the nation at large, the unfolding Watergate revelations present a profound challenge to the people's sense of trust in their government. Even before Watergate, however, many leaders in our national political life just outside the Presidential orbit may well have had to come to terms with a fundamental unease about the course of the Nixon administration.

This unease did not have anything to do with suspicions of wrongdoing. Rather, what has been at issue is the question of the commitment of the Nixon administration to the underlying legitimacy of government agencies and their rules, the media and their criticisms, cabinet-level officials and their linkages with interest-group constituencies, Congress and its Constitutional prerogatives, or the rest of the Republican party and its political needs.

An Occupation Army

In successive waves over a five-year period, President Nixon has attempted various schemes to govern the executive branch in the manner of a small army of occupation garrisoned amid a vast and hostile population.

The first major Nixon administration reorganization pulled two trusted lieutenants—Secretaries Shultz and Finch—out of day-to-day departmental responsibilities and brought them into the White House. The second move was to change the name of the Budget Bureau and strengthen its powers over government departments. Third, there was a noticeable slowdown in the staffing of the top levels of departments whose programs are given a low priority by the administration. And, finally, there was an effort to

9

move people without any notable background, experience, interest, or qualification into top levels of various government agencies, apparently to provide listening posts for the White House.

Programmatic commitments appear to lie at the heart of the Nixon administration's seeming distrust of many parts of the national government. It is a fairly reliable rule of thumb that government agencies retain forever the political coloration that they have when they are founded, given their central missions, and initially staffed. Undeniably, also, the great expansions of federal agencies have taken place under Democratic Presidents. Thus a Republican President is bound to feel at least a little as though he is surrounded by career-long Democratic bureaucrats, all hot in pursuit of the basically Democratic objectives of their housing, education, welfare, transportation, urban development, and science programs.

A Matter of Degree

Once written into law and placed in the charge of a government agency, of course, it can be argued that programs are no longer Democratic or Republican programs but simply government programs, and whoever runs the government is obliged to see to them. This rather simple-minded, traditional view was sharply challeged by the Nixon administration decision to dismantle the Office of Economic Opportunity while the law embodying the agency was still in force. It is uncertain how this questionably legal maneuver struck the leaders of other government agencies, but to the OEO staff itself the attack must have seemed flagrant and somehow outside the rules of the game.

Leaders of Congress have expressed themselves in similar terms on the issues of impoundment and executive privilege. It is not that the Nixon administration, in asserting executive privilege and in impounding funds, has done unprecedented things. It is that it has done these things to an unprecedented degree, so much so that a matter of degree is transformed into a difference in kind and has an impact on the normal relations of comity and trust between Congress and the Presidency.

As we all know, the Constitution ordains that Congress and the

President were meant to do battle. In the end, their capacity to do business at all rests upon a set of mutual restraints and accommodations, because in the last analysis, either branch can do the other in.

A Question of Politics

It is a matter of the utmost sadness that serious people in Washington and elsewhere could begin, in the summer of 1973, to speak unflinchingly of ultimate sanctions, and specifically of the impeachment or resignation of the President. Before Watergate, it is now clear, the mutual accommodations and understandings that must exist for orderly business to be done between Congress and the President were deeply eroded.

There was the ludicrous and intemperate claim of executive privilege for virtually everybody in the executive branch and on virtually all issues. There was the matter of impoundment—for example, of all public works projects added by Congress to the budget as presented by the President. Likewise, grant and loan programs for water lines and sewers, open spaces, and public facilities were impounded, apparently to coerce the Congress into enacting the administration's special revenue-sharing bill. And there was the attempt to cancel the Rural Environmental Assistance Program.

What is at issue in all of these actions is not whether they represent good public policy or even whether they were legal. Rather, the question is whether they were good politics. The answer must be framed not only in terms of the goals of national constituencies and interest groups and how much the President wants to gratify them, but also in terms of whether or not the President thinks he needs to get along with Congress.

Using Up Credit

The Nixon administration attacks on newspapers, on television commentators and the networks, and on the so-called "elitist" Eastern press—somehow these, too, got out of hand. Again, different observers might well draw somewhat different bills of particulars. Some would include as unwise the attempts to get injunctions enforcing prior restraint on publication of what turned out to be innocuous Pentagon Papers. Others remember the petty and futile exclusion of the *Washington Post*'s Dorothy McCardle from coverage of routine White House social functions, and the clumsy investigation of Daniel Schorr of CBS, followed by the patently dishonest rationalizations of the White House press spokesman. Somewhere in between these were the famously abusive speeches of Vice-President Agnew, or opaque references to "ideological plugola" by a White House functionary, accompanied by not-so-opaque administration plans to exert political influence over public broadcasting.

Less noticeable to casual readers was the fact that, well before Watergate, President Nixon was also using up sizable amounts of credit with Republican party leaders. There is always an election-year competition for campaign funds between Presidential candidates and other party standard-bearers further down the ticket. In this contest, the Presidential candidate—especially an incumbent—usually wins. It is then up to him to take the initiative and spread any extra cash around to help the party win some key Senate and House races, once he is fairly certain that his own campaign can be paid for.

This Mr. Nixon apparently neglected to do. Moreover, in his low-profile campaign he made few personal efforts to help fellow Republicans. Now that they are able to see the uses made of some of the money that could have paid for more conventional campaign expenses, it is no wonder that not a few Republican stalwarts are angry.

"Peace at the Center"

Some of the disagreeable relations between Mr. Nixon and the rest of official Washington are, as I have indicated, the result of programmatic differences. His dismantling of the President's scientific advice apparatus, for example, can be explained as simply a wish to rid himself of spokesmen for an interest group whose interests he did not want to gratify. Likewise, his dismissal of the American Bar Association as a clearinghouse for future Supreme

Court justices came only after the relevant committee of the Association found fault with a couple of his prospective nominees. Other problems are evidently the inescapable product of Mr. Nixon's work style. His intense desire for "peace at the center," for orderly, private, unharried decision-making, thrust a great burden on his most intimate staff. Not only have they had to protect the President, ruthlessly filter the stimuli to which he is subjected, meanwhile bringing him options and decisions to make, but they have also had to face outward, to deny access to Congressmen, cabinet officers, and others whose responsibilities include shares in the ordering of various aspects of the public business. As time has gone on, it has become evident that there has been too much "peace at the center."

The Washington Subculture

A major by-product of the extreme insularity of this President has been a growing inability to come to terms with the ongoing subculture of official Washington, that noisy little world inhabited by Congressmen, agency heads, journalists, interest-group leaders, party dignitaries, lawyers, embassy folk, and others, some of whom have been harshly dealt with by the Nixon administration. Of course, these few thousand people are not "the" people, those whom Presidents address on television and who vote by the millions in national elections. But does this mean that official Washington consists of nothing but "nattering nabobs"?

Some of these nabobs are themselves duly elected officials under the Constitution. Others are employed at activities contemplated under statutes of the U.S. government. Still others are doing work that manifestly aids in the proper discharge of governmental functions.

Can a President govern effectively or at all if he systematically alienates himself from most of the rest of official Washington? Can his feelings of alienation, or those of his closest advisers, lead to excessive suspicion, to a frame of mind that encourages the taking of extraordinary precautions, to worries about political opponents that verge on the prurient? If Mr. Nixon's style of work

13

tended to alienate him from official Washington before Watergate, could we reasonably expect that the trauma of Watergate would decrease his alienation from this indispensable community sufficiently to restore to him the capacity to govern?

These sorts of questions have no easy answers, and as time has gone on, and revelation has piled upon revelation, it has been harder and harder to find people in Washington outside the inner moat of the White House itself who could give an optimistic answer.

Indeed, the only cause for optimism in this entire dismal business is the thought that there is something sturdy and enduring about the system of checks and balances that was written into the Constitution, and that at least to some degree, the checks have checked and the balances have balanced in such a way as to bring home to the President, and conceivably to his successors, the fact that legitimacy in our system proceeds not from electoral mandates alone, but also from the mutual accountability of political leaders. The political process in America occurs not once every four years but continuously. That is one valuable lesson of Watergate.

Persons who value the proper working of American political institutions, and who see in their proper working a marvelous instrument of democratic self-government, are bound to view the unfolding events of Watergate with repugnance. For it is precisely because we Americans are so numerous, so diverse, and so liable to disagree that we must nurture with particular care a government whose leaders are subservient to law, hedged by custom, protected from arbitrary and impulsive acts by inner restraints and by institutionalized rules. That is the public trust that has evidently been so abused and which must be restored.

2

The Election of 1972

In each Presidential election year, the temptation for a political scientist who has written a book about Presidential elections to sound off is—apparently—irresistible. As the events of the year unfold, stray thoughts begin occurring, and before long an article has emerged from someplace and is looking for a publisher. This happened to me nine times in the 1972 election season. Three were published in the *Washington Post*, two in the *Wall Street Journal*, and four were not published at all. The circumstances surrounding the writing of each are described in headnotes. They are presented chronologically; one of the few things rational people can cling to in an election year is the regularity imposed by the calendar.

As readers will see, there are substantial risks involved in engaging in election year punditry. This is especially true for professors, who cannot hide behind the ritualized Philistinism that journalists, no matter how august, generally cultivate. Our only conceivable claim to the attention of the readers of the popular press is that we are presumably experts. Experts are supposed to be able to see into the future better than ordinary mortals; it is therefore immensely gratifying when an expert takes a pratfall.

I have had the experience myself. It is music to my ears when colleagues in the psychology department complain about their kids, or economists lose money on the stock market. The day Julia Child's apple tart turned out mushy was a banner day for me. There is plenty of amusement of this sort for readers of the next few pages, who will observe that for quite some time I thought the Democrats would win the 1972 election, and that their nominee would be Senator Edmund Muskie.

This did not, I am happy to say, blind me to the weaknesses of either proposition, and readers will find a pretty fair running explanation of why things turned out as they did in articles claiming that things would more likely turn out otherwise. This provides some uncomfortable vindication of Francis Bacon's wise remark that truth arises more readily from error than confusion.

DILEMMAS OF A FRONT-RUNNER

This article was written in March 1971, after I had spent most of an afternoon trying to convince several of Senator Muskie's campaign management staff to announce Muskie's candidacy as soon as possible. The idea behind this recommendation is described in the article, and is that a man whose main asset is his popularity in the public opinion polls ought to try to shove his rivals who have the assets of money, interest group support, and so on, out of the race before they nibble him to death.

At the time nobody was contemplating an early demise for Muskie's chances, and so this advice—in retrospect very good advice—was ignored. Moreover the scenario it sketched was so implausible that none of the newspapers to whom I offered the article were interested in publishing it. This freed me to do considerably less well later on.

Suppose an "unannounced" candidate for the Presidency says in some public place, in this year of "unannounced" candidates, that he has been "brainwashed." Can the fact that he is unannounced save him? Conceivably it can, if nobody hears him say it. But if nobody is listening to him, how can he line up the money, the staff, the friends and allies, and the enthusiasm he needs to make a run for the Presidency? This is a puzzle that will confront an increasing number of Democratic hopefuls, ranging alphabetically from Bayh to Yorty, as 1971 wears on.

Political commentators have already, with premature weariness, begun to take notice of the progressive lengthening of the Presidential campaign. Like the professional basketball and baseball seasons, it is taking more and more time to launch political candidacies, and periods between elections that used to be spent in hot stove league speculation—or in the business of governing— are increasingly devoted to the contemplation of the openings of campaign headquarters, the formation of committees, forays hither and yon about the country, jockeying for headlines, and so on. This is one of the consequences of the progressive democratization of the nomination process: the more people a candidate has to convince, the longer it is going to take.

A whole new phase of Presidential election campaigning has been developing—the pre-announcement phase, when Presidential hopefuls test their chances presumably without embarrassing themselves or overcommitting their possible supporters in case they fail. This period, like later phases of the campaign, has characteristic properties that confer strategic advantages on some candidates, and disadvantages on others.

In general, the conventional wisdom has it that the earlier the candidacy, the weaker the candidate. Nobody sticks his neck out early unless he has to, unless a waiting game is sure to be fatal. This is, as it happens, only partially true. It certainly does explain why John Kennedy felt he had to announce early and run hard in every primary in 1960, knowing as he did that without a massive show of popularity it would be very hard to overcome the bias that then obtained against nominating a Roman Catholic. It also explains why Senator McGovern, very much in the shadows of better-known Democrats, has chosen to announce early this year.

But these are not the only conditions that call for an early announcement. Consider the situation of Senator Edmund Muskie, commonly considered the present Democratic front-runner, and hence by the conventional wisdom the man who least needs to commit himself at an early date. In Muskie's case the conventional wisdom is extremely (though perhaps not fatally) misleading.

The central tasks for any Presidential candidate in preparation for the national conventions is to find and mobilize support within the party among state and local leaders, interest group spokesmen, prospective delegates, and party activists. This takes money, time, and a network of political aides—speechwriters, brain trusters, advance men, and so on. Different candidates are differently situated with respect to these necessities of life. The main—virtually the only—resource Muskie has in bringing allies to his side is the widespread expectation, fortified by public opinion polls, that he can come closer than any other Democrat to beating President Nixon.

In addition, Muskie is widely admired both in the party and in the country for his dignified and effective Vice-Presidential campaign in 1968. But this does not have quite the resonance with party leaders that the Kennedy name still commands—despite Senator Edward Kennedy's firm disclaimers of interest in running. And Muskie does not begin to have the ties with labor leaders and other powerful Democrats that Senator Hubert Humphrey has built up over his years of tireless service. Furthermore, in Gallup trial heats restricted to Democratic respondents both Kennedy and Humphrey run about as well as Muskie.

How, then, can Muskie protect—or possibly enhance—his position as the Democratic front-runner? There are clear disadvantages for a candidate whose main strength is his popularity waiting out the primaries, and nobody expects Muskie to do that. But the primaries present a formidable hurdle for a candidate with limited financial resources. And Muskie is particularly attractive to independents, who do not vote in Democratic primaries. The sheer number of primary elections is growing, and the field of prospective candidates likely to pop up in one or more of them is fairly large.

Thus Muskie may find himself squeezed in California between Jackson and Yorty on one side and McGovern and Bayh on the other. He may have a hard time wringing an unequivocal result out of Wisconsin and Oregon, where by state law all probable candidates must be entered. Financial exigencies may cause him to wish to concede South Dakota to McGovern without a fight. And so on. Nobody doubts that, barring some unforeseen accident of fate, Muskie will be able to do reasonably well in a reasonable number of primaries and thus arrive at the convention with a respectable contingent of delegates. But if he arrives with only that, will it be enough to overcome the pull of party leaders toward the magic Kennedy name, or their long-term loyalty to Hubert Humphrey?

It may in fact be enough. Nevertheless, for Muskie to bank on the probability is to tempt fate. An alternative, less passive, strategy is available to him. This strategy entails doing what he can to increase his visibility to Democratic activists well ahead of the March primaries. If he can achieve greater visibility, this should be reflected in increases in his public opinion poll ratings—since at early stages in a campaign high standing in polls is more a measure of name recognition than anything else. Nevertheless, a sufficiently high standing in the polls would carry an unmistakable message to party leaders. It might well start at least a small pre-primary bandwagon that would bring a few more early commitments and a few more dollars into the Muskie camp. These, moreover, would quite likely be diverted from the campaigns of smaller fry whose presence in strength in the primaries poses a significant threat to the Muskie candidacy.

Thus, if this argument has any cogency, the central strategic problem facing the Democratic front-runner at the present time is how to increase his visibility, how to reach beyond the well-informed stratum of inside-dopesters and newshounds who "already know" he is in the race. Other than going over Niagara Falls in a barrel, the logical thing for an unannounced candidate to do if he wants to increase his visibility is to increase his news coverage by announcing.

Whether or not Muskie will actually pursue this strategy is another matter. It does run against the conventional wisdom, which means that somebody is bound to interpret an early announcement not as prudent management of the one major resource Muskie has but as a sign of weakness. It may expose the candidate to more hustling around the country than he may find congenial, or necessary. It poses formidable organizational problems of finding sensible things to say on every last issue that blows into the headlines between now and November 1972—instead of six months from now and election day. And he runs the risk of saying something embarrassing. But there are already too many people listening for that to make much difference. Meanwhile party activists are bound to begin wondering why somebody who doesn't necessarily like the heat seems to be edging his way into the kitchen.

This essay, written in collaboration with Aaron Wildavsky, kicked off the 1972 election season for me in high style. It is a straightforward application of the solidest, most reliable information about the behavior of voters of which I am aware, harnessed to cautious assumptions about the impact of events.

That, of course, was the problem. At the time we wrote, George McGovern was nowhere to be seen on the public opinion popularity charts. The cautious, "reasonable" assumptions we had made about events turned out to be seriously out of whack. Nevertheless, reading the essay today seems to me instructive. It underscores what I believe to be a truth about recent Presidential elections that is sometimes hidden—that Republicans don't win them unless the Democrats lose them.

The current Las Vegas odds favor the re-election of Richard Nixon against the most likely Democratic nominee, Edmund Muskie by 8 to 5. "Jimmy the Greek" Snyder, the Las Vegas businessman who establishes these odds, is reported in the press to have arrived at this conclusion by a complex process, "based on delegate strength, financial backing, staff organization and poll ratings. He surveys political writers in all states, but keeps a particularly sharp eye on the bellwether states of Ohio and Illinois."

Despite all this work, we believe Mr. Snyder has his money on the wrong horse. By our reckoning, the Democratic favorite, Senator Muskie, should be able to beat President Nixon in November, and he, not Mr. Nixon, should be regarded as the favorite. The evidence leading to our conclusion is easily available to any careful reader of the newspapers, and its theoretical basis is reasonably common knowledge among political scientists.

The elements of our argument are these:

1. Democratic voters in Presidential elections normally outnumber Republicans.

2. The probability is low that 1972 will see a dramatic departure from the normal.

3. Indeed, most of the short-run factors capable of upsetting the normal pattern of voter behavior actually favor the Democrats.

For the last 30 years, the public opinion polls have been telling us that Democratic voters outnumber Republicans. About three-quarters of voting-age Americans profess a party allegiance; two-fifths lean Republican, three-fifths Democratic. Politicians of both parties generally recognize this. It is the source of the famous me-too Republican presidential strategy. It is also what Barry Goldwater bumped up against in 1964 when he pursued the strategy of providing "a choice not an echo."

Democrats' Numerical Superiority

Democrats, we know, are on the whole less well-off, less well-connected, and less well-educated than Republicans, and some or all of these characteristics makes it less likely that Democrats will actually turn out and vote. In normal times, this hurts Democratic candidates a little—but not enough to overcome the sheer numerical superiority of Democrats. Taking all voters—Democrats, Republicans, and independents—into account and discounting properly for their rates of actual turnout, the Michigan Survey Research Center calculates that in a normal year a Democratic candidate for President should receive 53 per cent of the vote.

Yet for 11 of the past 30 years a Republican has sat in the White House, and in three out of eight elections the Republican candidate actually won. It must be that some election years are not "normal."

Indeed they are not. Dramatic circumstances alter cases. One of the standard methods in American history for a hopelessly outnumbered party to overcome its handicap is to nominate a war hero. The recipient of years of non-partisan adulation, Dwight D. Eisenhower was the perfect Presidential candidate for a minority party. When shall we see his like again? Not, we suggest, in time for the 1972 election.

And even General Eisenhower, with his enormous prestige, could not transform the American party system; Congress, even during the Eisenhower Presidency, was for only two years outside Democratic control. Despite the irresistible impulse to vote for Ike in 1952 and 1956, the basic Democratic tendency of the American voter came through in Congressional elections.

This accounts for two out of three deviations from the Democratic column in the last thirty years. What about the third? Most American voters—even under the new rules—are old enough to remember the election year of 1968. Neither Mr. Nixon nor Mr. Humphrey was an overwhelming, Eisenhower-like figure. But the year was far from normal: two tragedies of enormous significance befell the Democratic party. First, one of its leading Presidential contenders was assassinated. This embittered legions of his friends and followers, and removed from the scene a leader who could have helped stake out a new party position on Vietnam in time to have a meaningful effect on the campaign.

Instead, the tragedy of the Kennedy candidacy led directly to the tragedy of Chicago. Where normally a newly nominated candidate can expect a boost in his public opinion rating as the result of party leaders' joining ranks to say nice things about him, Hubert Humphrey's rating dropped disastrously. Nobody had a good word for him. Thus the usual process of opinion leadership through which party activists transmit their enthusiasm for the candidate to others was badly short-circuited. Lacking their customary cues, the party faithful were not mobilized. By the time they realized a Republican might actually win, it was too late.

Can Republicans in 1972 count on the Democratic party's tearing itself apart as it did in 1968? Even a maimed and crippled Democratic party, desperately short of funds and torn by dissension came within a hair of winning the election of 1968. Our conclusion is that the Democrats cannot possibly be worse off in 1972, and in all probability they will be much better mobilized and more united.

Smaller-scale, short-run forces seem equally unlikely to give Republicans comfort. Take the matter of election-year issues. The Nixon administration is working hard to take the sting out of the problems of the economy, and undoubtedly will try to do more as time goes on. But as of now, inflation and unemployment worry more voters than any other set of issues. These are traditionally issues that put voters in the mood to vote Democratic. They activate those mainstays of the Democratic coalition, the labor unions. And on public opinion surveys, the Democratic party is identified as the party of prosperity, the Republicans as the party of the rich.

What about foreign affairs and the war in Vietnam? Traditionally, the Republican party is seen by the voting public as the party best able to handle foreign policy issues, while the Democrats are identified as the party of war. President Nixon's planned travels to Peking and Moscow, if they are not calculated to remind people of these things, nevertheless seem well designed to do so.

In this, however, Mr. Nixon may well be in for an unpleasant surprise. The well-publicized announcement of his trip to China failed to give him the temporary boost in the public opinion ratings that dramatic Presidential announcements in foreign affairs have elicited in the past. Moreover, despite Mr. Nixon's efforts to wind down the war, the Republicans, not the Democrats, are now seen as the party of war. Gallup reports that voters now say that the Democratic party is better able to deal with the Vietnam war by a margin approaching 2 to 1.

The Youth Vote

What about the impact of youth? Among voters between the ages of 18 and 21 most are uncommitted or independent, and many will not vote. Among those who profess a political preference, the Gallup Poll reported in October 1971 that 35 per cent said they were Democrats and 14 per cent Republicans. This squares with reports from other sources.

Third-party candidates are another short-run factor. Here the major consideration is George Wallace. Because of his strong ties to a single region, Mr. Wallace can pose a threat in the Electoral College. But to whom? It seems reasonable to suppose Mr. Nixon would have carried most of the states won by Mr. Wallace in

1968. If Mr. Wallace runs again in 1972, he can damage Mr. Nixon's chances in the South. Can he take just enough blue-collar votes away from the Democratic candidate in the North to tip one or more industrial states toward Nixon?

This outcome is not wholly implausible, but it does presuppose that blue-collar workers will be voting their social philosophies rather than their pocketbooks in a year when the economy is sluggish and unemployment, while falling, still high, when labor unions are extremely active, and when the Democratic party is likely to give them an opportunity to vote for Edmund Muskie.

A third party on the left might conceivably deprive the Democratic candidate of his winning edge. None of the main available prospects, however, seems to constitute a serious force.

This brings us to the strengths and weaknesses of the probable candidates of the major parties. Mr. Nixon has been in the public eye more than twenty years and for the last three has been President. Though a very visible figure, personal popularity has escaped him. Senator Muskie, on the other hand, emerged from relative obscurity in 1968. By surviving the campaign unscathed he established himself as a new face in American politics. Yet his visibility lagged significantly behind that of the President, Senator Kennedy, or Senator Humphrey. In April the Gallup Poll reported that both Messrs. Kennedy and Humphrey had been heard of by 94 per cent of the voters, whereas Senator Muskie fell a full 10 points behind. After Mr. Muskie's announcement of candidacy, his visibility jumped 5 points and from this position, still well behind President Nixon in visibility, Mr. Muskie ran even with Mr. Nixon in both the Gallup and Harris Poll trial heats.

In horse-races with other Democratic hopefuls, Senator Muskie does about as well as Senator Kennedy and Senator Humphrey with partisan Democratic voters, but heavily outscores them with independents. This suggests a source of strength in the general election if Senator Muskie becomes the Democratic nominee. Further, in the process of making the race for the nomination, he is not likely to become less well known.

Can we anticipate that as Mr. Muskie approaches Mr. Nixon in visibility that he will lose rather than gain the votes of the uncommitted, that he will reverse his steady progression in the polls? It is possible, but, we think, unlikely.

A Democratic Victory?

Although Senator Muskie is clearly the Democratic front-runner, should he falter, most of the same arguments work in favor of other Democratic hopefuls as well.

Because these signs, when read together, all point to a Democratic victory it is hard for us to see how the odds come to favor President Nixon. It is true that Mr. Nixon enjoys the incumbency of office. This gives him visibility and the chance to make some of the issues. It also saddles him with other issues, not of his own making, The Republican party seems likely to be well financed; the debt-ridden Democrats, underfinanced. In order for money to have a strong influence on the final result, it is not enough for there to be great differences between the two parties. The less well-off party must be so handicapped that it cannot make its candidate visible, cannot move him from place to place, and cannot campaign. Badly off as the Democrats are, they are unlikely to be that badly off.

Thus Jimmy the Greek's odds seem to us wrong. It should be a prosperous year for sportsmen who like to bet against Las Vegas.

This article is possibly one of the most embarrassing things I have published. It reveals a stubborn incapacity or unwillingness on my part to grasp what the new participatory rules and the logic of the situation were doing to the chances of the various Democratic candidates. I caught on fairly soon thereafter and, as a Democrat, became rather pessimistic about the implications of what the Democratic party was doing to itself for the general election.

All this talk about delegates "thinking about second choices" and "appealing to a broader spectrum of voters" clearly stamps the analysis as anachronistic in the context of 1972. It took me slightly less than a month to figure that out.

In the aftermath of the Wisconsin primary two propositions are now being accepted as conventional wisdom. The first is that the Democrats are tearing themselves apart and that President Nixon's chances of re-election have been enhanced. The second is that the primaries are destroying the chances for nomination of Senator Edmund Muskie, whose candidacy is now generally regarded as on the ropes. Neither proposition will stand up to much close examination

Florida and Wisconsin didn't help Muskie, to be sure, but analysts haven't given adequate weight to a few underlying facts about primary elections. For one thing, centrist candidates are handicapped in a crowded field. With a big menu to choose from, voters scatter their choices widely. Second, primary electorates are quite unrepresentative of party voters in general elections. In primaries, it's ideologically committed partisans who turn out, and the more ideological candidates—not the ones in the middle—reap the benefits. Thus the Democratic primaries don't tell us what all Democrats want, just what some of them want. Moreover there is no way to tell what the second choices of any of these voters would be like. Yet sooner or later the Democratic party will have to choose just one nominee to run against Richard Nixon. In order to have a hope of winning, the candidate they finally settle on will have to draw support not merely from the 30 per cent of the party voters who are most liberal or from the 22 per cent who are most reactionary but from a fairly wide spectrum of Democrats. So, over the slightly longer run, being in the center is important to a candidate's chances.

So far the main lesson of the primaries has been that several possible Democratic nominees are closely matched as far as primary electorates are concerned. To analysts who like to report unequivocal results, the idea of such a fair contest must seem intolerable. The messages they have been sending have made the financial backers of several Democratic hopefuls jittery, since some of them, obviously, are backing eventual losers.

It's much too early, however, to count Muskie out. It is certainly true that he has committed one or two tactical blunders, the most important of which was his late announcement of candidacy. Now he is spread much too thin and, by the very nature of his central position, comes across indistinctly on short notice to audiences in the primary states. What is a disadvantage in the early primaries, however, may turn out to be a blessing at a national convention when delegates start thinking about their second choices and about appealing to a broader spectrum of voters in an attempt to beat President Nixon. Muskie's main problem, and it may prove insuperable, is to stop a stampede away from him of overimpressionable souls who are misreading the primary results to date.

While the primaries have exaggerated Senator Muskie's weakness, they have done the opposite for George McGovern and George Wallace. There is no reason to disbelieve the polls that say that neither of these hopefuls has overwhelming support among voters in general or even among Democrats. The "smashing" victories both have achieved thus far have fallen well short of majorities even among sharply biased primary electorates. Senator McGovern can surely claim, however, to be in the process of consolidating his grip on the left-wing activist element of the

Democratic party. There is something remarkable about this achievement, since McGovern is in so many ways more moderate than the bulk of his more passionate followers. It seems plausible to assume if the party turns to a centrist candidate for the Presidential nomination that his showing in the primaries will bring Senator McGovern's name prominently into Vice-Presidential consideration.

Of all the major candidates the one least affected by the early primaries is Senator Hubert Humphrey. It is clear that he enjoys substantial reservoirs of strength among black voters and in organized labor, both at the core of the Democratic coalition. While many strongly ideological voters find his candidacy distasteful, other Democrats, with only slightly longer memories, count Humphrey as one of the foremost modernizers of the Democratic party. Nobody doubts that he will be a force to reckon with at the national convention. Still, he has not moved into anything like an unequivocally leading position in the wake of Muskie's poor showings in Florida and Wisconsin.

Does any of this warrant the proposition that President Nixon has been gaining in relation to the eventual Democratic nominee? In spite of equivocal primary results, the Democrats do not seem to be tearing one another limb from limb. So far the level of discourse among serious contenders for the nomination has been civil. Certainly we have heard nothing like the harsh words the Kennedy forces used against Hubert Humphrey in West Virginia in 1960, or that Lyndon Johnson spoke against John Kennedy at the Los Angeles Convention. So it is premature to say that the Democrats have been doing themselves irreparable damage.

Meanwhile, there are signs in the primaries themselves that a Republican should treat as quite ominous. One significant advantage Republicans have traditionally held over Democrats has been in the superior capacity of the GOP to turn out voters at the polls. Turnout, however, so far, has been quite high in the Democratic primaries, much higher than in the hotly contested year of 1968. If Democrats turn out in the general election to the extent they have turned out in the primaries, the President might well be not just defeated, but defeated decisively.

The figures are clear in New Hampshire, where in 1968 only 35 per cent of those turning out for the primary voted Democratic. In 1972 the comparable figure was 43 per cent. In Wisconsin, home of the cross-over, 60 per cent of the voters voted in the 1968 Democratic primary. This year the figure was 80 per cent.

Primary elections are notoriously difficult to interpret. Because so much depends on them, they are often given panicky misinterpretations. A cautious look at the primaries so far suggests, however, that President Nixon may be in for some real trouble in the general election, and that the report of Senator Muskie's death has been slightly exaggerated.

PRIMARIES, POLLS, AND
DEMOCRACY

In the article immediately following we see the germination of the idea that George McGovern could actually win the Democratic nomination. At the same time I quite obviously remain impervious to the claim by McGovernites that this outcome reflected the inexorable will of the people. Anybody at all can claim that nobody loves them but the people. And if they can win a few elections where not many of the people turn out, they can usually get a few of the media folks to believe them. At this point, for reasons given in the article, I wasn't having any of that.

One striking anomaly has arisen in this election year that voters concerned about democracy—and not just Democratic voters—may wish to ponder. This is the curious discrepancy between what the primaries seem to be telling us and what the public opinion polls seem to be telling us about whom Democratic voters want to be their standard bearer. How can a substantial number of primary elections manage to produce a Democratic front-runner who at the same time is tied for third place in the affections of Democratic voters, according to the Gallup poll? Are the polls wrong—or are the primaries wrong?

A reasonable case can be made for both propositions. Take the public opinion polls. Early in a Presidential election year they are relatively changeable, and more than any other thing what they measure is name recognition, the relative visibility of candidates, and not the stable or well-thought-out preferences of committed voters. This explains why George McGovern has been moving up in the affections of voters and Edmund Muskie has been moving down. As Muskie has dropped by the wayside the coverage he has received in the media has subsided, and this has immediately been translated into losses of first-choice support among Democratic voters.

Meanwhile, as McGovern has picked up a few important primary victories, he has gotten more and more favorable attention from the media. As he has received more attention and become better known, his popularity has increased in the opinion surveys.

An interesting picture of ordinary Democratic voters emerges from this analysis. As among possible candidates of their party, they are, within limits, relatively indifferent. What determines the ebbs and flows of the preferences of large numbers of these voters is not ideology or convictions or assessments about the probable effectiveness in office of one candidate or another, but the images that the media project of men winning or losing in primary elections.

Thus one explanation of why McGovern isn't ahead in the polls is that his image hasn't yet caught up with his performance in the primaries, but in due course it will. When McGovern began campaigning, over a year ago, he was literally invisible to survey respondents. Today 17 per cent of all Democrats prefer him over all other alternatives. Tomorrow, who knows?

This is one possible explanation of the discrepancy: that it is too early to take the polls seriously because they are not recording "real" preferences of people who have really made up their minds.

Another way to explain the discrepancy is to argue that it is the primaries, not the polls, that are wrong. It is now fairly certain that whatever good things we may say about primaries, they do not provide a very representative sampling of Democratic opinion. Their defects in this respect are legion. Sometimes Republican voters cast ballots in Democratic primaries. In Wisconsin this year, for example, 80 per cent of the voting on primary day took place in the Democratic primary, in a state that went only 43 per cent Democratic for President in 1968. Not every state makes cross-over voting as easy as Wisconsin, but it is far from a negligible factor in primary elections.

Then there is the matter of how big the menu is. It makes a difference whether voters are choosing between two candidates, as in Illinois or three as in Pennsylvania, and twelve, as in some of the early primaries. As my colleague Aaron Wildavsky says, "Who wins is determined by how many play."

Likewise the sequence of elections is important. If Tennessee, Florida, and Indiana had occurred successively on the first three Tuesdays of the primary season, George Wallace, not George McGovern, would be the man to beat. If they had all occurred on the same Tuesday, Wallace might be entirely out of it.

Finally, there are the known characteristics of voters in primary elections. As a timely article by Austin Ranney in the March 1972 *American Political Science Review* reports, primary electorates do differ from the voters who turn out in general elections by being somewhat better off, better educated, and better connected. They are also more ideologically committed.

This combination of characteristics of primary voters, when combined with the characteristics of primaries—their timing, sequence, number of choices, and the effects of cross-overs—could quite possibly produce a string of victories widely hailed in the press as notable for a candidate who falls well short of being the favorite of a majority of Democratic voters. If something like this is what has happened, then of course the primaries are not giving a good indication of Democratic preferences.

We have no way of knowing for sure which of these interpretations is correct; probably both are to at least some degree. And both interpretations cast a shadow over the earnest attempts by the Democratic party to make their nominating process this year responsive to ordinary people. Both interpretations suggest that ordinary Democratic voters are, as usual, taking a back seat to political activists. Under the spur of the McGovern Commission guidelines, it is much harder for party professionals, fat men with cigars in the back room, to simply decide who national convention delegates are going to be. Now prospective candidates have to rely on two other sorts of fat cat: people with money and people who control the media. Money can buy candidates the attentiveness of voters, and the battle for attention is what a primary election or an early public opinion poll is all about. It is fatuous to suppose that prospective candidates can actually engage in lengthy discourse with voters about the complexities of public problems, or discover what is really on their minds as they barnstorm through primary states. Rather, the best they can hope for is to create a favorable image for themselves, and in doing this, it is essential to enlist the assistance of the media.

We have a fairly good idea what the cigar-smoking fat men in the back room thought about when they decided whom they wanted for President: Who can win? With whom can we do business? Who can run the country without disgracing the party and ruining its chances for further victories? Because they are harder to locate, it is more difficult to tell what the people who raise the money for candidates want. For example, it is reported that a young man whose main claim to distinction seems to be that his father has earned a lot of money for him to play with, has pledged $300,000 to the primary election campaign of one Democratic candidate—with whom he presumably agrees. In 1968 this same person is reported to have made a substantial offer of money—which was refused—to the Humphrey camp in exchange for various concessions on public policy. This illustrates the problem: now that enormous amounts of money are needed by candidates before they can hope to be nominated, to whom is the nominating process really "open" and "responsive"? Are there more or fewer democratic constraints upon the new class of activists as compared with the bosses, professional politicians, and party leaders who used to dominate the process? These are questions for which populist ideologies may have ready answers but, for small d as well as large D democrats, are they the right answers?

THE NUMBER ONE ISSUE

This article was written just before the California primary when McGovern-Humphrey rivalry was at its most intense. Very few of the campaign workers on either side knew that for a long time these two Senators were next-door neighbors in suburban Washington, and that they have through the years for the most part been friends and allies. Instead, naturally enough, they concentrated on the ways in which Humphrey and McGovern differed. And what more salient issue than the number one issue of hair?

Can it be merely an accident that Senator William Proxmire (D., Wis.) dropped out of the Presidential race just before announcing that he was undergoing hair transplant treatments? Or that Senator Harold Hughes (D., Iowa) got rid of his beard before announcing for the Presidency? Or that Senator Philip Hart (D., Mich), who kept his beard, did not announce for the Presidency at all? I think not.

Something there is in American politics that doesn't love hair. Hair is suspicious; you can curl it, straighten it, dye it, even conceal things in it. Each of these acts has political significance.

Remember the late Senator Robert A. Taft (R., Ohio), upstanding, no-nonsense Robert A. Taft? He, even he succumbed to the problem of hair, carefully taking lengthy strands from the northeast corner of his head and combing them meretriciously toward the southwest. If Robert Taft could thus deceive the American people what can we expect from lesser mortals?

What indeed? And so it is no wonder that in this more enlightened, more alert time somebody has gotten wind of Hubert Humphrey. Does he or doesn't he? Only his hairdresser and 60,000 McGovern workers know for sure.

And yet even here there is room for doubt. How is it, for example, that with all the charges of Humphrey hair-dying from the McGovern camp, the chiefest of McGovern chieftains, looking and sounding suspiciously like Harpo Marx, says nothing? Is he unwilling to express himself on the gravest issue yet to surface in this campaign? Or is his mind on higher things?

Though unrecognized, hair has been the number one issue in American election campaigns for some time. Recall the anxiety in the camp of candidate John F. Kennedy in 1960 as he strove to overcome Vice-President Nixon's shorter haircut. The story of the 1960 campaign is basically the story of hair, with Kennedy turning the tables on Nixon in their first and decisive televised debate by shaving just before air time. What beat Nixon, as every schoolchild now knows, was ineptitude in concealing his five-o'clock shadow. Pundits agree, moreover, that this was as it should be, since a candidate who cannot manage a five-o'clock shadow certainly cannot be expected to manage the country.

Even farther back in American history hair has claimed center stage. Abraham Lincoln's beard, for example, is second only to Richard Nixon's in intrinsic world-wide significance. Henry Adams records the sentiments of contemporaries about Thomas Jefferson's "gray neglected hair," and James Madison's "powder on his hair, which was dressed full over the ears, tied behind, and brought to a point above the forehead, to cover in some degree his baldness . . ."

As the election season progresses we shall expect to see more, not less, of hair. For it is increasingly clear that the candidates this year have forgotten—or never learned—the lessons of the only successful Presidential hair strategy of modern times. This was brilliantly put into effect by that most underrated of Presidential campaigners, Dwight D. Eisenhower.

IS McGOVERN ANOTHER
GOLDWATER?

Strictly speaking, Senator McGovern did not do as badly in 1972 as Senator Goldwater did in 1964–by a tiny margin. But if this article is right, he should have done a lot better than that. McGovern is indeed in his style and sentiment closer to the center of American politics than Barry Goldwater. But in various ways and for various reasons he failed to capitalize on that advantage.

If anything can stop George McGovern's drive for the Democratic Presidential nomination it is the argument among party regulars that he is a Democratic Goldwater. No loyal Democrat wants to go through a comprehensive defeat in Congress, gubernatorial races, and state legislative elections such as the Republicans suffered in 1964 by putting Barry Goldwater at the head of their ticket. And there are enough superficial similarities to give a prudent Democrat pause.

Like Senator Goldwater in 1964, Senator McGovern trails in polls conducted among members of his own party. After a year of steady campaigning, Mr. McGovern was barely visible to American voters at large, and was the first choice for President of a derisory 6 per cent of Democratic voters. After several notable successes in primary elections, he began to gather strength among Democratic voters in the polls, but up to the eve of the California primary he still has no decisive edge over his main rival for the nomination, Senator Humphrey. If anything, this shows less strength than Mr. Goldwater showed among Republicans during the 1964 primaries, because Republican voters split their first choices among a number of possible candidates, including Senator Goldwater, who held his own in the polls though he was ideologically sharply divergent from most of the other possibilities of that year.

Like Senator Goldwater, Senator McGovern's greatest strength lies among those drawn to party activism by ideological commitment and policy. Mr. Goldwater's rallying cry "in your heart you know he's right" finds an echo—not a choice—in Mr. McGovern's slogan "Right From the Start." For both candidates a sizable part of their core constituency exists because these voters believe that the candidates are "right" on the issues and "right" for them ideologically.

A third similarity is that both men learned to work the nominating process better than any of their opponents. Senator McGovern's successes in the primaries have overshadowed the diligent and enthusiastic work by his supporters in states holding district and state conventions. These efforts have in many areas borne fruit, and a sizable number of McGovern delegates will appear at the convention from non-primary states. This was also a source of Goldwater strength.

Can we infer from these three important similarities that if the Democrats nominate Senator McGovern they are in for the fate that awaited followers of Senator Goldwater in 1964? Perhaps. But additional consideration should also be weighed in the balance.

For example, Senator Goldwater was not merely the candidate of ideologues, he was himself relatively inflexible ideologically. Senator McGovern is a far more moderate man. In 1968 he was never tempted by the thought of a fourth party, and indeed he endorsed the Humphrey nomination immediately. Even as the pre-convention campaign this year has proceeded he has toned down and moderated many of his positions in attempts to broaden the base of his support, and there is no reason to expect that this process would not continue if Mr. McGovern were the nominee. This contrasts sharply with Senator Goldwater's behavior in 1964: he never really tried to unite his own party, much less appeal across party lines. Senator McGovern seems likely to make strenuous attempts to do both.

Finally, the fact that there are many more Democratic voters to begin with is important. No Republican can merely unite the Republican party and expect to win a Presidential election; as the leader of the minority party, he must do somewhat better than that, and appeal disproportionately to independent voters and at least a little to Democrats.

Because Democrats are much more numerous than Republicans in this country, the Democratic standard-bearer who unites his own party is much closer to his goal than his Republican counter-part. Thus simply because he is a Democrat, Mr. McGovern starts from a somewhat stronger position than Mr. Goldwater did in 1964.

From a viewpoint within the Democratic party, Senator McGovern in 1972 may look a lot like Senator Goldwater did to Republicans in 1964. This does not mean, however, that he will perform as Mr. Goldwater did in a general election. It is more likely, in fact, that if nominated he will do a lot better than that.

PROMISES, PROMISES

By June of 1972 I had already begun to crystallize a rather gloomy view of the forces that seemed to be moving in the Democratic party. From somewhat accountable elites the burden of leadership was shifting toward somewhat less accountable elites. The resources of the former consisted mostly in their occupancy of high public office. The resources of the latter seemed to me to consist mostly in the skill and wherewithal to manipulate symbols and make promises to primary electorates.

Political responsibility in America, as I see it, entails a two-dimensional commitment. Not only must a public leader, to act responsibly, engage in mutually instructive interactions with his electorate, but he must also fulfill elite expectations attaching to his role. A good Congressman, for example, to me is not merely somebody who can get re-elected, and who knows how to make speeches his constituents like to hear, and who shows up and votes right. Being a good Congressman takes a lot more than that, even though only insiders are ever likely to know who qualifies and who does not. But it also means such things as going to committee meetings and pulling your weight, understanding the policies and the agencies that your committee supervises.

There does not need to be a tension between one sort of responsibility and the other. But frequently there is, and especially for Presidential candidates, who have to reconcile their promises with what they know they can deliver.

It is one of the weaknesses of our political system that these tensions exist, but as near as I can determine, they are probably unavoidable, given the disparity in attention, information, and concern between elites and masses in this enormous country. The basic commitment of an educator, of course, is to the reduction of this difference, but along the way one cannot help railing at the size of the problem.

It is now more than halfway through our quadrennial silly season and the voice of the candidate is heard in the land. What is the voice saying? It is making promises, promises, over television, on billboards, wherever two or three are gathered together. Presidential campaigns have always been a time for promises. Nowadays, because of the extension of the primary election season and the proliferation of primaries, the nuances of what candidates say and the theatrics of how they say it matter more and more. This is true because in a primary election all the candidates are members of the same party. Voters, who in a general election can use their party identifications to tell which side they are on, must strain during a primary to catch other clues that can help them differentiate among Presidential hopefuls. The candidates themselves, most of them, have spent the last few years agreeing with one another on nearly everything, and working in harness against the designs of the opposite party in Congress.

But in the primary election season, they must change. Each one tries to emerge as different, as unique, as indispensable, or voters will never find their names on the ballot. And they must somehow satisfy the newsmen who follow them doggedly around the track, hungry for any moment that departs from the routine, searching for signals that will predict success or failure. And so candidates go out among the people and make speeches and promises.

My first proposition is, then, that it is increasingly the case that campaign promises are necessary. Voters need them to distinguish among candidates in primary elections. Newsmen need them to write about during the long pre-convention season. Candidates need them to have something to say.

But as campaign promises increase in volume, they do not necessarily increase in their predictive value. That is, they may tell us very little about what candidates will do or can do once they are elected to office. Sometimes this is true simply because the promises themselves are vague. Did John F. Kennedy "get this country moving again"? Did Richard Nixon "bring us together"? How can we tell? Slogans like these are susceptible to so many alternative interpretations that they may rightly be said to have no meaning at all, and therefore no capacity to predict what newly elected Presidents will do in office.

Another type of campaign promise also has this problem. This is the promise which a President cannot redeem single-handedly, but only with the co-operation of others who may be differently situated in the political system. This applies to all promises that entail substantial new legislation. There is a general rule that can be formulated with respect to such promises: the more a candidate promises, and the more radical or change-oriented his promises are, the less he is likely to deliver.

Why is this so? The reason is embedded in the check and balance character of our political system. The more any one political leader wants, the more he must give away to get it. Nobody, not even a President of the United States, has unlimited political resources. And so Presidents, like everyone else in the political system, must bargain. Bargaining means giving away some things in order to get other things. And it means that in order to deliver on a small number—conceivably a very small number—of substantial changes in one area, a President may have to give up the rest of his program.

Concretely this means that a candidate who promises to revamp the tax structure and also the welfare system, who wants to decriminalize drug use and make drastic cuts in the defense budget, will probably, if elected, have to settle for a lot less than a candidate who promises to move more cautiously in any or all of these areas.

Suppose, for example, a newly elected President announces a sharply reformed tax program. Under the Constitution an announcement is not enough to put this program into effect. It must travel to Capitol Hill, where Congressmen and Senators—who are also elected officials and who have made their own promises—must legislate. Congress changes all the time. Some senior Congressmen succumb to old age. Others have been lured into retirement by the recent upgrading of the Congressional pension plan. Still others leave in pursuit of higher office. Even so, we already know enough about the composition of the next Congress to guess at the fate of a sweeping tax reform. It will encounter tough sledding. Such a proposal at a minimum will receive very sharp scrutiny. Its capacity to raise adequate amounts of revenue will be elaborately tested, especially in the light of budgetary commitments new and old. All those interests and groups on whom new burdens would fall will be heard. And, just possibly, some tax reform might emerge, but almost certainly not a comprehensive reform.

Would such a result constitute delivery on a promise to sweep the cobwebs out of the tax structure? Or would it be precisely the sort of piece-meal, crabwise, incremental step that our more modish campaign orators denounce?

There is a real dilemma for democratic politics embedded in this highly probable scenario. Should campaigners promise a lot, deliver a little, and trust that the short memories of American voters will prevent widespread disillusionment? Or should they make more modest promises, attempt to educate voters to the realities of national government, and risk being outflanked by orators with more attractive but less candid slogans?

It is pretty clear how our political system is tilting these days: it is rewarding easy answers. A sizable number of voters in primary elections is evidently attracted to the polls by the prospect of "sending them a message" of generalized dissatisfaction. The candidate who asked for trust in himself and in the political system did dismally in early primaries while the hopeful who made an anti-establishment claim to be "Right From the Start" has done extraordinarily well.

In 1964, our fading memories should remind us, the American people also had an opportunity to vote for a candidate who appealed for votes because "in your heart" you knew he was "right." This does not mean that Senator McGovern is a Democratic Goldwater. It should serve to indicate, however, the high value Americans put on moral superiority when they go to the polls. One of the natural advantages of a relatively unknown and untested candidate, it appears, is the willingness of voters to turn their hopes and anxieties into votes for him on the grounds that he is outside the party establishment and hence presumably not responsible for their feelings of malaise.

There is another possible perspective on the Presidential nomination process, one that lays emphasis on Presidential selection as a means of getting control of the government. From this perspective the important thing is not how good you feel as you emerge from the voting booth on primary day but rather whether public policy can be changed over the long run in directions you favor. People who take this view must ask themselves hard questions not only about what the candidates are saying but also about what they can do and what they have done. Such a train of thought places less weight upon lonely voices and symbolic gestures and more weight upon administrative skill, demonstrated hospitality toward programmatic innovation, and capacity to bargain legislatively and with balky bureaucrats. This would also lead voters to ask where a candidate's commitments have been when the limelight has been off as well as what kind of vibrations he gives off when the limelight is on. If they were to do so they would discover, for example, great disparities between Senator McGovern and Governor Wallace, and a wholly different set of similarities and differences between McGovern and Senator Humphrey.

These sorts of similarities and differences have been crowded off the front pages and seemingly out of the consciousness of voters in the the excitment of an endless string of primary elections. Yet when all of the fanfare dies away, as it eventually must, the person we pick to be President has to govern for the next four years. Will his promises forecast the results he eventually gets? Will anyone remember what he promised and whether he delivered? And will they learn from the experience?

THE STRUCTURE OF POLITICS
AT THE
ACCESSION OF GEORGE McGOVERN

At the time, nobody noticed how Senator McGovern's handling of the Eagleton fiasco gave the lie to the McGovernite dogma that freedom from the interest groups of the Democratic coalition conferred untold advantages. I am particularly pleased at the title of this essay, which is a pun on the title of the superb book by Lewis Namier which established in British historiography the vogue for understanding national politics through the detailing of the social constraints upon members of Parliament.

The curious process by which Senator McGovern persuaded Senator Thomas Eagleton to resign as his running-mate tells as much about McGovern's relationship to political forces working in America as anything that has happened so far in this surprising election year. McGovern strategists have time and again asserted that the old interest-group coalition theory of how to glue the Democratic party together is wrong. Their argument is that it is now possible to reach ordinary voters directly, to speak to their discontents, and to mobilize their support without the mediating endorsement of notables—mayors, state party leaders, labor union officials, and so on.

Because Senator McGovern did not come close to winning a majority of votes in the primary elections, it is possible for academics and analysts to dispute about how well this theory actually served him. As a short-run practical matter, however, nobody argues with success, and so it is now fashionable to view the electorate as so many separate grains of sand, atomized and directly attentive to the candidate himself. This is generally regarded as tremendously liberating for a candidate, who no longer has to take strict account of the opinions and desires of party bosses and interest group leaders. What has really happened, of course, is that McGovern seems simply to have succeeded in substituting one set of mediating devices—and one set of outside opinions—for another. In reality no candidate speaks directly to more than a handful of voters. In bypassing the strategy of assembling a coalition of interest groups, McGovern has placed his candidacy squarely at the mercy of the news media.

This is not necessarily a bad thing; Americans take for granted a level of objectivity and professionalism in their political journalism that citizens of most of the nations of the world would envy. Nevertheless, the elite American news media do display one property that makes excessive reliance on their good will hazardous for any public figure: they tend toward convergence both in their interpretations of big stories and in their recommendations about what political leaders ought to do.

Consider the big Eagleton story of a week ago. In rapid succession most of the leaders of press opinion crystallized around the following elements of the episode: that Senator Eagleton should have been more forthcoming in private with McGovern about his medical history and that McGovern and his staff should have been more careful in checking out Eagleton's background. It apparently went without saying (although the matter is at least debatable) that no one with Senator Eagleton's health background ought even to be considered for the Vice-Presidency, and so McGovern's early protestations of support for Eagleton were regarded as false and disingenuous. In short order most of the influential news media were clamoring for Eagleton's resignation from the ticket.

A Presidential candidate differently situated from McGovern might well have been in a position to carry through an early intention to stick with Eagleton. At least meaningful opinions other than those expressed through the mass media could have been solicited. An "old politics" candidate, one with firm linkages with blocs of voters through traditional party organization and interest group channels, would have been able to take counsel with party leaders and allies around the country and arrive at an independent determination of his course of action.

This sort of independence is, as we have seen, not open to someone in McGovern's position. No candidate whose only real contact with voters is through his image in the mass media can afford to stay out of step with widespread editorial opinion for very long. Thus it appears that McGovern has seized independence from one set of institutions for mediating between candidates and the people only to have thrown himself into the arms of another set.

Reasonable observers may disagree about whether this is a good or a bad turn of events. What seems increasingly apparent is that there is no such thing as an unconstrained Presidential candidacy. The field of forces surrounding different candidates may vary, but no candidate can enjoy the benefits of a nation-wide campaign in his behalf without absorbing certain costs as well. Evidently this is as true for George McGovern as it is for any other candidate, new or old.

WAS NIXON THE FAVORITE?

Just after election day, nearly a dozen people from around the country sent Aaron Wildavsky and me copies of the eight-month old Wall Street Journal *article in which we had claimed that the odds favoring President Nixon were wrong. And so we prepared the following response—never printed—for the* Journal.

Everybody knows that you wrap fish in yesterday's newspaper. Everybody, that is, but the readers of the *Wall Street Journal*, who, in the last few days, have been sending us numerous copies of the *Journal's* editorial page of last February 23. Surely there are some who do not remember that vintage edition of this newspaper. Over our names there trumpeted the following headline: "Is Nixon the Favorite? Don't Bet on It." In that apparently immortal article we argued that the then Democratic front-runner, Senator Edmund Muskie, and not President Nixon should be regarded as the favorite to win the Presidency.

What went wrong? By popular demand, we will attempt to deal with that question. But first, let us recall briefly what the article said. It said, simply, that as long as there were more Democrats than Republicans in this country, strategists for both parties should assume that, all other things being equal, Democrats should beat Republicans in national elections. When they did not, we argued, something special would have to intervene. In 1952 and 1956, the something special was pretty clearly Dwight D. Eisenhower, a military hero of tremendous non-partisan popularity. In 1968, it was the drastic, violent disintegration of the Democratic party, the assassination of a leading contender, the rise of George Wallace. Were these phenomena likely to repeat themselves in 1972, we asked, and in the same way?

Governor Wallace, we speculated, if he ran in 1972 as a third party candidate, as he was then threatening to do, would hurt the Republicans in the South. In 1968, the labor movement proved that by dint of hard effort they could cope with the Wallace threat to the Democrats in the North. A pistol shot in Laurel, Maryland, in May 1972 put an end to that problem in political analysis. When bullets start flying, rational calculation is not the only casualty, but it is an important one.

Then there was the matter of President Nixon's popularity. With several Democratic hopefuls—Muskie, Humphrey, Kennedy—coming close to him or even running slightly ahead in the polls, he was no Eisenhower, we said. And, indeed, the nature of his 1972 landslide seems to bear that estimate out.

What a peculiar landslide it was! In 1936, when Franklin D. Roosevelt won 60.8 per cent of the vote, the Democratic party gained eleven seats in Congress and six seats in the Senate. In Johnson's 1964 landslide of 61.1 per cent, Democrats picked up thirty-eight Congressmen and two Senators.

These, however, were Democratic landslides. Evidently, when Republicans win the Presidency—even by large majorities—very little land actually slides. In 1956, when Eisenhower won his landslide of 57.4 per cent, the Republicans lost two Representatives and one Senator. The figures for 1972 are equally startling. Richard Nixon won 61 per cent of the vote. Yet Republicans gained only twelve seats in Congress (six in the South, where party alignments have been changing) and actually suffered a net loss of two Senate seats. Moreover, more people apparently stayed home and failed to vote at all than ever before in American history. This is surely not the enthusiastic outpouring of sentiment that we associate with a landslide.

One hypothesis remains to be considered, and that is that our article was quite true on the day it was published and that it was not the Republican candidate who turned people on but the Democratic candidate who turned people off.

There seems to be some justification for this view. At the beginning of the year Senator McGovern was not well known, and he never established a public image that could withstand such difficulties as his espousal and then withdrawal of the $1000 wel-

49

fare scheme linked to what seemed to be a confiscatory tax plan, his offer to "beg" Hanoi for peace, or the well-publicized uncertainty after his nomination surrounding the leadership of the Democratic party. None of these small fiascoes amounted to much, of course, except as background music for the unfortunate Eagleton episode, from which the McGovern candidacy never seems to have recovered.

It is possible that a better-known candidate could have withstood some or all of these blows which harmed Senator McGovern's credibility as a candidate so much. It is even conceivable to us—although even less likely—that a Democratic Presidential candidate might have survived the hostility of a major part of the leadership of organized labor. The McGovern candidacy, at any rate, could not.

All this is, in a way, terribly unfair to George McGovern. Everyone makes mistakes, especially in campaigns, especially when he loses. Retrodiction beats prediction, as politicians (as well as professors) soon learn. McGovern's difficulties, we believe, were not primarily personal but were caused by his location in the Democratic party. The intense but narrow constituency which gave him his success in his run for the nomination forced every one of his bad moves once he became the party candidate. It was not regular Democrats but McGovern die-hards who applauded his willingness to abase himself before Hanoi; they loved the idea of soaking the rich; they (and not the hard-hearted hard hats or the evil ethnics) toyed with refusing to campaign for him if Eagleton remained on the ticket.

Looking at the Congressional results again, it seems possible to start another line of speculation. What if the Democrats had nominated a Presidential candidate who had not won the election but who had done, let us say, ten points better than McGovern's 38 per cent? Could William Spong's Senate seat in Virginia have been saved? Could Democrats have elected Nick Galifianakis to the Senate from North Carolina? (Jimmy the Greek made them both clear favorites just before the election.) Could Ed Edmundson have won in Oklahoma? Barefoot Sanders in Texas? All of them had opponents who ran not against them but against George

McGovern. And all were given better than a fighting chance—indeed some were rated as ahead—by political analysts in their home states.

Much the same speculation holds for the House. Might not John Monagan have survived in Waterbury, Connecticut, with a little more help from the top of the ticket? Andrew Jacobs in Indianapolis? It is in the nature of history that we will never know the answer to these speculations. But it is at least as plausible as any argument we have heard to say that the real story of the 1972 election was this: not that President Nixon won an overwhelming victory, but that Senator McGovern's Presidential candidacy more or less single-handedly staved off a Democratic landslide.

If this is even partially true, then how could the Democrats possibly have been so self-destructive? Earlier in the year—on May 25 to be exact—one of us wrote an article ("Primaries, Polls, and Democracy") for the editorial page of the *Wall Street Journal* that sought to explain how. Nobody has sent us a copy of that article in the mail, however. We assume readers have used it to wrap fish.

3

Social Stratification
and
American Life

Once in a while I plague my sociologist friends by announcing that sociology as a discipline has no distinction other than the claim that social stratification causes everything: what people eat, what they wear, whom they vote for, how they talk, what work they do and what reward they get from it, how they go crazy and how they are treated once they go round the bend, and so on, and on. Anthropology, of course, can be distinguished from sociology (and everything else) by the fact that anthropologists claim that kinship causes everything. My idea of a renaissance man of the social sciences is somebody who believes that social status and kinship are the same thing.

Sociology and anthropology, along with psychology, are social sciences that focus on causes; like economists, political scientists define their turf in terms of effects, and search eclectically for causes that will account for the patterns of politics that they observe. One obvious point of intersection between the concerns of political science and those of sociology is the study of the influence of patterns of social stratification on political life.

Much of the scholarly research that has been done on this topic has emerged in the form of local community studies. Although I

53

have contributed my share of essays to this branch of the literature, I reproduce none of them in this volume, and instead stick faithfully to the theme of social stratification and national politics. Here, peculiarly enough, very little scholarly work of quality has ever been undertaken. And so we must turn to the work of journalists to find competent contemporary accounts of the ways in which the main institutions of American life outside the public sector that bear upon the American pattern of stratification operate.

Within the public sector a formidable literature is building up on Congress, and the main appellate courts and the Presidency are never far from academic scrutiny. One of the central insights of the sociological imagination, however, is that there is no hard and fast line between allegedly public and private institutions in their impact upon the lives of ordinary people, and therefore in principle in order to come to grips with the social organizations that affect the real world we live in there ought to be studies of business corporations, law firms, labor unions, and so on, comparable in richness and scope to the studies we have of Congress or the Supreme Court.

Although there are not such studies, even by social scientists who have clamored the loudest that they ought to be done, close attention to the writings of any of a large corps of serious American journalists will uncover a sizable number of first-rate accounts of the internal politics of ostensibly non-political organizations. I had the pleasure of writing fairly extensive reviews of two such efforts. The first is a description by Peter Prescott of the Choate School. In the few years that have elapsed since Prescott published his book, Choate, like other private preparatory schools, has undoubtedly undergone change. Nevertheless, even if what Prescott describes is no longer fully true, it does give a far better basis for us to assess the claims widespread in sociological circles about the sort of civic indoctrination that takes place in such institutions.

Tom Wolfe I regard as a significant and serious social commentator with a sharply etched, and little understood, theoretical perspective all his own. I don't know if it is a pity or not that he refuses to present himself or his work in this light, and instead dons the cap and bells of the so-called para-journalist. That is his own business, and a pretty good business it must be. Reading a lot of his essays at one sitting persuaded me, however, that he has an over-all intellectual strategy, and reprinted below is my attempt to describe what I think that strategy is.

Both these essays review works that engage the question of how the stable pattern of reward in society—its stratification pattern— affects the lives of its inhabitants.

A WORLD OF THEIR OWN*

For many years now, we have been hearing that elite private preparatory schools are the seedbeds of power in America, and not merely places where people of high status and income (and a few others) send their boys to get a secondary education. In the often-echoed words of C. Wright Mills, the prep schools are supposed to be "a selection and training place of the upper classes . . . a force for the nationalization of the upper classes . . . a prime organizing center of the national upper social classes."

With phrases like these rolling off so many tongues one would have thought that quite a bit was known about what prep schools are actually like, and particularly how they go about their sensitive tasks of selecting and training America's power elite. But it is not so; like a good many institutions in contemporary American life, prep schools have been little studied, understood, or written about.

So far as I know, *A World of Our Own* is the first more or less objective report to see print on an American private preparatory school. Thus, like Xavier Rynne's book on the Vatican Councils or Gay Talese's on the *New York Times,* part of its fascination is in the predictable revelation that an institution whose outer shell is familiar enough also has rather complicated inner workings. What grips all these authors is the struggle for institutional power: who has it, who wants it, what is done with it, and what ought to be done with it.

Like Talese (and, it is rumored, Rynne), Peter Prescott is an alumnus of the institution he writes about: in 1953 he graduated from the Choate School of Wallingford, Connecticut. Fifteen years later he returned to Choate and, securing permission from the headmaster, hung around, asked questions, and recorded what he could of the life of the school as seen through the lives of

* Review of Peter S. Prescott, *A World of Our Own: Notes on Life and Learning in a Boys' Preparatory School* (New York: Coward-McCann, 1970).

some of its 570 students and 80 faculty, almost all of whom live on the Wallingford campus throughout the school year.

What he was looking at is, of course, a total institution, that is, an institution which by design totally absorbs the time and attention of its inhabitants. Like prisons, mental hospitals, and ships, private preparatory boarding schools are hard to get into and hard to leave, sufficient unto themselves, and very jealous of outside distractions.

On these points Choate is quite typical. A young student quotes the headmaster of Choate: "You don't need anything outside. Everything is inside the School." Here is the headmaster's response, in part, to a student who suggested that day passes be given to younger students on Saturday so that they could go to New Haven: "Frankly, I don't see how we can open ourselves to a mass exodus to surrounding cities on the weekends without taking a great deal less responsibility than we take for our students. . . . [J]ust to go and wander around New Haven seems to me unconstructive." Part of a dialogue between the Headmaster and a member of his faculty at a faculty meeting Prescott attended went this way:

> Headmaster: . . . "Were *you* here over the weekend?" Master: "Yuh, I was." Headmaster: "I understood that you were not!" Master: "I was here Friday afternoon, Saturday, and, uh, yesterday," Headmaster: (absolutely icy now, words cutting like blades): "*Not* Saturday night. Not over the weekend when you could have been helping with the house." Master: "I was in the house Saturday night for a while, yuh." Headmaster: "Oh, David." Master (frightened): "I was! I drove out here Saturday evening!" Headmaster: "Well, maybe. Perhaps." (He moves slowly down to [the master] and stresses his words carefully.) "Let me tell you that the structure you see that is built here is built by the blood, sweat, and tears of a lot of men who are working like dogs here, day in and day out. And if others are not willing to pull their weight in the boat, there's a strong feeling that they don't have the same vote and quite the voice in affairs as the men who are working within the basic structure. . . ."

As I have said, Prescott is fascinated by power within the institution. These quotations may give some small hint as to where that is located, and so, perhaps, it is time to introduce the Captain Ahab of Prescott's account, the Headmaster, Seymour St. John, in 1968 the 55-year-old successor to his father in the post he has himself held since 1947. Prescott says, "The man's vitality, his chemical attraction, is astonishing. His eyes sparkle; his gaze is steady . . ." What is his white whale? It is very hard to say, because in spite of the enormous flood of words that oozes out of the Choate establishment to justify their stewardship of the school to parents, alumni, each other, and the world at large, what they are after, their goals, are in Prescott's view, quite vague:

> When someone at Choate is sure he need not define his terms, he can talk for a long while about the School's values without touching upon anything of substance.

Prescott is far more sympathetic to St. John than Lytton Strachey was to Thomas Arnold, yet out of his reporting comes much more than a whiff of the eminent Victorian: "the worship of athletics and the worship of good form"; "first, religious and moral principle; secondly, gentlemanly conduct; thirdly, intellectual ability." (The quotes are from Strachey and Arnold, respectively.)

Choate has compulsory chapel, every day, and masters take attendance there.

> "Chapel," St. John, an ordained Episcopal minister, tells the new boys their first evening at school, "'is a central part of our school lives." Decorum is important, even in approaching the chapel. "Boys should be quiet as they approach the building," the *Student's Handbook* says, "and carry on no conversation as they enter." Nor can one keep one's hands in his pockets. . . .

There are a lot of other rules: "No opening windows when room is too warm instead of lowering heat." "No dragging boxes or trunks downstairs without carrying them."

Athletics is compulsory. The whole school moves in a body to Deerfield for the Big Football Game. "No blue jeans will be allowed: 'House masters will make a check,' St. John says, 'table masters will make a further check, bus masters will make a final check.' " Prescott says: "Choate, like many schools, has a long history of finding a special mystique or moral worth in athletics. The basic premise is: *Team sports build character*, and the unspoken, but essential corollary attached to it is: *Character is built in direct ratio to the degree of competitiveness and violence involved in team sports.*" (Prescott's italics.)

There is a great deal more in the book that suggests (though St. John denies it) that however ill formulated the shape of the mold, Choate is out to mold men. Some of the students think it is a Procrustean bed:

> Item from the *Choate News* . . . "Speaking for the black students at Choate, Harold Ray asked the Headmaster whether his goal was for all black students to be assimilated into the "upper middle class" values of the School.
>
> Mr. St. John: "Will you define middle class values?"
>
> Ray: "The whole system of the School; mandatoryness—chapel, sports."
>
> Mr. St. John: "The answer is yes."

Prescott's account suggests that a significant feature of Choate today is the growth of critical thinking about preparatory school life by members of the student body. This certainly contrasts with the recent poll that showed the vast majority of Etonians favoring the continuation of corporal punishment (on themselves!) or with my own memories of a less repressive prep school, where student leaders conformed unquestioningly to administration views on most imaginable subjects (not that many subjects were, in fact, imaginable). People who didn't like school were simply disregarded as having a "negative attitude," and were referred to by students and faculty alike as belonging to a disloyal 15 per cent of rotten apples in the barrel, as being incorrigible and unconstructive. This is still St. John's rhetoric, which he uses less to stigmatize students caught smoking pot or beating up on smaller boys than persons in the student body and faculty who listen carefully to what he says and want to enter into dialogue with him about his educational premises and policies. This sort of conversation comes hard enough to St. John when it is initiated by members of his faculty; Prescott heard students collectively told more than once that if they had any serious reservations about Choate they should leave, that only long years and hard sacrifices entitled students or faculty to question the educational goals or practices of the institution in any public way. This was certainly not a good enough answer for some of the junior faculty, but very little came of their haphazard attempts to think through a tenable educational philosophy of their own.

Perhaps one of the central weaknesses of a place like Choate is that its very enclosure and insulation prevent the adults in the place from having a very sophisticated, complicated, subtle, or rich set of expectations about the possibilities of being adult in the outside world. It seems to me that fairly broad and generous and fully operative conceptions of adulthood are a necessary prerequisite of any acceptable philosophy of secondary education—and it is precisely these sorts of conceptions that the insularity of preparatory school life seems to forbid its leadership and faculty.

Ultimately, it cripples: many faculty at Choate told Prescott they felt intimidated by St. John, confessed themselves unwilling to breach his formidable defenses, to speak up at faculty meetings, to challenge practices—compulsory chapel, excessive emphasis on athletics, overscheduling of students and faculty alike, morbid fascination with punctuality and breaches of the rules against smoking—that many of them felt were harmful to good education. Why were they intimidated? Many said, incredibly, that they feared for their jobs, jobs that in the booming economy of the late '60s paid an average of $7500 a year, plus a couple of thousand dollars more in fringe benefits, in exchange for eighteen-hour days, six-and-a-half-day weeks, the neglect of home and family, and no hope of tenure. Is it dedication alone that keeps educated men in boom times silent at the thought of losing such a situation?

None of this, and nothing in Prescott's book, answers the question that at least some outsiders will want answered—namely, how places like Choate train up America's power elite. Prescott is inclined to credit Choate alumnus John Kennedy's charge that private preparatory schools in fact do considerably less than they should or could do about civic education in general and the political awareness of their students in particular. I think this is true; the political concerns of prep school students who have them are mostly focused *inside* the institution, on student affairs, not outside. When they leave, they are about as knowledgeable on and motivated to pursue political questions as when they arrived. What merit there is in the notion that prep schools train the power elite can more readily be understood by invoking Sophie Tucker's law—"rich is better"—as an antecedent cause of both prep school attendance and eventual appearance in some letterhead or directory designated as a nesting place of adult power elite members.

The final question that one must ask is whether *A World of Our Own* is true. Much of it is straightforward reporting, direct quotations and so on, with eye-witnesses present. Yet there are bound to be those who will regard Prescott as having imposed rather severely on the hospitality of the School. As his year of field work wore on, and crises, conflicts, and difficulties arose within earshot, misgivings seem to have set in. He was asked, and declined, to let Choate's trustees read the book before publication. He speaks admiringly in the text, and gratefully in the acknowledgments, of two young dissident masters who left Choate. As Prescott says, "Choate likes to speak of itself in the optative, not indicative, mood." Because it is so likely that he will be accused of plunging a dagger into Alma Mater's long-suffering back, I think it worth recording that in my view Prescott has written a thoughtful and scrupulous book. He looses his cool, makes unfair remarks, or takes cheap shots very rarely—only just often enough to establish that the even-handedness that characterizes the bulk of this book's tone was won at the cost of some effort.

The fact that many readers will find this an unflattering portrait of Choate may be accounted for by a divergence between the educational and social values of Prescott and many of his readers, on the one hand, and St. John and his allies on the faculty and board of trustees, on the other.

Prescott acknowledges that Choate is, so far as he can tell, an excellent example of the type of institution it is. He does not quite confront the possibility that there may be inherent limitations on the genus private boarding preparatory school so serious that the issue is not whether the place would work to his satisfaction if St. John were less old-fashioned or more permissive but rather whether, given Prescott's own set of adult values, a place like Choate is defensible at all. It would have been intriguing to see Prescott take the question head on. My view is that he has earned the right to do so by the appropriate blend of sympathy and detachment with which he wrote this book—and, one assumes, burned his bridges in Wallingford.

DROP OUT, TURN ON, FAIL*

Divide the whole world into foxes who know a little bit about a lot of things and hedgehogs who know one big thing, and journalists working on general assignment will come out foxes every time. Or almost: Tom Wolfe (Ph.D. Yale, in American Studies) is a glaring exception. He knows one big thing, and the three volumes of his work now in print—two collections and one expansion of pieces originally written mostly for *Esquire* and *New York* magazine—are all about that one big thing, again and again.

America, says Wolfe, is increasingly a land of people who have learned how to beat the status game by dropping out of the big society-wide sweepstakes based on jobs where practically everybody loses. The post-World War II American on the whole has enough money to avoid starvation and with what is left over he has available the option of buying his way into smaller "status spheres," pockets of people larger than primary groups who create little worlds based on stylized, expressive behavior—sometimes including a code of etiquette, esoteric skills, an argot, and distinctive modes of dress.

Most of the pieces collected in Wolfe's three books are ethnographic surveys of these little subcultures. His earlier collection, *The Kandy-Kolored Tangerine-Flake Streamline Baby* was about the little worlds of stock car racers, the designers of the multistory neon signs in Las Vegas, a teenage pop-record tycoon, a disk-jockey, the builders of customized autos, the nanny mafia. In *The Pump House Gang* Wolfe visits surfers, teenage "hair boys," motorcyclists. In addition there are long pieces on Robert and Ethel Scull, who beat the odds in the big status game by collecting pop art, Hugh Hefner, "king of the status dropouts" who rarely leaves the sybaritic little world he has created in the house

* Review of Tom Wolfe, *The Electric Kool Aid Acid Test*, and *The Pump House Gang* (New York: Farrar, Straus and Giroux, 1968).

63

he owns, and Carol Doda, who made it in the night club business by enlarging her breasts (which she refers to as "them") with silicone.

Several articles are about England; they suggest that Englishmen are still hung up on their old monolithic status system and haven't learned how to—as Robert Scull says—"enjoy." "Mid-Atlantic Man" is a fable about a middle-class Englishman in the advertising business who tries the dodge of going American. Wolfe says:

> The American has always gone English in order to endow himself with the mystique of the English upper classes. The Englishman today goes American, becomes a Mid-Atlantic man, to achieve the opposite. He wants to get out from under the domination of the English upper classes by . . . going classless. And he goes classless by taking on the style of life, or part of the style of life, of a foreigner who cannot be fitted into the English class system, the modern, successful, powerful American.

In this particular fable, Mid-Atlantic man fails: Englishmen see through him and the rich Americans discover they can get a genuine upper-class Englishman to sell out for the same price the Mid-Atlantic man is asking.

Why has Wolfe got it in for the English? Because their status system still works, still oppresses the middle classes. A second fable chronicles the anxieties of a teen-age London society girl and also has a dire outcome. Lower-class Englishmen on the other hand, led by the Beatles, seem to have found a way out. Wolfe visits a nightclub that operates in a London cellar to catch the lunch-hour trade of teenagers that make up the bottom of the English white-collar work force.

> There is hardly a kid in all of England who harbors any sincere hope of advancing himself in any very striking way by success at work. Englishmen at an early age begin to sense that the fix is in, and all that work does is keep you afloat at the place you were born into. So working-class teenagers, they are just dropping out of the goddam system. . . .

What they are dropping into is "The Life": Edwardian clothes, tremendous style-consciousness, noisy rock music that "messes up your mind":

> . . . down in the cellar at noon. Two hundred and fifty office boys, office girls, department store clerks, messengers, members of London's vast child work-force of teenagers who leave school at 15, pour down into this cellar, in the middle of the day for a break. . . .

Back to America. Wolfe's most ambitious effort to describe a dropout status-sphere is his treatment of the San Francisco hippie scene through a book-long look at Ken Kesey and his Merry Pranksters titled *The Electric Kool Aid Acid Test*. Wolfe emphasizes the cult-like quality of Kesey's group, and explores the ways in which this particular status-sphere, which totally absorbs its participants, is highly dependent upon the elaboration of a belief system. Thus, a serious dedication to dropping out of the mainstream has for at least some Americans become a religious experience.

There is a long chapter in *The Pump House Gang* on Marshall McLuhan, also a high priest. If McLuhan is right, television is undermining the social order by making the new generations being raised on it more tactile, more spontaneous, more associative and less linear and logical in their cognitive organization than the generations for whom the main medium was the printed word. On the other hand—and this is something Wolfe does not mention—if, as McLuhan claims, television is turning the world into a global village and reducing fragmentation, the creation of little status-spheres becomes more difficult and less likely.

Wolfe gives a good exposition of the main lines of McLuhan's thinking, even without looking too carefully at its implications for his own big idea. Of more interest to Wolfe is McLuhan himself, poised between the two worlds of English Lit and big-money prophethood.

There are a number of other worthwhile observations in Wolfe's various collections, but almost all essentially embroider his main theme: The possibilities fed by affluence and mass communications for making it in the status structure of America are fragmenting, exfoliating, burgeoning. Unlike Nathanael West, who also wrote about the expressive potential of modern Americans, Wolfe views these status spheres with great sympathy, sees them no more as opiates than success in the square world would be. Somewhere, in the tangle of Wolfe's unremittingly flamboyant prose, which sometimes works and sometimes doesn't, I sense the beginnings of a horse laugh at the expense of Karl Marx.

4

Congress

When Gerald Ford, Minority Leader of the U.S. House of Representatives, became Vice-President, it was duly noted by at least one senior savant of the Washington press corps that Ford had never in his long Congressional career had his name as principal sponsor on a major piece of legislation. Readers were invited to draw their own conclusions: Was Ford's dereliction due to laziness? To insufficient concern for the public weal? To lack of influence with his fellow legislators? Question marks hung in the air.

I will now impart what is apparently a secret about the House of Representatives: major pieces of new legislation become the property of the committee chairmen who handle them. It is the chairman's name that normally goes on the bills that become famous laws. If you are not a chairman, your name generally does not go on major legislation, no matter how fertile your ingenuity, how vigorous your initiative. Minority leaders do not serve on committees and hence do not qualify to be chairmen. Before Ford was Minority Leader, he served on the House Appropriations Committee, which has the crucial job of legislating the annual budget for the U.S. government, but which never initiates new laws of any other kind.

This is a mild example of a phenomenon that puzzles academic students of Congress—namely, the extent to which Congress is a thing apart, isolated up on Capitol Hill, away from the rest of the government, and from the bulk of the press corps, especially the editors, bureau chiefs, and famous columnists who shape opinion.

There is no question that this gap exists. I was astounded one day to hear the man who is perhaps the most famous journalist in America say to a group of freshman Congressmen that he felt as though he needed a visa whenever he crossed Seventh Street on his way from "downtown" Washington on up to Capitol Hill. He went on to say to these newly elected Representatives that this illustrated the extent to which the Congress (and not his august self) was out of touch with the mood of the country.

Well, that is surely one way of looking at it, but not the only way. For more than a decade a few political scientists and a few journalists have specialized at looking at the world from the point of view of Capitol Hill, and have taken Congress as their special responsibility. It is not an easy responsibility to discharge because it demands something very few academics can provide—namely, a continuous presence in the halls of Congress for the purpose of monitoring the tides of opinion and activity that ebb and flow there.

Most scholars sooner or later tire of this; on Capitol Hill there are special facilities and provisions for accredited journalists but none for scholars who must tramp the hallways like tourists when they are not taken under the wing of some kindly Congressman. So, wearying of the chase, we retreat to our universities and attempt to write down what we have learned; meanwhile our friends and acquaintances in Congress fall by the wayside, configurations of power and pressure flex and shift, and our anecdotes go stale and out of date.

This accentuates the challenge that all academic Congressional specialists feel, to seize somehow from our experiences on Capitol Hill something of lasting value. This drive toward generality colors even occasional and ephemeral writing on Congress, and is especially noticeable in the full-blown case study that appears at the end of this chapter.

The chapter opens with a contribution I made to a symposium

marking the fiftieth anniversary of Time Incorporated, and it sounds many of the themes that recur in the selections that follow: Congress is an organization. The behavior of the people who work there becomes comprehensible once we understand how the organization is designed, how it shapes, grants, and withholds incentives, and how the goals of individuals intersect these patterns of incentive. Then also, we can make a more intelligent assessment as to how well Congress is doing its job in the political system.

These sorts of perspectives inform the review essay on books by William White and Richard Bolling, both of whom are writing about the House of Representatives, Congress's less visible but far more interesting half. And they make comprehensible an otherwise mind-boggling collection of odds and ends that a Congressional subcommittee once published on the uses of social science. This collection makes little sense until viewed in the context of an organizational imperative—in this case the needs of Congressional committees to assert themselves in relation to subject-matter jurisdictions.

Like other social institutions, Congress has its private heroes, and a cluster of short reviews celebrates the service of three of these: Robert Taft, Paul Douglas, and Clem Miller. Miller, more evocatively than any Congressman in modern times, undertook the task of educating his constituents to the realities of Congressional life. Douglas and Taft, through the inner strength of their characters and the high intelligence they applied to the analysis and exposition of public problems, earned an extraordinary measure of esteem from their colleagues in the Senate. Like all organizations, Congress has only limited use for individualists. Like most interesting organizations, its members nevertheless paradoxically reserve their highest regard for those among them who are somehow larger than the mold that is necessarily a comfortable fit for most of them.

Two schemes for changing Congress next receive attention, and both, predictably, are analyzed from the perspective of their organizational consequences. The chapter concludes with a descriptive case study of influence processes in the House on the occasion of the selection of a Majority Leader.

DOES CONGRESS KNOW ENOUGH
TO LEGISLATE FOR THE NATION?

The short answer to this question is, of course, No. Most of the problems facing the nation, and consequently Congress, are manifold, complex, and intractable. They are rooted in hard facts of nature as well as "sown in the nature of man," as Madison wisely said. It is doubtful that anyone knows enough to prescribe measures that can be counted upon to ameliorate many of these problems. It is no wonder that Congress fails to do so; indeed, mankind receives little enough comfort from all its other elected officials, from bureaucrats, judges, pundits, and professors. Does Time Incorporated know enough to pronounce its weekly benediction upon the nation? There is a short answer to this question, too.

So let us be modest in our demands as well as our expectations. If each of us recognizes that there are bound to be profound limitations upon the cognitive capacities of people organized into any system of activity, of whatever design, we are better prepared to assess the ways in which the special organizational imperatives of Congress limit and enhance its capacity to collect and deploy knowledge for its benefit and for that of the nation. And we can search for ways of improving the knowledge-seeking and knowledge-using capabilities of Congress from within the four corners of a more secure understanding of the peculiar sort of organization Congress is.

I

Part of this understanding can be had by asking what sorts of information Congress is best at seeking out and employing. Three kinds of information come readily to mind, and all three suggest how closely information-gathering and -using processes are tied to the mainsprings of the organizational life of Congress.

First, Congress is extremely good at finding out who wants what and how badly. Congressmen go about discovering this in a variety of ways: for example, by attending legislative hearings, by receiving lobbyists, and by reading their mail. It is a central duty of a legislative body in a democracy to find out who wants what and how badly. It also falls to legislative bodies to go well beyond ascertaining this sort of information in determining outcomes. Some observers believe that persistent failures by Congress to enact this or that measure which by some criterion has wide-spread popular support demonstrates a failure of cognition. In my opinion, cognition is rarely the problem. More often such "fail-ures" can be attributed to two other phenomena: first, an aggrega-tion process in which Congressmen tend to discount unmobilized and unfocused opinion—such as, for example, would be reflected in a nation-wide public opinion poll—and to weigh much more heavily opinion that is focused, mobilized, and urgently pressed upon them.

That the wants of "how many" should be discounted against "how badly" some people want things may or may not be a flaw in democratic practice, depending upon the kind of democratic theory in which you believe. There is no doubt, at any rate, that Congressmen do this, and they do it in part because of their problems of simple survival. Mobilized and focused opinion is opinion that moves voters; simple expressions of preference on a poll may or may not be. Congressmen must appeal to voters every second year and Senators every six. To ignore mobilized opinion is to ignore voters; to attend to mobilized opinion is to give voters what many believe to be their due regard. In any event, a popularly elected official who persistently fails to attend to this opinion cannot long remain invulnerable to challenge—if not in a general election, then in a primary—and in consequence over the long run Congress does tend to reflect those strands of opinion in the electorate which are well mobilized and highly focused. Likewise, over the short run Congressmen come to be disposed to be attentive to opinions which have these character-istics.

A second source of "failure" to reflect certain kinds of opinion in legislation over the short run can be accounted for by structural characteristics of Congress. Even the crudest muckraker knows that a central feature of the Congressional system is the committee structure, a device for dividing the work of Congress by subject matter and creating special enclaves of power and expertise. The committee system and the seniority system by which the populations of committees are stabilized are customarily the focus of much dissatisfaction. Complainants were right in asserting that home rule for the District of Columbia would have hard sledding so long as John McMillan of South Carolina chaired the House Committee on the District of Columbia. My point here is that it was not a lack of knowledge or information on McMillan's part but rather the firmness of his convictions against home rule, and his use of power, that stymied home rule.

A second realm of information-gathering in which Congress does well has to do with the monitoring of the executive bureaucracies. Here Congress operates on two levels: a continuous flow of communication from constituents to individual Congressmen and Senators makes it possible for members of Congress to monitor the delivery of services from bureaucracies to the public. The fact is, of course, that most members pay little personal attention to the ordinary run of constituent casework that comes through the office. Nevertheless, the information is always there, and a flash flood of complaints about the Veterans Administration or the Marine Corps or the Social Security Administration may well pique the interest of a Congressman in ways that an ordinary rainfall of complaints would not. Some people would argue that this continuous flow of intelligence constitutes a significant bulwark of the plain citizen against the growth of arbitrariness in the federal bureaucracy, and thus in a sense the humble case work of Congressmen provides an informational basis for the exercise of the central Congressional responsibility of checking and balancing the executive branch.

At a somewhat more exalted level this process of monitoring executive agencies also goes on, and this of course is through the legislative processes of authorization, appropriation, and confirmation themselves. Here the much-maligned committees play their crucial role. Because they are organized by subject matter and are assigned supervisory roles over explicit and limited parts of the executive branch and because they are manned by a substantial number of Congressmen who expect to remain in Congress and in due course receive the blessings of seniority in the form of subcommittee chairmanships, it is possible for Congress to develop a sizable cadre of persons having subject-matter competence approaching expertise. This artifact of the Congressional division of labor is not a sufficient condition for effective checking and balancing, since the will and the energy to do so must also be present. But it is a necessary condition. Most critics of Congress fail to see this; it is a fatal mistake. The committee system is the foundation not only of Congressional power but of Congressional competence. Consequently, as we shall shortly see, to improve Congressional competence we must improve, not cripple, Congressional committees.

A third type of information-gathering that Congress does well is embedded neither in the needs of Congressmen to survive nor in the Congressional division of labor but in the further ambitions of members of Congress. Many Representatives look forward to being Senators or Governors. Senators have in recent years increasingly cast sheep's eyes at the Presidency. Those so situated, and sometimes others as well, seek and exploit information about issues and policy innovations that can win the loyalty of national publics and the attention of the news media.

We are all increasingly aware of the desire of members of Congress to be known as "Mr. Health Care," "Mr. Science," "Mr. Crimebuster," and so forth. My point is that the adoption and pursuit of these roles entail a significant investment in information-gathering. In order to create or adapt to a national public on a given issue, Congressmen must become knowledgeable about that issue, be capable of defending their positions and of taking new initiatives.

In these three broad ways, then, the organizational imperatives of Congress, the needs of Congressmen to survive and enhance their careers, create capabilities in the gathering and the deployment of knowledge.

II

As I have said, the conditions which give rise to these capabilities are necessary conditions; remove needs for electoral survival, pathways for ambition, the division of labor, or the capacity to check the routines of the bureaucracy and the corresponding Congressional information-gathering activities would wither. Necessary conditions, however, are not sufficient conditions.

Many thoughtful observers believe that in the day-to-day experience of Congress these conditions are in fact insufficient to produce adequate information relevant to Congressional policy-making. Two complaints about Congressional knowledge are so common that any serious address to the problem must face them. They are: 1) Congress is usually outgunned by the experts from the executive agencies, and consequently lets its prerogatives in shaping legislation lapse; 2) in many subject matter areas, Congress is immobile and ignorant because the Congressmen in charge of those sectors are immobile and ignorant and wish to remain so. This may come about for four reasons: senility or ineptitude of committee chairmen; the opposition of chairmen to legislation in the field; the corruption of chairmen by outside interests; or collusion between chairmen and executive agencies.

The two complaints are linked. Congress is by no means necessarily outgunned by executive agencies in the policy-making process when the opposite of these conditions obtains. That is, when committee chairmen are able and intelligent, when they favor legislative activity, when they want to pursue an independent Congressional course of action, the means are in general readily at hand for Congress to do the intelligence-gathering it needs to do. To all those acquainted with Capitol Hill the instance of tax policy will spring to mind. It is doubtful that any agency embodies more knowledge than the professional staff of Congress devoted to this field. Moreover, it is the established practice of the House Ways and Means Committee systematically to co-opt the expertise of the executive branch when they deal in their own way with tax matters.

It would be possible for the close observer of Congress to enumerate similar information-gathering activities regularly engaged in by other Congressional committees and subcommittees. The Daddario subcommittee of the House Science and Astronautics Committee, for example, commissioned studies by the National Science Foundation and constituted and regularly met with an advisory group of senior experts in the area of their responsibilities. I note also the recent establishment of an Office of Technology Assessment as an agency of Congress. I assume Congressmen and Senators will watch this new agency closely to see whether it lives up to its promise and becomes an analogue in its field to the staff of the Joint Committee on Internal Revenue Taxation.

I have been painting such a rosy picture that readers will be entitled to ask how it happens that there are so many complaints. One answer is this: It must be borne in mind that what I have been describing is a set of capabilities that Congress possesses only as a collective entity. As individuals, Congressmen by the dozens may well rightly feel at the mercy of their ignorance. The Joint Committee on Internal Revenue Taxation does not work directly for *them*, after all, but rather for the small fraction of members directly charged with writing tax policy. Yet they all must vote on tax measures. Most of them will have at one time or another to pretend to knowledge of what they are doing in this area. And in this private knowledge-gathering enterprise, over the vast range of policies, individual Congressmen and Senators are mostly on their own.

This creates a tension between two clear organizational imperatives: Congressmen and Senators must specialize, or else Congress loses the capacity to shape policy that expert knowledge alone grants. On the other hand, Congressmen and Senators must be generalists, because they believe—and for good reason—that this is what their constituents demand of them.

The resolution of this dilemma that I have in general favored comes down hard on the side of specialization: we must educate constituents to more reasonable expectations of their representatives. We must help them to see that the demand for the illusion of omnicompetent Congressmen is a demand for the reality of an incompetent Congress.

Members of Congress are entitled to smile at this prescription; indeed they are entitled to ask how someone who claims to have taught in a university these last few years comes to place such confidence in the efficacy of education. There is no real answer to this objection except this: alternative solutions entail much higher costs and risks, most significantly the risk of rendering the legislative branch utterly impotent.

III

I believe Congress can do more than it has done to systematize the gathering of specialized information in the manifold areas where they must act. Although taxes and some aspects of science policy may be bright spots, there are plenty of subjects on which Congress is less impressively prepared. On another occasion I made the point that in some respects Congressional knowledge fell behind that of the executive branch in those areas where the executive was most energetic in adopting professional standards of data collection and analysis. Adopting professional standards means submitting to the rules and practices and craft norms and constraints of a professional community. It is such communities which decree, for example, what respectable economics is— regardless of the politics in whose service the economics is harnessed. In consequence of this commitment to professionalization by the executive branch Democratic administrations must find Democratic economists, and Republicans, Republican economists, to do their economics for them. The age of debate about economic policy is surely not over, but the age of patent medicine economics in national politics—at least in the executive branch— is.

Many bright young economists now have the opportunity early in their careers to serve a tour of duty with the Council of Economic Advisors. There is no reason why Congress cannot tap the same pool of talent and in much the same way if it chooses to do so. The same is true of operations researchers or defense analysts. Instead of hearing from experts occasionally at hearings, the relevant committees and subcommittees could hire them for two-year periods, let us say, and gain a much greater familiarity with the thoughtways that underlie expertise. This can also give Congress continuous access to technically advanced criticism of executive proposals, more sophisticated insight into alternatives, and more sensitive awareness of emerging problems in the world.

In saying this, I am, of course, suggesting that what Congressmen need on the whole is not information but regular opportunities for self-education. There is, after all, no special training for being a Congressman or a Senator. Members of Congress must define their jobs their own way and learn what they need to learn as best they can. I think it is remarkable that as many members know as much as they do, given the severe constraints on their time and energy. I do believe that they can do better as knowledge-gatherers and analysts, but only one who has considerable respect for the capacities of Congressmen, as I do, is likely to think the effort is worthwhile.

How to move toward professionalization of Congressional knowledge-gathering and analysis? Ultimately, as I have more than hinted, the problem is one of committee staffs. These are uneven in quality and expertise, reflecting most of all their loyalty to the chairman and to the political goals that he sets for the committee. Those chairmen who want to move in the direction I have indicated on the whole know how to go about it. One device they have occasionally used that makes especial sense to me is to constitute a panel of expert—and if possible, distinguished—professional consultants to monitor the output of the staff from the standpoint of its professional adequacy. These chairmen, however, are only a small part of the problem, at least as an outsider sees it.

More common by far is the following complaint: Frequently the conditions for immobility and incompetence that I enumerated above are met. So a final question remains—how might Congress be encouraged to minimize senility and ineptitude among its committee chairmen, the opposition of chairmen to legislative activity, the corruption of chairmen by outside interests and collusion with executive agencies?

The best answer I have heard to this cluster of problems was one given a few years ago by Representative Morris Udall. To decrease the influence of outside factors on committee chairmen, increase the influence of inside factors. Udall suggested subjecting all committee chairmen to an automatic, non-discretionary election, by secret ballot, in the party caucus that precedes the opening of each Congress. Chairmen would be automatically slated against the two next ranking committee members so an element of choice would be present, but seniority would also be given its due. It was anticipated, of course, that most chairmen most of the time would pass this hurdle without difficulty. Only those chairmen hopelessly out of step with the majority of their party in Congress or definitely incapable of doing the job would be likely to be replaced in this process. But the mere existence of such a mechanism might reasonably be expected to encourage chairmen to build their alliances within Congress more broadly, and hence more responsively. Some elements of this proposal have been enacted by House Democrats, but not all of them. Although it is fairly clear that a more honest reflection of Congressional sentiment on the performance of chairmen can be obtained with a secret ballot, so-called public interest lobbying groups have opposed the secret ballot in caucus because it makes it harder for them to keep score on their friends and foes. The automatic, non-discretionary feature is also missing, thus gratuitously stigmatizing those Congressmen who initiate an election in any particular case. So we have not had a full test on the majority side of the efficacy of Udall's ingenious plan.

Congress has moved slowly but on the whole more effectively in related areas. A gratuitous Supreme Court decision in *Powell* v. *McCormack* places the establishment of an automatic Congressional retirement system beyond the reach of any enactment short of a Constitutional amendment. It is within the power of Congress, however, to restrict the holding of chairmanships to persons below a certain age. Quite understandably, more progress has been made on the carrot than on the stick side of this problem; Congressional pensions are now sufficiently generous—as they should be—to help senior members contemplate voluntary retirement with equanimity, and even pleasure.

This paper has ranged far enough even in a short space to

suggest at least some of the dimensions of the problem of Congressional information-gathering, processing, and use. At the heart of the discussion, as I see it, we must keep the hard fact that Congress is an organization that runs according to a powerful set of imperatives dictated by the nature of our Constitutional order, the character of our party system, the vast scale of our land, and the heterogeneity of our people. Schemes for reforming Congress must first of all come to an understanding of the logic of its organizational structure. This is as surely true for those who despair of Congress as it is for the somewhat smaller, more select group of us who are eager to see Congress prosper.

REPRESENTING THE HOUSE *

Fresh from his recent triumph as the election-year Parson Weems of his long-time friend Lyndon Johnson, William S. White now turns his magisterial attention to the House of Representatives. But, if we can believe his former colleague, Russell Baker of the *New York Times*, White's credentials for the task are somewhat tarnished. "The snobbishness of the Senate is not limited to its members but extends to hangers-on," wrote Baker in *An American in Washington*. "Newsmen who cover the Senate may look down upon an occasional assignment in the House as beneath their stature. William S. White, the distinguished columnist and authority on the Senate, has boasted, only half-jokingly, that he has never set foot on the House's side of the Capitol." This is clearly not quite true: White admits to moments of cozy intimacy with fellow Texan Sam Rayburn, and occasionally gives vent to patronizing references to "this old House" of which he denominates himself "a close, and on the whole, a fond observer" for eighteen years, "during which I have had intimate knowledge . . . inside as well as . . . outside."

Nevertheless, White makes plain that his affections remain with the Senate. Able members of the House, he suggests, ought to be "promoted" to the Senate, which is "the better legislative body by and large, since "it can always outthink the House if it puts its mind to it." However, his attempts to give meaning to judgments such as these—which are in their pristine state vacuous—founder. His case for the comparative unimportance of the House rests upon such items as:

(1) The argument that the House really has no influence upon matters of national security policy. Yet, White admits that the power of the purse in defense matters is crucial and the powers of

---

* Review of William S. White, *Home Place: The Story of the U.S. House of Representatives* (Boston: Houghton Mifflin, 1965) and Richard Bolling, *House Out of Order* (New York: E. P. Dutton, 1965).

the relevant House Appropriations Subcommittee (fortunately headed by a Texan, George Mahon) are most vital of all. He resolves this seeming contradiction with a stunning disclosure: "Defense is by the deepest possible definition a home affair; and the House is the home of home affairs."

(2) The bald implication that at national party conventions Senators are more important than Representatives. The memory of Speaker John Nance Garner's role in nominating Roosevelt in 1932 ought to have given White pause. Even more recently, in 1960, Representative Stewart Udall won the Democratic delegation of Arizona in behalf of John Kennedy away from Senator Carl Hayden, who was boosting Mr. Johnson. Presumably, examples can be multiplied on both sides of the argument, but even if White were correct, it would have no necessary bearing on the collective powers of the House.

(3) The assertion that while the Senate gives talented junior members room for maneuver, the House does not. In fact, junior members are given important work to do in both bodies only if they are very lucky and very resourceful. In another connection, White himself instances Richard Bolling in the House, who, though very junior, became very influential with Speaker Rayburn's assistance. To prove how the Senate recognizes great ability instantly, White offers Mr. Johnson, who similarly enjoyed Rayburn's assistance (and that of President Roosevelt) earlier in his career, and later made his way in the Senate with the aid of older Senators, and not, as White blandly asserts, "simply by virtue of a high capacity for personal leadership." White's preoccupation with the Senate is, in short, debilitating rather than illuminating, for the Senate is not used as a means of making operational so much as tenuous moral comparisons.

This hardly leaves room to discuss what is ostensibly the subject of the book. On the House, White is quite uninformed, even about the most obvious details. His account of the normal operations of the House legislative process in one short chapter is both skimpy and ludicrously wide of the mark. Sprinkled throughout are oversimplifications, inaccuracies, and blunders on a variety of topics. On Congressional districts: "One rarely finds [one-party districts] in any essentially urban area of the country." On elementary points of history in the large: "The humility of the House, taking it as a whole, has been one of its outstanding characteristics nearly from the beginning, is so now, and no doubt ever will be" (War Hawks of 1812? Reconstruction?), and history in the small: "Never in all history has a topmost House National reached the Presidency save for James Madison . . ." (Polk? McKinley? Garfield?). On procedure: the Education and Labor Committee is assigned the jurisdiction for medicare; the Republican Committee on Committees is alleged to come crucially under the influence of Ways and Means.

There is a persistent confusion between personal qualities of politicians and their political positions. The "Above Average," as White describes him, is sometimes the abler, more enlightened member, sometimes the more senior member. Sometimes, it is impossible to tell which; but it is clear that, whoever he is, only he has the potential for a share in that small portion of greatness White allots to the House. The "Average" member gets White's pity, but for the oddball "Non-Average" he reserves a special scorn, as is only due the "young or youngish lawyer," the "academician diverted to elective politics," the "quasi-professional writer" who is "always a reformer and Liberal with a capital L," who goes "by rattling subway to the meeting place of the American Veterans Committee or perhaps of Americans for Democratic Action."

It is indeed hard to see how any right-thinking American can fail to avert his eye from the repellent picture White paints of the advocate of reform. And so it is to the author's credit that although he finds them sadly wanting in practicality, he does consider certain proposals for reform briefly upon their merits before dismissing them.

In particular White defends the system of seniority, which, he avers, is the very "synonym" of "experience, capacity, earned prestige, personal influence through personal power." The Rules Committee, he suggests, is essential for a number of reasons, the most curious of which follows: "I assert in complete confidence and without hesitation that [on the occasion of General Mac-

Arthur's farewell address to a joint session of Congress] had an influential member suddenly offered from the floor a resolution condemning [the] President of the United States, and calling on General MacArthur to lead this nation forward, it could have been a bad moment for constitutional government in the United States. It could have been, that is, but for the existence of something called a Rules Committee. . . ."

The fact is that the rules of the House and Senate reveal no method by which any business at all can be considered in a joint session of Congress. Joint resolutions, separately passed by each chamber, to take effect must have the President's signature—an awkward procedure for a resolution designed to depose a President. The probability of any such act as White contemplates must be rated as very low. And all this regardless of the existence of the Rules Committee, by which he sets so much store.

That Mr. White should attempt a book on the House was inevitable, one supposes, after the spectacular success of his Senate book. But he has not written a book about the House at all. Rather, this is a chronicle of his biases, in favor of the Senate, Texans, and whatever political machinery happens to be on hand at the moment, and against liberals and reformers.

On the other hand, Representative Bolling gives ample evidence that he knows the House; that he loves it as he finds it is less obvious. As one of the most intelligent and articulate liberal reformers in the House, Bolling is perhaps overly concerned to offer a description of House operations sufficiently discouraging to sustain his indictment of the House as "ineffective in its role as a coordinate branch of the Federal government, negative in its approach to national tasks, generally unresponsive to any but parochial economic interests. Its procedures, time-consuming and unwieldly, mask anonymous centers of irresponsible power. Its legislation is often a travesty of what the national welfare requires." But he really does not support these charges. To have done so would have required quite a different sort of book.

There is no real discussion of the substance of issues in *House Out of Order*; rather, it is a book about political strategy and tactics which, at its best, is frankly autobiographical. Bolling describes at length his activities in the fights surrounding the Landrum-Griffin bill, the Civil Rights bills of 1956 and 1957, and the packing of the Rules Committee in 1961. These are highly personal accounts which quite properly emphasize Bolling's own perspective. They also reflect faithfully Bolling's characteristically cryptic style of exposition which sometimes leaves out basic information. Even so, they are the best part of the book, and one wishes Bolling had given us more of them.

The main thesis of the book is that the Speaker and the Majority Leader—the "Leadership"—are weak and the committee chairmen are strong, and that this is a bad thing, because the Leadership, as elected representatives of the majority party, is entitled to prevail in conflicts with men whose claim to high influence is based primarily upon luck and longevity. During most of Bolling's tenure as a Representative, many Democratic chairmen have been more conservative than either their party leaders in the House or the majority of Democratic members. This leads Bolling to favor a type of Congressional reform that would vest greater committee appointment power in the hands of the Speaker, subject to the ratifying vote of the caucus.

The probability is slight that this proposal will be enacted by any House Democratic caucus in the near future, but this is of less moment than the validity of Bolling's diagnosis. There is much merit to the general argument that in recent years the House has been a conservative force in American politics. But also over this time, a number of techniques have been worked out to cope with these facts of life—techniques that Bolling himself has been known to apply effectively. One of these has been the extensive use of the Democratic Study Group, an organization of between a hundred and two hundred liberal House members. This group circulates reports on substantive issues, has set up an informal whip system, arranges for some campaign support for its members, and on many crucial occasions has consolidated liberals behind well thought-out parliamentary strategies. Another technique for neutralizing conservative strength has been the manipulation of the committee assignment process through the Speaker so as to tip the balance on key committees and give liberal legislation a better chance to reach the floor.

Although Bolling does not say so, over the last few years power in the House has been pushed by these and other means steadily toward the Democratic leaders of the House and away from the more conservative committee chieftains. Each of the three key committees—Rules, Ways and Means, and Appropriations—has since 1958 taken at least one major swing to the left. Customarily, episodes of liberalization take place at the opening of Congress, when simple majority rule within the caucus governs party decision-making. In 1961, the Rules Committee was packed with what on most issues has proved to be a reasonably durable administration majority. Two years later, the caucus placed two liberals on the Ways and Means Committee over the opposition even of the Leadership, which, Bolling suggests, had made a bad bargain to support one conservative Southerner in return for Southern help with the 1963 resolution—which won by a large margin—permanently enlarging the Rules Committee. Over the last few Congresses, the membership of the Appropriations Committee has become steadily more liberal. In 1963, seats were given to members from New Jersey and Connecticut that previously had been held by members from Arkansas and North Carolina. Since the death last year [1964] of Clarence Cannon, the entire subcommittee structure of the committee has evolved in directions generally more favorable to Presidential budgets.

This year, with a net gain from the last election of perhaps forty new administration votes on the floor, the rules of the House were changed, giving the Speaker greater power to expedite floor consideration of measures he favors. Some House insiders assert that these most recent changes would not have been so easy to achieve had not Bolling's more drastic proposals also been widely circulated and in the minds of many Democrats. And so, in a small way, this book served as a political weapon whose main thrust could have been blunted by a more thoughtful or accurate interpretation of events like those it was designed, in part, to influence.

House Out of Order also serves as a kind of public announcement of a change in Bolling's role from agent of the late Speaker Rayburn to outspoken critic of the system of power as it is, at least in theory, presently constituted. Where Bolling was once, as Rayburn's man, unsympathetic to proposals of structural reform, he now hoists his own reform banner. This move is bound initially to cause some uneasiness among those of his colleagues who have been reform-minded all along; and it remains to be seen how Bolling will fit into the ranks of liberal Democrats, now that his relationship with Rayburn, which afforded so much scope for his talents, can no longer define his role within the House.

CONGRESS LOOKS AT
SOCIAL SCIENCE*

Naïve professors may have the impression that "publish or perish" is the law only of the academic jungle. But it's publish or perish for Congressional committees, too. The annual hassle over the appropriation for the House Un-American Activities Committee, for example, is these days mostly a fight over its printing budget. Committees hold hearings and publish reports in part as a way of announcing an interest in a topic and of asserting jurisdiction over it.

Recently, social science has become a hot topic around Congress. Senator Mondale has a bill to set up a Council of Social Advisers. Senator Harris has decided to push for a Social Science Foundation separate from the National Science Foundation. A similar idea was recently sponsored in the House by Representative Dante Fascell. Meanwhile, Representative Daddario's subcommittee of the House Committee on Science and Astronautics—which formally has oversight jurisdiction over the NSF—has a bill (which passed the House but died in the Senate in the last session of Congress) that explicitly broadens the mandate of the NSF in social science.

All this shows a vastly increased concern—and mostly sympathetic concern—on Capitol Hill for social science. The high level of interest is remarkable in view of the social sciences' minute share—about 3.5 per cent—of the federal research budget. But lawmakers have come a long way since the establishment of NSF

* Review of *The Use of Social Research in Federal Domestic Programs*. A staff study for the Research and Technical Programs Subcommittee of the Committee on Government Operations, U.S. House of Representatives. Harold Orlans, ed. Vol. 1, *Federally Financed Social Research, Expenditures, Status, and Objectives*, Vol. 2, *The Adequacy and Usefulness of Federally Financed Research on Major National Social Problems*, Vol. 3, *The Relation of Private Social Scientists to Federal Programs on National Social Problems*, Vol. 4, *Current Issues in the Administration of Federal Social Research* (Washington, D.C.: Government Printing Office, 1967).

in 1950, when minimal support for "hard" social science was gingerly included, or the dark days of the Reece committee, whose chief counsel had so many unpleasant things to say about private foundation support for social science research.

One of the earliest harbingers of a more enlightened legislative attitude appeared in the work of the specially constituted House Select Committee on Government Research, which, under the direction of Carl Elliott during the 88th Congress, looked into the entire range of government-sponsored research. On the social sciences, the Elliott committee's final report in 1964 said:

> We are concerned lest the natural sciences continue to overshadow the social sciences . . . [B]asic research in general, while greatly in need of support, is difficult to defend because of the intangible nature of its results; and . . . particularly basic research in the social sciences is currently undersupported. That this is true can perhaps be best explained by the observation that poor social science research is easier for the layman to identify and ridicule than are biological or chemical or nuclear research. . . . We are persuaded that in the world of our probable future, our ability as a nation to compete will depend to a great extent on the efficacy of today's research into our grave social and economic problems [*88th Congr., 2nd Session, House Rept.* No. 1941, p. 45 (1964)].

In a sense, Representative Henry Reuss's subcommittee on research and technical programs of the House Government Operations Committee is the organizational successor to the disbanded Elliott committee; the Reuss subcommittee was organized in 1965 in response to a recommendation of the Elliott committee, and some of the Elliott committee staff went over to the Reuss group when it began. There is, however, some jurisdictional ambiguity between it and a number of other permanent House subcommittees. As an earlier *Science* observer noted:

> . . . congressional committee preserves are balkanized and jealously guarded. Medical research was out of bounds because it had long ago been preempted by Representative L. H. Fountain (D—N.C.), head of the Government Operations Subcommittee on Intergovernmental Operations. Atomic energy was similarly beyond reach. . . . Similar sovereignties reduced the choices in other fields, and, as a

consequence, the Reuss subcommittee had to choose its subjects with a view to avoiding trespass [D. S. Greenberg, *Science Vol. 150,* 1566 (1965)].

The present "staff study" of the Reuss subcommittee has to be read in the light of this organizational background. Despite the formidable bulk of this study, it appears to be less a serious work of evaluation than an opening shot, a grand jury presentation on the basis of which hearings can be held, and an exploration of the possibility that a subcommittee position on social science can be carved out and defended.

The report is thus best understood as a four-volume appendix to the three-page press release that accompanies it. This latter document has already attracted favorable notice in the *Wall Street Journal* and *The Reporter*, and bears a curious relation to the study proper. The release contains comments and conclusions predominantly critical of government-supported social science research; the study itself provides only the most meager justification for these comments and much material tending to modify or even refute them.

The opening sentences of the committee press release read:

> Many federal agencies and university social scientists have been more interested in the pursuit of knowledge for its own sake than in the use of research to evaluate or to improve programs directed to the nation's major social problems. This divorce of much social science from the study of issues actually confronting the citizen and society reflects both an academic preference and a failure of federal agencies to understand how social research can help them.

The release goes on to describe these two sentences as "findings" of the report and to cite a large number of other "critical comments." Where, the diligent reader may wonder, in the four volumes of this "study" may these "findings" be found? Has the author of this report conducted a study of the "interests" of some scientific sampling of social scientists in order to ascertain the relative degree of their commitment to pure knowledge versus social problems? The answer is no. However, volume 3 of the report does contain a remarkable array of more or less relevant testimony. More than fifty social scientists responded to a question put to them by the subcommittee which read, in part, "Some concern has been expressed lest the increased emphasis on technical problems of their disciplines decrease the interest of academic social scientists in practical issues of public policy. Is this concern warranted?" Only six respondents agreed in the slightest. A few were unresponsive. The remainder disagreed with varying degrees of qualification, elaboration, and vehemence.

Readers clearly have ample warrant to wonder about the empirical justification for other "findings" revealed in the press release and widely publicized by the subcommittee. But what of the "study" itself?

It consists of motley and disparate materials. For instance, there are statistical data on federal expenditures for social research, the result of a subcommittee request to various federal agencies. The subcommittee request and all agency responses are printed verbatim in volume 1. The remainder of that volume (pp. 80–379) would be known in the college publishing business as "readings": material snipped from a large number of published sources containing comments on federally supported social science research, including such matter as three Presidential addresses "on the role of the intellectual in government." Volume 2, 635 pages long, is once again mostly a scissors-and-paste job including such old favorites as Durkheim and Sutherland on crime, Harvey Perloff and Wolf Von Eckhart on cities, and so on. This volume also includes verbatim reprints of responses by sixty-one social scientists to a twelve-item subcommittee questionnaire that begins: "What is your opinion of the general quality, scope and nature of the research now being sponsored by the Federal Government in [one of six areas: crime, education, poverty etc.]?"

On to volume 3! Six hundred and five pages. Once more, mostly readings. Max Weber on "objectivity." C. Wright Mills. Merton. Moynihan. A veritable plum-pudding of "findings." But given the distinction, and in some cases the antiquity, of their sources, these findings are not properly attributable to the subcommittee's work. In this volume, the subcommittee's original contribution consists of the responses of fifty-odd social scientists and research administrators to a 21-item questionnaire. Item 2 has already been quoted. Item 4 goes: "What can your professional field contribute today, on the basis of present knowledge, in helping the nation to cope with its domestic social problems? Please comment briefly."

Volume 4, along with still more readings, interoffice memos, and legal texts, offers responses of natural scientists, government agencies, university research administrators, and foundation executives to a more restricted but not more focused list of questions, such as, "Who shall make policy for the social sciences in the executive office of the President?"

Given the ramshackle structure of the report proper, it is perhaps no wonder that neither the rather ill-humored introductory summaries to each volume by editor Harold Orlans of the subcommittee staff nor the committee press release do the report justice. Nor can this attempt to summarize in brief compass the mass of undigested, unevaluated, and unsupported testimony the subcommittee has jumbled together in these four volumes. But at this stage it is perhaps not inappropriate to observe that the subcommittee has permitted to be published at public expense a work that is not likely to be widely cited as an exemplar of federally financed social research.

A VOICE FROM THE FLOOR*

Two weeks after his book was published, Representative Clem Miller perished, at forty-six, in the wreck of a small airplane high in the mountains of his home district, the First of California, where he was campaigning for his third term in Congress. The book he has left behind is a fitting memorial. It gathers together the newsletters he wrote with characteristic verve and spontaneity to a selected number of friends and neighbors back home. The letters are not the usual pastiche of self-serving comments and stale jokes that many Congressmen send out, but thoughtful essays on the way things are in the House of Representatives.

The extraordinary aptness of his portrait of the House, which Miller sketched from month to month during two terms in office, invites generous quotation. Here is how he describes the ways in which multiple demands on a Congressman's time undercut the legislative process on the House floor:

> . . . So much of what occurs on the Floor is routine. There are only rare occasions when circumstances *demand* one's presence. Thus, what is of overriding significance gives way to what is immediate. The competing interests, the endless details of congressional routine, take hold. Members are called to the Floor for a quorum call as the afternoon's debate begins. Soon, nearly everyone arrives to answer his name. Most stay for a while, listening and chatting. Then, inevitably, the drift begins. Pages hurry up and down the aisles with sheaves of messages, calling a congressman to argue with an executive department on behalf of a constituent, or to tell a garden club delegation why he favors the Shasta daisy for the national flower. Or the Member goes downstairs for lunch, or over to the Senate, or downtown to a conference. . . . Almost without volition, he finds himself back in his office trying to keep up with the mail, interview-

* Review of Clem Miller, *Member of the House: Letters of a Congressman*, edited, with additional text, by John W. Baker (New York: Scribner's, 1962).

ing and being interviewed by a stream of callers. Now, he is too far away to get back to the Floor for a teller vote.

Miller's observations draw the reader into the web of the Congressman's world, showing why things are as they are instead of the way they "ought" to be. The supreme value of this lesson is that it should come from a self-confessed liberal idealist who shared most of the policy preferences of those who habitually condemn Congress in the most scathing terms. The author makes it quite clear that the first job of anyone who would deal successfully with Congress is to understand how it really works. And understanding demands an appreciation of the role of ritual, symbol, and precedent in House affairs, a grasp of the reasons for the specialization of functions, and of the necessities for comity among the specialized committees. One can begin to see how it comes to pass that the House is ruled by an oligarchy of elders which fluctuates in size and power depending upon external circumstances. Miller writes of the leaders of the House:

> Yes, they lead, but they lead only because they win. If they cannot be certain of winning, they don't want to go. Latent power, negative power, is so much better than power committed that lacks victory as a capstone. Hence, the legislative timidity of the Congress. . . .
> Hence the great time lags for the consideration of legislation . . . while the Leadership waits for the pressures to build . . . Hence, the distaste for short cuts . . . distaste for battle just for the sake of battle, distaste for the Discharge Petition, and for Calendar Wednesday, and for the Democratic Caucus.

Understanding the House also means seeing its strength as a social institution that educates its young and shows them what they may and may not do. Congressmen share certain experiences that to a degree separate them from other men—the crucible of running for elective office, the rigors of campaigning that bind them together.

> These people, these congressmen [Miller observes,] have all been through the mill. They have returned from the indifferent cruelties of the political wars. They may have been saddened by the failure of friends to understand as much as they were outraged by the indigni-

ties suffered from their opponents. Elections are unrelenting and painful.

Those who have survived this ordeal soon acquire a certain wariness about what it takes to get a bill passed: "The congressman may seek to take the castle by scaling the walls in open combat or by a sapping operation under the moat." A particular tactical problem may require the greatest subtlety: "Here is the choice: If he is silent, perhaps the Senate will restore the item to the bill. If he speaks up and is beaten, he will *never* get it back. And the chances of winning are better than 500 to one against."

Only rarely does an edge of exasperation show through Miller's humorous and tolerant tone, as when he speaks of the problems of keeping the Democratic party in the House together:

> It takes organization. It takes discipline. And these Democrats do not have in large measure. Discipline works in a democracy if it is understood. Indoctrination and organization are weak on the Democratic side. The Democrats don't meet to talk things over, to be persuaded, to be sold. We don't meet in caucus because Leadership fears that it would irreparably breach the tenuous links with the South. So we go our own way. . . . the Republicans caucus, lock horns, knock heads, and show up to vote in season and out . . .

But Miller rarely bothered with recrimination in his search for a formulation that will explain what is actually going on:

> Members will frequently, and even customarily, follow a committee chairman against their own best interests and against the dictates of friendship or reason . . . The committees with their chairmen are like a string of forts. The northern coalition, as the attackers, are spread out, with poor communication and hence poor co-ordination. They have no base of power from which to menace the chairmen on the one hand or to discipline their members on the other.

For Clem Miller, the key to politics was understanding, not moralizing. His was a mind that ruminated upon the classic questions of politics: What moves men? What prizes do they covet? When are they hesitant? When bold? What leads them to affection? To animosity? Despite the tragic brevity of his writings and his life, despite the frustrations of just causes lost in the most intractable of political milieux, Clem Miller's book is a salute to the fundamental decency of his colleagues in the House and a testament to the sharpness of his sensibilities and the precision of his mind.

MR. REPUBLICAN *

On a sloping lawn near the U.S. Capitol there stands an imposing hundred-foot tower, a memorial to Senator Robert A. Taft, Republican of Ohio, placed there by unanimous act of Congress two years after Taft's death in 1953. No other member of Congress, past or present, is so honored. In 1957, a special bipartisan committee of the Senate selected Taft as one of the five most significant figures ever to sit in the Senate. Both these signal honors attest to the special esteem in which Taft was held by his colleagues. Son of a President of the United States, several times himself a Presidential hopeful, and leader of his party in Congress, Taft inevitably would attract the attention of a biographer.

It was by no means inevitable, however, that Taft would receive a fair or sympathetic hearing at a biographer's hands. Most of his colleagues respected Taft for his intelligence, his mastery of facts, and his analytical power. Few of them liked him, however, or even knew him well, and many found him stubborn, narrow-mindedly ideological, and cold. "Taft has the best mind in the Senate—until he makes it up," was a famous remark. He is remembered today for the Taft-Hartley bill, a law regulating labor-management relations enacted over President Truman's veto and widely regarded by union people as anti-labor. Taft denounced the Nuremburg trials as ex post facto and encouraged Joseph McCarthy in his assaults on the reputations of persons linked with the State Department. He was the foremost conservative politician of his time, yet he regularly sponsored bills for federally subsidized housing and aid to education. He opposed the excessive interventionism of the Marshall Plan but supported General MacArthur in Korea. As a member of the Yale Corporation he deplored the employment of left-wing professors but demanded that they be left strictly alone in the pursuit of their work. He was

* Review of James T. Patterson, *Mr. Republican: A Biography of Robert A. Taft* (Boston: Houghton Mifflin, 1972).

strongly partisan, a party regular, and highly conventional in his address to most questions, yet fiercely self-reliant and independent in his drive to master issues and present them in his own way. He wrote all his own speeches. And for all his conventionality he was never a religious man. He was for years an undisputed leader in an institution known far and wide as the world's most exclusive gentlemen's club, yet in his personal relations he was relentlessly unclubable—awkward, shy, and brusque.

James T. Patterson has done even-handed justice to this remarkable mélange of characteristics, neither forcing an interpretation upon recalcitrant contradictions in his subject's character, nor permitting an undue fascination with warts to obscure the main features of Taft's portrait. Patterson, whose previous work was on the conservative coalition in Congress, enjoyed the full co-operation of the Taft family, and exclusive access to a formidable treasure-trove of family documents. In addition he seems to have combed through or interviewed every other plausible source for letters, diaries, and recollections. Although he has written an authorized biography, it is nevertheless an independent work of scholarship.

Two features in particular distinguish the book: Patterson shows a remarkably thorough grasp of the dynamics of Congressional politics and of national politics more generally throughout the entire sixty-year period of his narrative. And he is absolutely fair-minded in discussing the activities of Taft and his contemporaries. It is now fashionable in historical writing to commit the sin of anachronism, in which the historian parades his knowledge of how things turned out—plus his presumably superior moral insight—so as retrospectively to weigh and judge the acts of his subjects. By scrupulously refraining from any such nonsense Patterson has immeasurably enhanced the value of his book. He has also produced a well-informed and illuminating portrait of a significant American and the politics of his times.

IN THE FULLNESS OF TIME *

Paul H. Douglas is certainly one of the most remarkable public men of our time. Born and brought up a rural New Englander, he became a champion of Middle Western city dwellers as Senator from Illinois from 1948 to 1966. An indefatigable and independent crusader for lost causes in the Chicago City Council, he got his start in politics from the Kelly-Nash machine, and was boosted to the Senate by Jack Arvey. A deeply committed Senatorial supporter of liberal programs, he passionately attacked wasteful governmental spending. A Quaker, he enlisted in the Marines at age fifty, requested combat, and was wounded and decorated in World War II. A University of Chicago intellectual, he was a tireless grass-roots campaigner—especially in the small towns of downstate Illinois.

Amid these and other contradictions, it is perhaps most remarkable that Douglas himself has always seemed to observers to be all of a piece—not a conventional politician, surely, or easy to categorize or predict, but nevertheless possessed of a firmness of character that embraces disparate impulses and influences and resolves them in a definite and individual way. This is a quality that sometimes goes by the name integrity. From first to last in a long life of public service Paul Douglas has been conspicuous in his display of that singular quality, and it is apparent in his memoirs as well.

There is no need to labor a comparison between memoirs of the kind Douglas has produced and the ordinary run of politicians' recollections. I do not recall an American politician ever saying in a public place as Douglas does, "I have always feared the emergence of some of my father's traits in me" (p. 5), and yet it is hard to believe that in the dead of night some other American public figures might not also harbor such thoughts. As

* Review of *In the Fullness of Time: The Memoirs of Paul H. Douglas* (New York: Harcourt Brace Jovanovich, 1972).

a relatively young man Douglas found, "I had allowed my career and public concerns to crowd out family responsibilities. In later years I paid a heavy price for the tenuousness of my relations with the children" (p. 70). Here, Douglas speaks softly but directly to one of the serious hidden problems of public service in America. People who hang around politicians—especially in Washington—know this occupational hazard exists on a large scale. Yet it is rarely faced and almost never ventilated.

Small revelations of this sort do not occupy much of the book. They do, however, powerfully attest to the candor of the author, and give a special value to the highly individual comments he makes on less private matters.

For example, garden variety liberals, on reading this book, may be intrigued to find the furnishings in their pantheon slightly rearranged. Douglas pays a touching tribute to Herbert Lehman, Jerry Voorhis, and Frank Graham, in all of whom he found a strain of curiously admirable self-destructiveness. Ed Kelly, Richard Daley, and Jack Arvey, a somewhat less quixotic trio, also receive good notices. Douglas disliked Adlai Stevenson, on the other hand, and gives a view of Stevenson pretty much unavailable elsewhere.

Observant as he is of personalities, Douglas, more than most public men, was engaged in the life of the mind, until the age of fifty-six as a working economist and teacher of great distinction. Regrettably Douglas skips over the bulk of his professional life, thus depriving us of more than a glimpse of the University of Chicago during one of its golden periods. It is hard to believe that an enthusiastic participator like Douglas failed to swim in the mainstream of the corporate life of his department, his university, and the economics profession, but if he did, he gives no record of it here.

After 1948, when Douglas was elected to the Senate, the account is much fuller. Each of the myriad issues in which Douglas played a major role is recalled in impressive detail. During the 1950's a full-dress Douglas Senate speech on any topic, no matter how complex, was a special occasion. In his capacity to marshal evidence and march an argument to an inescapable conclusion

Douglas had few peers and no superiors. In his memoirs he retains the great teacher's gift of clarifying the main issues while describing their disposition by the Congress. Here, in the heart of his book, Douglas has created a valuable record of the vicissitudes of liberalism in the critical years of struggle that preceded the harvest of the 89th Congress.

Without those years of effort, I doubt that there would have been anything to harvest when the opportunity finally arose after the 1964 election. In remembering these years, Paul Douglas not only reminds civilized Americans of their enormous debt to him, but makes a fresh claim on their gratitude.

A NOTE ON THE PRESIDENT'S
MODEST PROPOSAL

Proposals to "up-date," "streamline," "modernize," or "reform" Congress are not exactly rare. At this moment the Joint Committee on the Organization of Congress is pondering reform proposals; the Brookings Institution has commissioned a number of studies bearing on the subject; so has the American Enterprise Institute; and the American Political Science Association has its Study of Congress. But it is no secret that much of the political steam has gone out of the drive for Congressional reform. This steam was generated in the heat of battle in the 86th Congress, where an overwhelmingly liberal Democratic majority was largely thwarted in its attempts to enact a program. Several years have gone by, and most of the programs lost in that year—and a good many others besides—are now law. Meaningful changes have been introduced piecemeal into the organizational structure, especially into that of the House of Representatives, without drastic institutional reforms.

There is a sense, then, in which the President's proposal in his 1966 State of the Union Address to amend the Constitution, provide four-year terms for Representatives, and elect the entire House and the President together, is something of a surprise.

It is also going to be a political Pandora's box. For no matter how uplifting the rhetoric with which this modest proposal is debated—and if the pieties uttered on the issue so far are any sample, this is going to be an excruciatingly uplifting debate—no man can tell what the political consequences will be if the amendment is enacted. Consider the following twelve predictions, each, in its way, entirely plausible and realistic:

Prediction 1

If enacted, the President's amendment will increase the independence of Congress from the executive branch. In the old days the job of the legislator was a part-time occupation. Frequent elections with their appeal for a renewal of public confidence made a good deal of sense when citizen-legislators lived most of their lives back home, and only briefly and intermittently met at the Capitol to do business. In those days, representation was all a representative did.

In the modern era, Congress meets in almost year-round session. The job of the legislator has lost its amateur standing. The professional legislator spends most of his time in Washington and, in an important sense, the controlling norms of his occupational existence are no longer clustered around the problem of "representation," where he is supposed to reflect the judgment of his local constituency on matters of national policy; as a matter of fact, on most issues his constituents have no guidance to offer him. Nowadays, the central role of the legislator is *deliberative.* In most respects his working life is determined by his committee assignment rather than his constituency case work. The norms that guide him are those imposed by the House as an institution.

Too frequent elections are a genuine disruption in the life of a deliberative body. They distract the member from the highly technical, and politically complicated tasks of formulating, enacting, and disapproving of programs and policies. Campaigning time is time spent away from the Congressman's modern-day job. Lack of a sufficiently long tenure in office means that newly elected members cannot build up expertise quickly; it discourages the recruitment of some of the ablest men, and it leads to the over-all weakening of Congressional influence in governmental policy-making.

The four-year term would, by increasing the stability of Congress, improve its capacity to organize its work, and hence would strengthen Congress within the political system.

Prediction 2

The amendment will increase the dependence of Congress on the executive branch. If all Congressmen must be elected in the same election as the President, the composition of the House is contingent to the maximum degree upon the Presidential candidates' popularity and programs. Individual Congressmen are mostly invisible to their electorates anyway. Only in the mid-term election does the popularity of candidates other than the President matter. By abolishing the mid-term election, Congressmen are cutting a tie to the electorate and staking everything on the local effects of the Presidential race. Hence the amendment increases the dependence of the House on the executive.

Prediction 3

The amendment will increase the technical proficiency and expertise of Congressmen on matters of national policy. By cutting down on the time they have to spend campaigning, Congressmen will get the chance to really dig in on matters of legislative importance.

Prediction 4

The amendment will make no difference in the technical proficiency and expertise of Congressmen. If length of term really mattered, then the Senate with its six-year term would be filled with subject-matter experts. But as a matter of fact it is not; and the House, even with its two-year term, has a great many. Apparently, length of term is nowhere near as important as the fact that the House, being much larger than the Senate, can divide its labor more efficiently, can assign members to one subject area and thus produce specialists.

Prediction 5

The amendment will decrease the costs of elections. It abolishes mid-term House elections; hence there would be no election expenses in those years.

Prediction 6

The amendment will increase the costs of nominations. The four-year term makes the prize more valuable, hence more people will contest nominations, driving up the costs to each contestant, and greatly increasing total costs.

Prediction 7

The amendment will increase party responsibility and facilitate coordination between the Presidential and Congressional wings of the party. With everybody running in the same year, it will be harder for Congressmen to avoid endorsing the Presidential platform. A President has a better opportunity to carry into office with him a House that shares his goals and policies.

Prediction 8

The amendment will make no difference in party responsibility. The distribution of safe House seats will remain roughly the same. Sectional and regional problems will be unchanged by the amendment. President Eisenhower could not carry Congress in 1956; and President Kennedy would have been much better off if he could have served with the House that was elected in the mid-term of 1958 than with the House elected with him in 1960. The amendment does not affect the seniority system, the committee system, or the Rules of the House, which from time to time have worked against party coordination between the House and the President.

Prediction 9

The amendment will increase the advantages of running in competitive districts. The four-year term makes *any* Congressional seat more attractive. It means that men in competitive districts will not have to spend all their spare time campaigning, as is now the case.

Prediction 10

The amendment will decrease the advantages of running in competitive districts. By hard work, a Congressman can turn a district that is marginal when he first wins his seat, and competitive between the parties for other offices, into a safe district *for him*. The mid-term election is one important instrument he can use for this purpose. It is an election where more attention focuses upon him and his incumbency. The election legitimizes overt politicking and publicity-seeking. It gives the Congressman an opportunity to mobilize his supporters and to make friends. The abolition of the mid-term election means that the Congressman from the competitive district is never on his own, but must always suffer the local consequences—whether for good or ill—of the Presidential race.

Prediction 11

The amendment will decrease the influence of local special interest groups. Because the number of elections is cut in half, the financial burden on Congressmen of campaigning is less, and therefore they need to worry less about compromising themselves to special interests in return for campaign funds.

Prediction 12

The amendment will increase the influence of local special interest groups. In a Presidential election year, most of the money that is raised nationally goes to national candidates and their enormous expenses. The Congressional candidate thus has to raise money for his own campaign primarily within the district. The needs of the national campaign make him *more* dependent rather than less dependent on local financial support.

The alert reader will see that not all of these predictions can be wholly true, for each is contradicted by at least one other. The "benefits" that are supposed to flow from this Constitutional reform, it appears, may or may not flow.

Senators, meanwhile, are certain to notice an important defect in the proposal from their point of view. The four-year term gives Congressmen a free shot at the Senate. Nowadays a Representative, in order to run for the Senate, must give up his chance to succeed himself, since he cannot also run for re-election to the House at the same time. In the off year, however, when there is no House election, he can challenge the Senator—and possibly beat him—without risking his House seat. It is not an idle threat; over one-third of the present Senate is populated by former Representatives. The administration's draft amendment meets this objection by providing that Representatives must resign if they run for another office. It will be interesting to see if this provision survives the markup in the House

Some observers are sold on the merits of the four-year term, but dislike the feature that ties Congressional to Presidential elections. In an extreme version of a revised proposal, the House could be elected entirely at the mid-term, thus thwarting the possibility of a landslide, such as occurred in 1932 or 1952 or 1964. This proposal also makes any sort of party co-ordination between the branches difficult because the House and the President would be working on completely different time-schedules. A less extreme proposal would preserve the four-year term but elect half the House every two years. This would create two classes of Congressmen: those always elected in the mid-term and those elected with the President. One wonders on what basis membership in these two classes would be distributed among the states. Would Southern Democrats and senior Republicans get all the off-year gravy?

A third possibility, which meets most of these objections, would be to elect Congressmen for staggered two- and four-year terms, thus periodically bringing each Representative up for election in Presidential years with elections at the mid-term interspersed. The main difficulty with this proposal is that it deprives the President of the opportunity to score heavily in the House when he is elected by a landslide, because only two-thirds of the House would be elected at any one election under the system.

All this sort of discussion proceeds upon the unacknowledged premise that we are reasonably sure of the role of the House in our scheme of government, and that Congressional elections are primarily a nuisance and not in and of themselves terribly meaningful. I suggest that they may be. They confer legitimacy upon the acts of government.

Our government, to be sure, receives the consent of the governed in many ways: by widespread obedience to law, by patriotic affirmations of all kinds, by the participation of people, groups and interests in all the various aspects of the political process. But in the political process, elections are especially important. They are highly formal and ritualized. They engage the attention and involvement of large numbers of people. They are often contested between well-organized parties. And so they elicit the commitment of citizens.

Frequent elections provide occasions for reaffirmation of commitment, and also for the channeling of discontent with the way the incumbent government is doing its job. With all the inconvenience they entail to Presidents who like very long sessions of Congress, and to Congressmen who find all of their time occupied by demands of some kind or other, I do not see how a stable, modern democracy that means to stay that way can do without frequent elections. The two-year interval, while it is certainly not a magic number, has one distinct advantage: it is on the books.

It is singularly puzzling that President Johnson, who has gotten so much co-operation from Congress, should advocate a change. He may, before debate on this matter is over, have reason to recall that the last time a President overtly tinkered with Constitutional checks and balances was in 1937 when Franklin Roosevelt came forward with a plan to "modernize" the Supreme Court.

Ask any man in the street what's wrong with Congress, and he will tell you the trouble is the seniority system. Don't ask him what the seniority system is, though, because chances are he won't be able to tell you. Most people are surprised, for example, when they find out that the Speaker is not the most senior member of the House, that the Majority Leader in the House is currently the 32nd most senior Democrat, and that his assistant actually outranks him by two places.* The same is true in the Senate: Democratic Leader Mike Mansfield is tied for 20th-ranked Senator, well behind his assistant, Russell Long. Republican Leader Everett Dirksen is the ninth-ranking Republican in the Senate. A few years ago, House Republicans removed their most senior member, the late Joe Martin, from the Leadership and replaced him with a more junior man. Then a couple of years later, they repeated the process; their current Leader is the relatively youthful Gerald Ford.

Out of all the decisions, big and small, that get made on Capitol Hill, only one set is determined strictly by seniority. This has

---

* The bare facts as recited in this and succeeding sentences in this paragraph were, of course, correct on the day this article was first printed (September 26, 1968) but have since changed: Senate Majority Leader Mike Mansfield endures, but his assistant is no longer Russell Long, who as a matter of fact was beaten out of the job by somebody quite junior to him, Edward Kennedy. Kennedy, in turn, was knocked off in a hotly contested election by Robert Byrd of West Virginia, also a relatively junior Senator. Everett Dirksen has been replaced by Hugh Scott, who is not the most senior Republican. On the House side, the Speaker was then John McCormack of Massachusetts; it is now Carl Albert of Oklahoma, who was Majority Leader. Hale Boggs of Louisiana, then Majority Whip, succeeded to the majority leadership (although he was senior to Albert) and was lost and presumed killed in an airplane over Alaskan waters. His successor as Majority Leader, Thomas P. O'Neill of Massachusetts, is a man of medium-high seniority.

Regardless of the details on the day this essay is read, the underlying principle should be clear: strict seniority does not determine who the party leaders of both houses of Congress are. These leaders are elected from and by the members of each caucus in each house.

to do with the committee assignments of Congressmen and Senators once they are appointed to a committee. Initial appointments to committees do not go by strict seniority, but by bargaining among individual members, their state party delegations, and the party committees on committees. The seniority of the member normally counts for only a little; the committee on committees is much more concerned about regional representation on the committee and the candidate's political experience and ideological position. Once a Congressman or Senator has a committee assignment, it is his. He can be persuaded, perhaps, to switch to a low-ranked position on a more desirable committee, but he is not subject to removal. When vacancies occur up the line, he moves up, and new-comers appointed after him sit below him at the committee table. Each party takes a side of the table, and has its own hierarchy of seniority. At the head of the table sits the chairman, the member of the majority party with the longest consecutive service on the committee. Next to him sits the ranking member, the minority party member with longest service. If at the next election the minority party wins enough seats in Congress, the ranking member becomes the chairman and the present chairman becomes ranking member. That, in a nutshell, is seniority.

Why all the fuss? Mainly, because committee chairmen have a lot of power. They are the executive officers of their committees. They hire and fire committee staff (not the elected members, who are appointed by committees on committees just as chairmen are, but professional and clerical personnel who do most of the day to day work of the committee). It is pretty much up to the chairman how fast bills are considered, and, outside of top priority items in the President's program, which ones. Committee chairmen sit on all conference committees between the houses, run the hearings that form the background of committee deliberations, and determine the number, the makeup, and the jurisdictions of subcommittees. When they want to, they can put their personal stamp on each and every bill their committee considers.

There are twenty-one standing committees in the House, sixteen in the Senate, and a few joint committees. Every bill debated in either house has first been considered in a committee; every bill introduced (over 10,000 a session) is referred to a committee in each House. Needless to say, most bills never emerge from committee. So the committees are powerful because everything that Congress does is filtered through them. And committee chairmen, who get to be chairmen by seniority, are powerful because committees are powerful.

So the question arises: considering the importance of committees in the Congressional process, isn't seniority a pretty haphazard way to choose committee chairmen? Defenders of the system claim that the haphazardness of the system is its great advantage. Consider some alternatives. Suppose the Speaker chose the committees and the chairmen in the House, as he did before the famous revolt of 1910 took the power to do so away from Speaker Joseph Cannon. In those days, members of the House used to complain about partisan manipulation and arbitrary treatment in committee assignments.

The same complaints were made in the early 1960's, when Senate Democrats got rid of seniority as an inflexible rule in the making of initial committee assignments. Senator Joseph Clark, among others, objected in a famous speech and then wrote a book about the Senate Establishment, as he called it, that was showing favoritism in passing assignments out.

This is the heart of the problem. Strict seniority as a method of determining committee rank selects chairmen by an impersonal, automatic process. Quite often, the results are entirely satisfactory. For example, nobody disputes the mastery of Wilbur Mills, chairman of the House Ways and Means Committee, over his committee's subject matter—which happens to be taxes. Sometimes, the results are unfortunate. From time to time a chairman of a major committee is physically incapable of carrying out his tasks. Leadership in such cases usually devolves *de facto* upon the next ranking member, but he can hardly exercise vigorous or innovative leadership. Sometimes the results are painful, as when a man deeply antagonistic to the legislation referred to his committee becomes chairman.

Presumably, incompetent or dissident chairmen could be avoided if some selection process other than seniority were used.

But it still would be up to the people who chose committee chairmen to decide whether they wanted strong committee leadership on each committee or not. And they might very well not.

A number of proposals have been made to modify the effects of seniority without doing away with it altogether. Two Congressmen, Morris Udall and Richard Bolling, have suggested plans for electing committee chairmen in the House by secret ballot. In the Udall plan the three most senior committee members of the majority party would automatically be nominees for chairman, thus preserving a certain amount of automation in the process and also giving due weight to the value of accumulated experience in dealing with the committee's subject matter. Members of the majority party caucus would vote by secret ballot. This would introduce an incentive for chairmen to be responsive to policies favored by rank and file party members. In Bolling's scheme the chairmen would be selected by the Speaker, subject to a vote of the entire party caucus. Both schemes are designed to remind each chairman of his responsibilities to the majority of the majority party in the House as a whole. Another variant would have the vote taken by committee members of the majority party, and still another would provide a vote by secret ballot by committee members of both parties. Of course this would encourage majority coalitions to cross party lines; in the past coalitions like these have often resulted in stopping legislation favored by the majority of the majority party. Thus advocates of different reforms operate from different premises about which majority is more legitimate: the majority of the majority party in committee or in the House, or the majority of the whole House.

Congress is one of the few legislatures in world history to use any form of seniority system to staff important policy-making posts. But Congress is also probably the most powerful legislature the world has ever seen. And the secret of its power, in the face of a powerful Presidency, a powerful court system, and powerful bureaucracies, is its method of dividing labor among committees that specialize in their subject matter. A seniority system gives a Congressman a great incentive to learn his committee's subject matter specialty. Naturally, job security does not always lead to competence, but job insecurity might well guarantee the opposite. And the seniority system does reward ability in enough cases to suggest that Congress might well be giving up some of its power within the political system if seniority was abolished.

If it were modified, however, the result would undoubtedly fall short of a catastrophe. Reform of the seniority custom would almost certainly play some part in any modification of the process by which chairmen were chosen.

But there is not much likelihood of sweeping change. Representatives and Senators start off their Congressional careers resenting the seniority system. But after a while, as one of them once told me, "it sort of begins to grow on you."

TWO STRATEGIES OF INFLUENCE
IN THE
HOUSE OF REPRESENTATIVES *

Political scientists seem to be fond of debating whether traditional political theory in America is dead or only sleeping.[1] Either way, there is no argument that the speculations which occupied thinkers of other days have been little used to illuminate current political behavior. The argument, when there is one, concerns whether it is even possible to use traditional political theory in this way. Regrettably, optimists on this point have not always demonstrated that they were right in supposing that traditional political theory could contribute to the understanding of present-day politics. But this does not mean that they are wrong.

A major obstacle to the use of traditional political theory in modern political science has been theory's long-standing concern with prescriptive statements. Prescriptions are not necessarily the best instruments for organizing information about the empirical world, since the preferences which they assert may not correspond to any observed (or even observable) events. However,

* This paper was originally presented at the annual meetings of The American Political Science Association, Washington, D.C., 1962. Several members of Congress, who I am sure would prefer to remain anonymous, read an early draft of this chapter and made many useful comments. I should also like to thank Lewis A. Dexter, H. Douglas Price, and Robert L. Peabody. Others who have been helpful include Aaron B. Wildavsky, Lewis A. Froman, Jr., Norman O. Brown, Luigi Einaudi, Joseph Cooper, Alan L. Otten, and Neil MacNeil. Research assistance was provided by a Ford Foundation grant to Wesleyan University.

[1] The phrase "traditional political theory" refers in this context to the history of political thinking rather than to any specific political doctrines. See, for example, David Easton, *The Political System* (New York: Knopf, 1953); Harry V. Jaffa, "The Case Against Political Theory," *Journal of Politics*, XXII (May, 1960), 259–75; Robert A. Dahl, "The Science of Politics, New and Old," *World Politics*, VII (April, 1955), 479–89; Dahl, "Political Theory, Truth and Consequences," *World Politics*, XI (October, 1958), 89–102; Norman Jacobson, "The Unity of Political Theory," in R. Young (ed.), *Approaches to the Study of Politics* (Evanston: Northwestern University Press, 1958), pp. 115–24.

prescriptions may in fact point to quite interesting and genuine dilemmas in the real world. In these circumstances, we have the option of converting the language of prescription to that of description if we desire to put traditional political theory to more modern uses.

The possibilities of this device have lately been explored by a group of students of the legislative process, using as their text the celebrated speech to the Electors of Bristol by Edmund Burke.[2] In this speech, on the occasion of his election as Member of Parliament from Bristol, it will be recalled that Burke undertook to state and resolve a recurring dilemma of the representative:

> Certainly, gentlemen, it ought to be the happiness and glory of a representative to live in the strictest union, the closest correspondence, and the most unreserved communication with his constitutents. Their wishes ought to have great weight with him; their opinion high respect; their business unremitted attention. . . . But his unbiased opinion, his native judgment, his enlightened conscience he ought not to sacrifice to you. . . . Your representative owes you, not his industry only, but his judgment. . . . Government and legislation are matters of reason and judgment, and not of inclination; and what sort of reason is that, in which the determination precedes the discussion; in which one set of men deliberate and another decide . . . Parliament is not a *congress* of ambassadors from different and hostile interests . . . but a *deliberative* assembly of *one* nation. . . . We are now members for a rich commercial city; this city, however, is but part of a rich commercial nation, the interests of which are various, multiform, and intricate. . . . All these widespread interests must be considered; must be compared; must be reconciled if possible.[3]

Six years after Burke spoke these words, he stood for election once again, and on the same topic said:

> I could wish undoubtedly . . . to make every part of my conduct agreeable to every one of my constitutents. . . . But . . . do you

[2] Heinz Eulau, John C. Wahlke, Leroy C. Ferguson, and William Buchanan, "The Role of the Representative: Some Empirical Observations on the Theory of Edmund Burke," *American Political Science Review*, LIII (September, 1959), 742–56.
[3] "Speech to the Electors of Bristol," November 3, 1774, *Works* (London: Oxford University Press, 1906), II, 164–66.

think, gentlemen, that every public act in six years since I stood in this place before you—that all the arduous things which have been done in this eventful period, which has crowded into a few years' space the revolutions of an age—can be opened to you on their fair grounds in half an hour's conversation? . . . Let me say with plainness . . . that if by a fair, by an indulgent, by a gentlemanly behavior to our representatives, we do not give confidence to their minds, and a liberal scope to their understandings; if we do not permit our members to act upon a *very* enlarged view of things, we shall at length infallibly degrade our national representation into a confused and scuffling bustle of local agency.[4]

A brief historical detour will suggest certain empirical problems related to Burke's position. Shortly after the second speech quoted here, Burke withdrew his candidacy, feeling he could not win. He and his constituents had disagreed over several matters, in particular his vote to free Irish trade from restrictions operating in favor of Bristol. Burke remained in Parliament, however, representing a pocket borough thereafter.[5] Although acting on his principle of independence from constitutent pressures was costly to him, Burke was clearly in a position to take a more luxurious stand on such a question than another member could who did not have the protection of a pocket borough and the party list.

This raises still a more general empirical point: Under what conditions will a representative be more likely to respond to the demands of "local agency"? When is he more likely to respond to a political situation as it appears to him in the light of his experience at the seat of government? Under what conditions will attempts to influence the representative through his constituency bring better results than attempts to influence him through the network of loyalties and affiliations he has built up through service in his deliberative body—and vice versa?

The United States House of Representatives is one laboratory for the exploration of questions such as these. Indeed, where the stakes are as high as they often are in House decision-making, it is not surprising that full-scale campaigns are mounted in order to

[4] "Speech at Bristol," September 6, 1780, *ibid.*, III, 2, 3, 4.
[5] *Ibid.*, and F. W. Raffety, "Preface" in *Works*, II, xiv–xv.

sway sometimes no more than a handful of marginal votes. But are these votes swayed from the inside or the outside? Do constituencies matter more or less than colleagues? [6]

Sometimes the answer is reasonably clear and unequivocal. Here are examples of *inside* influences at work:

> Representative Cleveland Bailey is a genuinely dedicated opponent of reciprocal trade. . . . [He] is unusual among members—probably unique—in that protection is *the* most important issue to him and that he creates the sense of having a deep felt conviction on the subject. In 1953–54 he went around and pled individually with a number of members to vote against reciprocal trade and for the West Virginia miners. One member put it, "He was rough, real rough. . . . I had to be rough with him." Another said, "In the 1954 vote, Cleve Bailey was worth 15 votes to his side easily." [7]

> The morning of one of the key votes on reciprocal trade [1955], Speaker Sam Rayburn attended a breakfast of the freshman Democrats in the House. I asked one of the Congressmen who was there about it. He chuckled: "Oh, you heard about that? . . . We'd just invited Mr. Sam to this breakfast. He turned it into a sort of speech and said he'd observed that *generally the new members got along better who went along*, but he didn't make any particular application—of course you could guess what he had in mind. . . ." [8]

On the other hand, it is sometimes possible to detect *outside* influences. The following example comes from the January, 1961, battle over the size of the House Rules Committee:

> It was learned that Representative Howard Smith, Southern leader and Rules Committee Chairman, has held several meetings in his office in recent weeks with representatives of the most powerful conservative lobbies in the country, trying to shape a campaign to beat Rayburn by applying pressure on members from home. The groups included the National Association of Manufacturers, the

[6] One approach to some of these questions was made by Julius Turner, who used the analysis of roll calls as his major source of data in *Party and Constituency: Pressures on Congress* (Baltimore: Johns Hopkins, 1951). See also David B. Truman, *The Congressional Party* (New York: Wiley, 1959).
[7] Lewis Anthony Dexter, "Congressmen and the People They Listen to" (Cambridge: Center for International Studies, Massachusetts Institute of Technology, Ditto, 1955), chap. ii, p. 14, chap. viii, p. 7.
[8] *Ibid.*, chap. v, pp. 4–5.

United States Chamber of Commerce, the American Medical Association and the American Farm Bureau. . . . Some members have reported heavy mail from business interests in their home districts. . . . On the other side, Northern Democrats have sent out an appeal to organized labor for help. Yesterday, Andrew J. Biemiller, chief AFL-CIO lobbyist, was at the Capitol trying to line up votes. . . .[9]

During the aid to education debate [a Roman Catholic Congressman] threatened to kill the public school measure by tagging on to it a parochial school amendment. [Presidential Assistant Lawrence] O'Brien appealed to [the Congressman's home district party leader] who immediately telephoned [the Congressman]. "Who sent you there, me or the Bishop?" he growled. "And who's going to keep you there, me or the Bishop?" [10]

At other times strong inside and outside influences are blurred together quite inextricably:

A newspaper correspondent told me: "Oh yes, you know those two boys [Congressmen] . . . well you know why Jack voted against the leadership? Just to oblige Joe to whom he's very close; Joe was afraid he'd be the only fellow from the state to vote against the leadership and he'd get into trouble with the leadership and the party organization so Jack went along with him to prevent his sticking his neck out all alone. . . ." [11]

The whip from the area told me . . . "Tom rather wanted to go along with the leadership, but he found Dave and Don and four other guys from surrounding districts were against the leadership, and he decided he'd better go along with them, because after all he's hearing a lot from his district against it, and how could he explain his being for it and Dave and Don and the rest being against it?" [12]

[9] Richard L. Lyons, "Pressure Rises as House Moves To Vote on Rules," *Washington Post*, January 31, 1961.
[10] *Time* (September 1, 1961), p. 14. The Congressman is not identified here, as he was in the *Time* article, first, because he denies the conversation took place (*Congressional Record*, 87th Cong., 1st sess. [August 29, 1961], p. 16318) and second, because the *Time* reporter's source for the quote told me that he had deliberately left ambiguous the identity of the Congressman, and, while the event really happened, the *Time* reporter was misled about whom it happened to.
[11] Dexter, *op. cit.*, chap. viii, p. 4.
[12] *Ibid.*, pp. 4–5.

The recent contest for the majority leadership of the House provides, as it happens, a rather good contrast between the two strategies of influence. In turn, the close examination of this case may begin to suggest answers to some of the questions posed above.

I

On January 10, 1962, the Democratic members of the House met in caucus in the House chamber and nominated John McCormack as their candidate for Speaker. Immediately following the conclusion of this business, Richard Bolling of Missouri asked that the agenda of the caucus be expanded by unanimous consent to include the selection of a Majority Leader, and Carl Albert of Oklahoma, his party's whip and the only Congressman put in nomination, was elected to that post. Thus ended a period of skirmishing for the Majority Leadership that had principally engaged Bolling and Albert from the time of Speaker Rayburn's death on November 16 of the previous year.

Most newspaper coverage of this event gave the impression that the battle between these two men was drawn on liberal-conservative lines. In Bolling's press conference on January 3 announcing his withdrawal from the race, newsmen repeatedly suggested that the contrast between them was predominantly ideological. A newspaperwoman asked, rhetorically, "Don't the liberals *ever* win around here, Mr. Bolling?" Another widely quoted colloquy went:

Reporter: "Mr. Bolling, do you regard your withdrawal . . . as a defeat for liberalism?"

Bolling: "Well, I consider myself a liberal, and at the moment I certainly feel defeated." [13]

Close observation suggests that the liberal-conservative distinction has only a limited kind of utility for understanding the Bolling-Albert fight for the majority leadership.[14] It is not necessary

[13] The best news coverage by far of this press conference that I saw occurred in the *Baltimore Sun*, January 4, 1962. See Rodney Crowther, "House Race Dropped by Bolling."

[14] Pursuit of this line of thinking at a McCormack-Albert press conference, January 9, visibly irked Mr. McCormack. "A reporter . . . caught [Mr. McCormack] at the door of the Speaker's lobby and asked him if he had asked for complete sup-

to base this conclusion on a *Congressional Quarterly* tabulation showing that Albert supported the Kennedy program 91 per cent of the time in the first session of the 87th Congress and Bolling 94 per cent—a fact continually cited by liberal supporters of Mr. Albert.[15] Equally significant are the facts, first, that Albert indeed had a great deal of support among members with impeccably liberal records of long standing and, second, that he was regarded at the White House as a genuine friend of the Kennedy program.[16]

If, then, the outcome of the Bolling-Albert contest cannot be explained by the usual ideological arithmetic one uses in analyzing the House, how can one explain what happened? In part, an explanation can be based on the strategies each of the main actors pursued. These strategies were in turn largely dictated by their respective positions and roles in the House during the final years of the Rayburn Speakership.

Often great differences in resources between political actors are largely nullified by the fact that resources are generally employed at low levels of intensity and with indifferent skill. In this case, however, resources on both sides were employed with considerable skill and finessse, and hence the outcome comes closer to reflecting a common-sense notion of the logic of the situation than might otherwise have been the case. It makes sense to describe the "cards" that each man held because, in this instance, the man

port of President Kennedy's program. The new Speaker drew back indignantly. 'I'm not trying to put words in your mouth,' said the reporter. 'Yes you are,' said Mr. McCormack, 'I've been voting for progressive legislation for 30 years. I'm not a one-year man. Why don't you wake up?' " Mary McGrory, "McCormack Speaks as His Own Master," *Washington Star*, January 10, 1962.

[15] *Congressional Quarterly*, XIX (November 24, 1961), 1893–94. This tabulation also shows that throughout their careers in Congress, the voting records of these men were quite close by several criteria.

[16] These statements, and many others throughout this paper, are based on interviews and observations gathered during the summer of 1961 and from December to February, 1961–62, in Washington. During these months I spoke on matters connected with the subject of this paper to over 100 Congressmen, Congressional aides, newspapermen, and others, and during the latter period, I conducted interviews with twenty-six Democratic Congressmen from all sections of the country on the Leadership selection process then going on. Quotations are from notes taken during these interviews, and are occasionally slightly altered so as to preserve the anonymity of the respondent. My work in the summer of 1961 was supported by a grant-in-aid from the Social Science Research Council, whose assistance is gratefully acknowledged.

who held the better cards made no more mistakes than his opponent, and, in the end, he won.

It is worth stressing that only part of the explanation can be given by referring to the roles and strategies of the main participants and to the different ways in which their demands were communicated to other House members. Two other significant variables can be sketched in only very crudely. This battle took place in the very core of an institution about whose habits and practices precious little is known, and, second, it engaged the participation of a great many more facets of the human personality than political decisions in the House normally do. The mysteries of how men interact with one another, of what leads people into enmity, jealousy, friendship, all seem to me to have played a very significant part in this contest. Obviously, the extent to which the outside observer can detect and extract meaning from these relationships is extremely limited, and this must inevitably weaken the plausibility and also the generality of the case I am about to construct, using, for the most part, more readily accessible materials.

II

The realization that Speaker Rayburn's health was failing seriously dawned on different members of the House at different times during the summer of 1961. That summer happened to have been an extremely hot and humid one in Washington. The House stayed in session continuously through the summer, one of the longest, bitterest, and most grueling sessions in the memory of veterans on Capitol Hill.[17] Over the course of this period, many members and observers, especially those who were close to the Speaker, could not help but notice the wasting of Mr. Rayburn's solid, imposing figure, the occasional, uncharacteristic wandering of his attention from the business of the House, his increased susceptibility to bouts of fatigue and irritability, the slowing of his gait.

[17] The session lasted 277 days, the longest in ten years. Late one especially debilitating August afternoon, an elderly Southern Congressman shuffled over to where I was standing just outside the Speaker's lobby, and confided that he was going to sponsor a bill that would abolish the final month of each session of Congress.

The House is, in the words of one of its members, a "Council of Elders." It honors age and places much power and trust in the hands of its most senior and oldest men. One consequence of this fact is the necessary, calm preoccupation of members—especially those just below the top rungs of power—with the inevitable occurrence of death. To that large fraction of members for whom the House is a career and a vocation, the longevity of members above them in the many hierarchies of the House—not the entirely predictable Congressional election returns in their home districts—is the key to the political future. This is not to say that members habitually rub their hands ghoulishly or enjoy the prospect of losing valued friends, but only that the norms and the rules of the House bring due rewards to men who accept the world as it is, who prudently make their plans and bide their time.

On the other hand, informal norms of the House also put constraints on members based on commonly accepted notions of decent behavior, decorum, and good taste. Hence it is impossible for an outsider to say when Mr. Albert and Mr. Bolling began thinking in any concrete way about the next step in their careers within the House. However, it seems safe to make two assumptions: First, that they each had entertained some general thoughts on the question of the Majority Leadership well in advance of the occurrence of an actual vacancy (on January 9) or probable vacancy (on November 16) in the position. Second, both men knew Speaker Rayburn well, and both undoubtedly guessed earlier than most members that his health had permanently disintegrated.

III

On Saturday, November 18, Sam Rayburn was buried in Bonham, Texas. Mr. Albert reports that he had planned to wait until the following Wednesday to begin his campaign for Majority Leader. "I was in my office in McAlester on Sunday night," Mr. Albert said, "when Charlie Ward [his assistant] came in and said, 'Bolling has announced for Majority Leader.' I heard it on the radio that night and saw a copy of the press release from my hometown paper before I announced myself. It was an Associated

Press report, and Bill Arbogast [who covers the House for AP] wrote the story."

As a result of this turn of events, Mr. Albert got into the race sooner than he had intended. Mr. Bolling had thrown down a challenge which he could ignore only at his peril. In addition, Mr. Bolling's action offered Mr. Albert an opportunity to run a campaign against him; rather than against any of the more popular or more senior members who had been mentioned for leadership positions.

To each side it appeared that the other had begun to make plans well before Mr. Rayburn's death. Observers partial to Mr. Albert noted that as long before as the previous spring, Mr. Bolling was being referred to in public as a prominent contender for a leadership post.[18] It was easy to infer that, at least in part, these references had been suggested or "inspired" by Mr. Bolling. On the other hand, observers partial to Mr. Bolling thought an alliance between Mr. Albert and the Speaker-to-be, John McCormack, was being announced when Mr. Albert, as his chief deputy, led the tributes on September 26, 1961, in honor of Mr. McCormack's twenty-one years as Majority Leader.[19]

It seems plausible to suggest that the signs and portents friends of both men were reading did not reflect conscious efforts by either man to organize a premature campaign for the Majority Leadership. Rather, each man appealed particularly to slightly different publics: Bolling to the press corps, Albert to various groups within the House itself. These groups may, without encouragement from either man, have initiated activity designed to facilitate their chances of advancement. "After Mr. Rayburn went home to Texas," Mr. Albert reported, "I had fifty or sixty members pull me aside and say to me, 'He's not coming back. Don't sit there and be done out of what you're entitled to.' But I refused to discuss the matter with them." Several members men-

---

[18] For example, Mr. Bolling was introduced to a large public meeting at the Midwest Conference of Political Scientists on May 11, 1961, as "the next Speaker of the House of Representatives."

[19] Mr. Albert's tribute on this occasion was much more elaborate than that tendered by any other member—save by Mr. McCormack's Massachusetts colleagues. See the *Congressional Record*, 87th Cong., 1st sess. (September 26, 1961), pp. 20084–96.

tioned that they had volunteered their support to Mr. Albert, and some, apparently, had attempted to persuade him to run for Speaker. "I would never do that against John McCormack," Mr. Albert said. "Mr. Rayburn and Mr. McCormack picked me and made me whip, and to run against Mr. McCormack would have been the act of an ingrate."

Two groups were especially partial to Mr. Albert: his deputy whip organization and colleagues in the Oklahoma delegation. "We make a fetish of the fact that if you scratch one Okie you've scratched all of 'em," one member told me. As soon as Mr. Albert announced that he would run for Majority Leader, the members of the delegation did whatever they could to help his candidacy. The deputy whips gave Mr. Albert a party after Mr. Rayburn had gone to Texas, and attempted, without success, to induce Mr. Albert to begin work on his candidacy at that time.

Mr. Albert's announcement to the press followed the report of Mr. Bolling's by several hours. As soon as the announcement was made, Mr. Albert sent off a telegram to all members asking for their support and began telephoning each of them individually. "I bet you he was on the phone four days running," one member said.

Mr. Albert's intensive telephone campaign began with the west coast members. "James Roosevelt [Congressman from Los Angeles] was the first man I called outside my own delegation," he said. By the end of the first day of telephoning, Mr. Albert thought he had all but five Westerners committed to him. "If I wasn't sure of a senior man in a delegation," Mr. Albert said, "I started with the most junior men and asked them directly to support me. Then I'd work my way up the line so that when the senior man said, 'I'll have to check with my delegation,' I would have something to report to him. Of course on a thing like this, you call your friends first, but I had no set, written-out plan. I don't work that way."

The reasons members gave for suppporting Mr. Albert are quite illuminating. They reflect two dominant themes, both of which illustrate the "inside" quality of his influence. On the one hand, Mr. Albert was his party's whip. Although there is no tradition which dictates that the whip shall be advanced to the Majority Leadership (as there is in promoting the Majority Leader to Speaker) many members felt that Mr. Albert nonetheless was "entitled" to the job by virtue of his six years service in the leadership hierarchy of the House. Some of them said:

> [From a liberal leader:] I made a commitment to Carl based on his years of service as whip, and the fact that he was in line for this job from the standpoint of his long service as whip.
>
> [From a Southwesterner:] Because I feel that he was entitled to it by reason of his effective part in the leadership of the House along with the Speaker and Mr. McCormack, I promised him my support.
>
> [From the elderly dean of a large delegation:] I am a firm believer in the rule that has governed the House for over 100 years, and that is that of seniority. If Congressman McCormack is to be promoted to the Speakership of the House on the premise of his seniority and being in line position, then obviously the Majority Leader and whip should pursue the same course.[20] I have had the honor of being a member of this great body for [many years] . . . and while I would be reluctant to say that the seniority process does not have some imperfections, nevertheless if any other procedure were to be applied, I am inclined to believe that rather a chaotic situation would immediately be evident.

A second theme illustrates Mr. Albert's personal popularity in the House. Many members could cite warm personal ties they had developed with Mr. Albert. The late John Riley of South Carolina said, "Carl Albert married a girl from Columbia, you know, and so he is practically a constituent of mine."

A Northern liberal: "I am in something of a special situation with Carl, since we're the only two members of the House who [belong to an exclusive, honorary organization]."

---

[20] Mr. Albert entered the House in 1947, Mr. Bolling in 1949, making them thirtieth (tied with nine others) and thirty-ninth (tied with nineteen others) in seniority respectively in the Democratic party in the House—not a very great difference. Mr. McCormack, on the other hand, was the beneficiary of a long tradition of advancement from Majority Leader to Speaker, and, in addition, after the death of Speaker Rayburn, was third in seniority. He had never served as whip, incidentally, prior to his service as Majority Leader, nor had Speaker Rayburn. Both Mr. McCormack and Mr. Rayburn had held office for so many years it is highly probable that most members were unaware of the differences in the customs pertaining to the advancement of the Majority Leader and the whip.

A Congressman from a border state said, "In all good conscience, I had to agree to support Carl because of his great help and encouragement to me [on a pet bill]."

A Southwesterner said, "As one of his deputy whips, I feel committed to Carl Albert."

A Southerner: "I committed myself to Carl Albert, who is my neighbor in the House Office Building."

Another Southerner: "My association with Carl Albert has been extremely intimate."

Three men who served with Mr. Albert on committees:

"Carl and I have sat side by side on [our] committee for fifteen years."

"Carl has been very kind to me in the committee work and has done several things for me which have been very important for my people. . . ."

"I sit right next to Carl Albert. . . . We have been close personal friends due to our connection on the committee. . . ."

Another member said, "Ordinarily I'm slow to make commitments, but due to a friendship with Carl which began when we were in the . . . Army together, I told him quite a while back that should he seek the position of Democratic Leader, I would support him."

And some members, not unexpectedly, combined the themes. For example: "He is not only my neighbor but a member of my committee, and with it all a fine, able, conscientious man who has been doing the dirty work for the leadership for a long time. . . ."

It was characteristic of Mr. Albert's "inside" strategy of influence that he used the telephone energetically and extensively himself to make personal contacts with members as quickly as possible. As whip, he was the custodian of a complete set of home, office, and district telephone numbers for each member.[21] One member said:

[21] Mr. Albert's administrative assistant said that this list happened to be in the Washington office while the telephoning was being done from McAlester, Oklahoma, where only the House telephone directory issued to all members was readily available.

Albert got on the phone and tracked me down in the frozen wastes of northern Rockystate the first day after the Speaker was buried. You wouldn't think politicians would fall for that, but many of them did. They were impressed by the fact that he'd called them first. As a result he was able to line up a lot of the members, including many Northern bleeding-heart liberals, in the first few days.

The principal argument which Mr. Albert used in asking the support of almost all the members I spoke with was the fact that he had already received a large number of commitments. This is instructive, because it evokes the almost obsessive preoccupation of Congressmen with "getting along" and not sticking their necks out unnecessarily. "This House gives out no medals for individual bravery," said one Congressman, "except posthumously."

Mr. Albert had an important further asset—the apparent backing of John McCormack. "I have heard McCormack say again and again that we have got to have a team player," one Congressman said. "I guess he means by that a member of his team, and I suppose he favors Carl Albert." I asked a newspaperman who was following the situation closely to tell me who the most important Congressman on Mr. Albert's side was, and he replied, "John McCormack." However, I could find no evidence that Mr. McCormack gave Mr. Albert any public endorsement.

Describing his campaign, Mr. Albert said:

> I didn't want to hurt Mr. Bolling's feelings. I never once threw knives or wrote mean things, although plenty of knives got thrown at me. I never once got on television. The sum total of my national publicity was a release when I got into the race and a release when I got up to Washington saying I thought I had enough votes to win. I refused to go on television although I was invited to go on most of the news and panel shows. I never mentioned Bolling's name at all. I never mentioned issues or anything. . . .

IV

Mr. Bolling's campaign, in contrast, followed an "outside" strategy of influence. As in the Rules Committee fight at the opening of the 87th Congress and on numerous other occasions where he had planned legislative strategy and tactics, he held aloof from direct contact with most members. "I seldom try to persuade people directly," he said. "Our districts persuade us—if we are going to be persuaded at all."

Bolling had an uphill battle on his hands. He was severely handicapped at the start by his unwillingness to do anything in his own behalf until well after the Speaker had died. "It's a funny thing that Dick was so dilatory," a friend said. Although he leaked an announcement of his candidacy for the Majority Leadership to the press on November 19, the day after the Speaker's funeral, it was not until November 28 that he sent a strikingly diffident letter to each of the Democrats in the House. This letter said:

> Just a note to confirm that I am running for Democratic floor leader and am seeking the support of my Democratic colleagues for that position. Reports during the past week have been encouraging and I am in this contest all the way.
>
> I am running on my legislative record and experience and hope that you will give my candidacy your consideration on that basis.

Several of his supporters expressed surprise at the mildness of this approach. The letter asked for "consideration," not support, and was not followed by an energetic telephone campaign. Furthermore, Bolling had waited twelve precious days after the Speaker's death before making his move. Why?

Answers to a question of motive such as this one—even the answers given by Mr. Bolling himself—are bound to verge on speculation. My guess is that Mr. Bolling's hesitancy had something to do with the relationship he had had with Speaker Rayburn. According to the reports of numerous observers who had no axes to grind, Mr. Bolling and the Speaker had built a bond of affection between them that went well beyond the usual political alliance.[22] Mr. Sam, who had no immediate family, was well known

[22] Friends of Mr. Albert note that Mr. Albert was Speaker Rayburn's personal choice for whip in 1954 and further suggest that Mr. Albert was also a close personal friend of Mr. Rayburn's. One influential Congressman said, "Mr. Sam thought the world of Carl Albert." But this same Congressman indicated that he thought Mr. Bolling's relationship with the Speaker was unique. Without excluding the strong probability that Mr. Rayburn had a high personal regard for Mr.

for his habit of adopting political protégés with whom he could develop a relationship of warmth and trust similar to that found in the family situation. This was, apparently, Mr. Rayburn's way of overcoming the loneliness that otherwise might well have overtaken any elderly bachelor.

The need to overcome loneliness was strongly ingrained in Mr. Rayburn from childhood. Mr. Rayburn is quoted as saying:

> Many a time when I was a child and lived way out in the country, I'd sit on the fence and wish to God that somebody would ride by on a horse or drive by in a buggy—just anything to relieve my loneliness. Loneliness consumes people. It kills 'em eventually. God help the lonely. . . .[23]

Mr. Rayburn's advice to Presidents Truman, Eisenhower, and Kennedy reflects the same theme. As he reported afterward, on a conversation with Mr. Truman just after the latter had become President:

> "You've got many hazards," I said. "One of your great hazards is in this White House," I said. "I've been watching things around here a long time, and I've seen people in the White House try to build a fence around the White House and keep the various people away from the President that he should see. . . ." [24]

His biographer and research assistant, D. B. Hardeman says, "Mr. Sam was . . . annoyed by inactivity. When he could think of nothing else to do at home in Bonham he would get out all his shoes and polish them. He dreaded holidays and Sundays because visitors were few." [25]

Albert (and, one supposes, several other members as well), the testimony of several knowledgeable and apparently unbiased observers was quite unanimous in indicating that for several years preceding his death Mr. Rayburn was particularly close to Mr. Bolling.

[23] David Cohn, "Mr. Speaker: An Atlantic Portrait," *Atlantic Monthly* (October, 1942), pp. 73–78. The quoted portion appears on p. 76. Mr. Cohn was a personal friend of the Speaker's. He comments on the quoted passage, "As he spoke, Rayburn relived the long, lean, lonely years of his childhood, and it was clear that he wished other children might be spared the bleakness of his youth."

[24] CBS News, "Mr. Sam: A Personal and Political Biography," telecast, November 16, 1961.

[25] D. B. Hardeman, "The Unseen Side of the Man They Called Mr. Speaker," *Life*, LI (December 1, 1961), 21.

Mr. Rayburn found it particularly congenial to work with younger men. D. B. Hardeman says, "Lyndon Johnson once confessed, 'The Speaker and I have always been very close but if we are not as close as we were once, it is because I'm almost fifty. If you notice, he never has older men around him.' " [26]

"I always liked the House the best," Mr. Rayburn said. "There're more people there, usually they're younger people, and as I've advanced in years, I've stepped back in my associations, boys, young people ten, twenty years younger than I. Their bodies are not only resilient but their minds are too. They can learn faster than the fellow advanced in years." [27]

One of the things which no doubt drew Mr. Rayburn to Mr. Bolling was the exceptional resiliency and quickness of the latter's mind. On this quality, friends and political enemies of Mr. Bolling agreed. He is an extremely "quick study," and had several other things in common with the Speaker:

"Bolling loves the House," a judicious, slow spoken Southern Congressman who knows him rather well told me. "He loves it and has studied it. He has read everything that has been written about the House and has studied its power structure. He has a brilliant mind."

Although nearly thirty-five years separated them, both Mr. Rayburn and Mr. Bolling were strongly committed emotionally to many liberal programs. Bolling refers to himself quite frankly as a "gut liberal"; *Time* magazine has aptly characterized Rayburn as a "liberal of the heart." [28] In addition, both men shared a high sense of rectitude in their work, treating the majority of their colleagues with reserve and judging them rather severely. This social distance which both men maintained was no doubt related in some complex way to the intensity of their feelings about political issues. It is instructive in this connection to note the tendency of both men to become laconic in public when dealing with prob-

---

[26] *Ibid.*

[27] CBS News, "Mr. Sam . . . ."

[28] *Time*, LXXVII (February 10, 1961), 12. What is significant there, I think, is not the placement of either man on an ideological spectrum so much as the high degree of personal engagement which the references to parts of the body suggest.

lems with which they had great personal involvement. Compare Bolling's prepared statement of withdrawal from the Majority Leadership race in 1962 with Rayburn's statement of withdrawal in 1934 from an unsuccessful race for the Speakership.[29]

In 1934 Rayburn said, "I am no longer a candidate for Speaker. There are no alibis. Under the circumstances, I cannot be elected." [30]

In 1962 Bolling said, "I am withdrawing from the race for Leadership of the House. Developments of the last few days have convinced me that I don't have a chance to win." [31]

Bolling privately expressed an unwillingness amounting to an incapacity either to "do anything" until after a "decent" time had elapsed after the Speaker's death [32] or to canvass for votes in his own behalf. The major portion of this burden within the House was carried by Representative Frank Thompson of New Jersey and a group of four or five others. The brunt of Bolling's campaign was, however, carried on from outside the House.[33] Ini-

[29] I was a witness to the events surrounding the composition of Bolling's statement of withdrawal, and am quite convinced that Bolling had no knowledge of Rayburn's statement. Rather, the striking resemblance between the two seems to me to illustrate a remarkable similarity in the style of the two men, not conscious imitation.

[30] Bascom N. Timmons, "Rayburn" (ditto, n.d.), part 4, p. 1. This series was supplied to certain newspapers at the time of Speaker Rayburn's death. Mr. Timmons is a newspaperman accredited to the House Press Galleries from a string of newspapers in the southwest. He is a Texan and was a friend and contemporary of Mr. Rayburn's.

[31] Rodney Crowther, *Baltimore Sun, loc. cit.* The psychologically minded would also no doubt find it relevant that Mr. Bolling's father died when he was in his early teens. However, anyone concluding from data such as have been presented here that either Mr. Bolling or Mr. Rayburn gave indications in their behavior of being emotionally crippled or lacking in control could not possibly be farther from the mark. The point here is simply that certain easily verified events and patterns in the lives of each man may well have predisposed him to like the other.

[32] Mr. Bolling's imputation of indecorousness (the news of which was communicated in such places as "Bitter Withdrawal," *Time,* LXXIX [January 12, 1962], 12) was resented in the Albert camp. In their view, Mr. Bolling had himself precipitated the battle by first permitting word to leak to the newpapers that he was a candidate for Majority Leader.

[33] One index of this is the apparent fact that Mr. Thompson is generally not too popular in the House (a fact of which both he and Mr. Bolling are aware). Mr. Thompson is an able and gifted man with extremely good political connections outside the House, both "downtown" and in his home state. (See Richard L.

tially, he had to decide whether to run for Speaker or Majority Leader—which no doubt also contributed to the quality of hesitancy in his campaign.

Factors pointing to the Speakership included the relative unpopularity of Mr. McCormack (1) with members, and (2) at the White House; but against this had to be weighed (1) Mr. McCormack's generally blameless voting record (from the standpoint of a pro-administration Democrat), (2) his long service in the second position, (3) the weight of a tradition which strongly favored the elevation of a Majority Leader, (4) Mr. Bolling's own relatively junior position, (5) the fact that Mr. McCormack, if he lost the Speakership, would remain as a Majority Leader not especially favorably disposed toward the program of an administration that had just done him in politically, and, (6) the fact that opposing Mr. McCormack would unavoidably exacerbate the religious cleavage in the House and the country which the fight over school aid in the last session had revealed.[34]

And so, Mr. Bolling decided to run for Majority Leader against the extremely popular Mr. Albert. In a straight popularity contest, Mr. Bolling knew he was "born dead." His role in the House had been quite unlike Mr. Albert's; indeed, several Congressmen contrasted them starkly.

A close friend described Mr. Albert's approach to the job of whip:

> The whip is more the eyes and ears of the Leadership than anything. On controversial matters, they like to know what the chances

Lyons, "Thompson Decision to Retain Seat Gives House Liberals Needed Lift," *Washington Post*, January 31, 1961.) But inside the House, he has a reputation for being sharp-tongued, supercilious, and too witty for his own good. He has a way of hanging nicknames that "stick" on friend and foe alike—to the delight of the former, the great chagrin of the latter. One political ally of Mr. Thompson's said, "He has got the reputation that whenever he is in favor of a bill, it is bound to lose. . . . Thompson is one of Bolling's major liabilities. I hear how the guys talk at the back of the room there [in the aisle behind the seats in the Hall of the House]. They say, 'Whose amendment is that? Thompson's? That guy? To hell with that!' And they vote it down." Another ally of Thompson's said, "Frank's always trying to talk silly with you when you're talking serious, and trying to talk serious when you're talking silly."

[34] See H. Douglas Price, "Race, Religion and the Rules Committee" in Alan Westin (ed.), *The Uses of Power* (New York: Harcourt, Brace & World, 1962), pp. 1–71.

of success are. . . . So the deputy whips count noses, and the whip's job is to evaluate the count—especially to assess the doubt-fuls. . . . Albert developed quite a genius for knowing what people would do. . . .

Another service he performed endears him to people. Carl's the kind of a guy everybody could find. He would talk to the leadership for [rank-and-file Congressmen].

A lot of these Eastern guys have a Tuesday through Thursday club. The whip takes the duty on of telling them if the signals change so they can get back here if they're needed.

He's done so many things for people. They trust him. They think of him, "Here's a man I can talk to when I need help." When the members go about picking a Leader, they want personal services, not intellectuals.[35]

I dare you to find a member of Congress who said Bolling had lifted a finger for him.

A supporter of Mr. Bolling's (for whom Bolling had, according to this member's testimony, lifted many a finger) saw the roles of the two principals in much the same light, although his evaluation of their roles was quite different:

Albert's approach to legislative matters is, well, everybody ought to vote his own district. . . . He brings his friends and his enemies in [to vote] both. . . . Why the hell get [a certain Southern Congressman] out [to vote]? He doesn't vote with us on anything. And he's a deputy whip! It's ridiculous. . . . The function of the whip [under Mr. Albert] is room service to members.

Albert was the whip, but Bolling was doing the whipping. . . . When the heat was being put on in the Rules Committee and all the other fights, it was Bolling putting it on, and he wasn't making any friends doing it.[36]

[35] Mr. Albert's friend may, in reflecting unfavorably on Mr. Bolling, have done Mr. Albert a slight injustice. Mr. Albert was an honor graduate of the University of Oklahoma and a Rhodes Scholar—neither of which makes him an intellectual, but they clearly don't disqualify him either.

[36] There are now several accounts of the 1961 battle over the Rules Committee in print, including a treatment of the episode in Price, *op. cit.*; the analysis of the vote by Cummings and Peabody in Robert L. Peabody and Nelson W. Polsby (eds.), *New Perspectives on the House of Representatives* (Chicago: Rand-McNally, 1964, 1971); a long chapter by Neil MacNeil in *Forge of Democracy* (New York: McKay, 1963), pp. 410–88; and a case study in the Eagleton series by William MacKaye.

Mr. Bolling was, as a friend of his described it, a "hatchet man" for Speaker Rayburn. This entailed a variety of activities on the Rules Committee, including monitoring the attendance of friends and foes, arranging for the disposition of bills, and keeping track of the intentions of the various (and numerous) factions in the House with respect to important legislation, in behalf of the Speaker. Occasionally, Mr. Bolling's job included putting the finger on members who were open to (or vulnerable to) persuasion, and he often had a crucial part in the process of persuading them—not always a pleasant task.[37]

Although Mr. Bolling is entirely in sympathy with policies espoused by liberals in the House, his position close to the Speaker precluded his joining in any formal way in the activities of the Democratic Study Group, the House liberal organization. As a friend of his put it, "Dick was aloof from the uprisings of the peasants."

"Bolling's got a sort of a chip on his shoulder," another member said.

"The thing you have to realize about Bolling," said an Albert backer, "is that he never bothers to speak to anyone else. I don't think Bolling understands politics."

Mr. Bolling's aloofness was, as I have suggested, probably something more than simply a reflection of his peculiar institutional position. A second friend of Bolling's said, "Despite a good deal of charm, Bolling just does not have a personality that inspires loyalty and friendship among men.[38] He's not a backslapping, how-the-hell-are-you type of guy. Bolling is personally quite pleasant, but reticent."

The late Clem Miller of California said, "Congress is a World War I rather than a World War II operation. You have to move huge bodies of men a few feet at a time. . . . Dick's spent the last few years divorcing himself from a base of fire. His job was right-

---

[37] See *Time*, LXXVII (February 10, 1961); William S. White, "The Invisible Gentleman from Kansas City," *Harper's* (May, 1961); Neil MacNeil, "The House Confronts Mr. Kennedy," *Fortune*, LXV (January, 1962), 70–73.

[38] Statements such as this one obviously are not intended to be taken with strict literalness. Most social scientists are agreed that the personal "qualities" of leaders vary according to the situation.

hand man to the Speaker. He came to Democratic Study Group meetings but always identified himself as an observer, not as a participant. He came in a sense to lecture us like small children rather than lead us in our councils. There was a good deal of hostility toward him in the Study Group as a result of that. The Study Group was set up as a foil for the leadership. You can't have your foot in both camps, and so Dick alienated the base of support that he needed in the House."

Another member, often allied with Mr. Bolling, characterized him as "totally unfriendly."

Mr. Bolling's personal situation within the House was further complicated by a common enough phenomenon. As a relative newcomer, as an extremely able member performing difficult tasks well, and as an intimate of the Speaker, Mr. Bolling was, in the opinion of several observers, the victim of a certain amount of jealous resentment.

"Jealousy is a big factor," one Congressman said. "Liberals have several characteristics that tend to make them ineffective, and vanity is one of them. They tend to be prima donnas." [39] Another said, "Dick is not a popular man in the House, no doubt a surprise to newsmen. For one thing, he's resented because of his ability."

Liberals were clearly not the only group of Congressmen susceptible to jealous feelings toward Mr. Bolling. His relative youth was offensive to some of his seniors. Mr. Bolling had risen very fast in the House and had been given many advantages by his friend, the Speaker. The record he had made thus far also suggested that, if elected, he would take many more initiatives than Mr. Albert and would more decisively challenge the powers of committee and subcommittee chairmen to control the flow and content of legislation—in behalf of programs for which many of these leaders had no particular liking.

Even to the superficial observer, Mr. Albert and Mr. Bolling are quite contrasting figures. Mr. Albert was fifty-three years old,

---

[39] Cf. a similar comment on Senate liberals by Tristam Coffin, "The Well Tempered Politician," *Holiday* (April, 1962), p. 107.

exactly on the House median; Mr. Bolling was only forty-five. Albert is physically probably the shortest man in the House and looks nothing like the collegiate wrestler he once was. He has a softly lined, friendly, gentle face which, says a colleague, "always looks faintly worried." Bolling is a tall, husky, quite handsome and imposing-looking man who gives the appearance of great self-confidence and looks very much like the collegiate football player he was. Mr. Albert in conversation is homespun, soft-spoken, emotionally unengaged, and low-pressure. A colleague says, "You could vote impeachment of the President, and it wouldn't bother Carl." Mr. Bolling in conversation is articulate, expansive, sophisticated, intense; in short, one would surmise, a rather more threatening figure to someone of average inclinations than Mr. Albert.

Mr. Bolling has far greater acceptance in the higher echelons of the "downtown" bureaucracies and surely in the press corps than almost any other Congressman, including Mr. Albert. Mr. Bolling is far more likely to spend his leisure hours among pundits, diplomats, and subcabinet officials than with Congressmen, a pattern which Mr. Albert reverses. Mr. Albert prides himself, in fact, in spending a greater proportion of his time on the floor of the House than any other member, where he is continually accessible to his colleagues.[40]

To a great extent, Mr. Bolling understood that a variety of in-

[40] See John M. Virden, "Little Giant from Bug Tussle," *Saturday Evening Post*, CCXXXV (March 24, 1962), 94–97; Paul Duke, "Albert's Soft Sell," *Wall Street Journal*, March 6, 1962; "Carl Albert, Nose-Counter from Bug Tussle," *Time*, LXXIX (January 12, 1962), 13. Certain other characteristics place Mr. Albert closer to the rank and file of Congressmen than Mr. Bolling. Mr. Albert was a small town boy, the son of a farmer and laborer, educated in public schools, and is a Methodist. Mr. Bolling was born in New York City, the son of a well-to-do physician. He grew up in comfortable circumstances and socially prominent circles in Huntsville, Alabama, after his father's death went to Exeter and the University of the South, has a Master's degree from Sewanee, and did further graduate work at Vanderbilt, and is an Episcopalian. If the script for this contest had been written by C. Wright Mills or one of his followers, Mr. Albert would have been the more "liberal" candidate and wouldn't have had a chance. (See Mills, *The Power Elite* [New York: Oxford University Press, 1956]). Mr. Mills carefully excludes Congress from his discussion of "the power elite" for reasons which seem to this reader designed to protect his thesis from evidence which would reject it.

stitutional and personal "inside" factors were working against him, and so he launched an "outside" campaign.

V

Bolling's task, as he saw it, was divided into several phases of activity. First, he had to stall the Albert bandwagon. Then he had to receive enough commitments to win himself. His primary targets were the big state delegations of New York, California, Illinois, and Pennsylvania. Secondary targets included getting a firm grip on his home state delegation and going after younger, liberal Congressmen and Congressmen who had substantial labor and civil-rights-minded constituencies.

His strategy for accomplishing these ends had two major features. First, he intended to draw as sharp a contrast as he could between himself and Mr. Albert on issues and sell the contrast as hard as he could through the mass media. Second, he set about "pulling strings" on members, a process which he had practiced before in legislative battles.[41] This entailed identifying the men and interest groups favorable to his candidacy who for various reasons could reach and persuade members of Congress. Naturally, the foremost among these would have been the President, but at no time was Presidential aid offered, and none was requested by Mr. Bolling.

The position of the White House in this battle was a complex one. While the mass media, on the whole, bought Mr. Bolling's contention that substantial differences in public policy separated him and Mr. Albert, the White House never did. It regarded both men as good friends of the Kennedy program, each having personal and political strengths and weaknesses. To intervene in

---

[41] An example of this process was given in *Time*, Vol. LXXVII (February 10, 1961) at the time of the Rules Committee fight: "*Time* Correspondent Neil Mac-Neil listened as two Rayburn lieutenants were running down the list of doubtful members. On one: 'The General Services Administration ought to be able to get him.' On another: 'The Air Force can take care of him.' A third? 'If you can get the Post Office to issue that special stamp for him, you've got him.' And a fourth? 'The United Mine Workers can get him.' And a fifth? 'Hell, if we can't get him we might as well quit. Go talk to him.' A sixth? 'No, but I'll fix that bastard.' " *Time* gives the strong impression that the two lieutenants are Bolling and Thompson.

behalf of one friend would have meant sacrificing another. For the White House to intervene and lose would have been disastrous for its prestige and legislative program. To intervene and win would have been more satisfactory but still would have involved (aside from the making of enemies) great exertion, the distribution of indulgences, and the "cashing in" on favors owed, all of which could otherwise be employed to improve the chances for passage of controversial reciprocal trade, medical aid, tax reform, and education bills. Several members of the President's official family were close to Mr. Bolling and were almost certainly partial to him, but none participated in the fight.

Mr. Bolling and his backers in the House concurred in the White House policy of non-intervention and in the reasoning behind it. The major inside advantage of their side, as they saw it, was a professional ability to predict outcomes accurately and to recommend appropriate strategies. They understood fully that the risks to the White House were great, the probabilities of success dubious. If they could come close to winning on their own, within perhaps five or ten votes, then their recommendation might change, since the White House could then probably put them over the top. But it is not at all certain that even then the White House would have been ready to move.

If the administration was inactive, other keenly interested bystanders were not. The AFL-CIO backed Mr. Bolling strongly and performed several notable services in behalf of his candidacy. Labor lobbyists made a complete canvass of possible supporters in the House and, in several cases, made representations in Mr. Bolling's behalf with members. The NAACP was also active. Roy Wilkins, national chairman, telegraphed 153 selected branches of his organization, "Bolling right on 26 civil rights votes, Albert wrong. Wire, write or call your Congressman. This could affect civil rights legislation for years to come." The Democratic Reform Clubs of New York City were also interested in Bolling's candidacy, as were some local and national political leaders around the country and at least one farm organization.

An example of indirect influence in Mr. Bolling's behalf was described by an Albert supporter, "I heard that President Truman, a neighbor of Bolling's and a loyal Missourian, called Mayor Wagner of New York to try and get the New York delegation to support Bolling."

Mr. Bolling was especially successful in enlisting the aid of the mass media. Since the civil rights battle of 1957, when he anonymously kept newsmen briefed on the confusing tactical situation within the House, Mr. Bolling has been extremely popular with the Washington press corps.[42] He is asked to appear on broadcasts and telecasts much more often than the average member. He counts many Washington correspondents, including several famous ones, as close personal friends.

Hence, it is not altogether surprising that he was able to gain the endorsement of the *New York Times* as early as December 11. On Sunday, December 24, the *Times* reiterated its stand, saying, "The conservative coalition of Southern Democrats and Northern Republicans would find it much more difficult to exercise its suffocating veto over forward-looking legislation with the imaginative and hard-driving Mr. Bolling as majority floor chief." [43]

Five days previously, on December 19, James Wechsler, editor of the *New York Post*, gave a strong endorsement to Mr. Bolling, in which he printed a long verbatim extract of a letter endorsing Carl Albert which Bolling had received from Judge Howard W. Smith, leader of conservative Southerners in the House.[44] Wechsler commented, "This is not to say Albert has faithfully followed Smith's gospel. He is a moderate, pleasant man whose voting record might be far more impressive if he came from a state more congenial to the advance of civil rights and less dominated by the natural gas interests. Despite their differences on a

[42] A Washington correspondent commented: "[Bolling] was a good news source and popular among newmen from the time he first got on the House Banking Committee and became even more popular when he was moved to Rules as Rayburn's obvious protégé."

[43] *New York Times*, December 24, 1961.

[44] This letter was sent in response to Mr. Bolling's November 28 request for "consideration" from each Democrat. Supporters of Mr. Albert were dismayed by the fact that while they had not solicited Judge Smith's support and Mr. Bolling had, the Smith endorsement was being used by Mr. Bolling against Mr. Albert with the press.

variety of matters, Smith is plainly confident that he can handle Albert; he is equally convinced that Bolling spells trouble. . . ." [45]

On December 29, Marquis Childs [46] and Edward P. Morgan both urged the selection of Mr. Bolling, referring once again to the Smith letter and to issues separating the two candidates. Mr. Morgan was especially vigorous in his commentary:

. . . where Bolling has been consistently for them, Albert has been basically against civil rights legislation, federal aid to education, full foreign aid and regulation of the oil and gas industry. It is reliably reported that one Texas Congressman told a Southern colleague that "with Albert in there, oil will be safe for twenty years. . . ." [47]

What of the outcomes of these activities? The relations between outside "pressures" and Congressmen have been variously described in popular and academic literature. There is an old tradi-

[45] James Wechsler, "Hill Battle," *New York Post*, December 19, 1961. Mr. Bolling's constituency is the Fifth District of Missouri, which includes most of Kansas City. Mr. Albert represents the thirteen counties of Oklahoma's Third District, an area known as "Little Dixie." This district is predominantly rural and is somewhat depressed economically. Its major products are timber, peanuts, cotton, and livestock. Several Albert supporters suggested that a generally liberal record such as Mr. Albert had made in the House was in some ways a more creditable performance for a man from a district of this kind than for a man from a big city. Although this argument has some plausibility, it should also be noted that several of the most respected southern liberals and moderates in the House have come from districts very similar to Mr. Albert's. Sam Rayburn himself was one such example. Others would be Carl Elliott of Alabama, Frank Smith of Mississippi, and James Trimble of Arkansas. This argument may, in other words, be an attempt to appeal to a popular stereotype which automatically classifies big-city districts as "liberal" and rural Southern districts as "conservative." But it may be that on the vast majority of issues coming to a vote in Congress, representatives from Southern, rural, economically depressed areas have constituencies as liberal as any in the country.
[46] Marquis Childs, "The High Stakes in House Battle," *Washington Post*, December 29, 1961—and elsewhere.
[47] "Edward P. Morgan and the News," American Broadcasting Company, December 29, 1961. The documentation of this case has never, to my knowledge, been made. I suggest that at the least the reference to Mr. Albert's position on federal aid to education would be difficult to defend.

tion which regards these relations as essentially nefarious.[48] Descriptively, the Congressman is sometimes thought to be a relatively passive creature who is pulled and hauled about according to the play of pressures upon him and whose final decision is determined by the relative strength of outside forces.[49] More recently, political scientists have become preoccupied with the qualities of reciprocity in the relations of interest groups and politicians. This literature calls attention to mutually beneficial aspects of the relationship and lays stress on the ways in which politicians may act to govern the outside pressures placed on them.[50]

My information on the impact of Bolling's outside campaign is necessarily incomplete. It is apparent at a minimum that a sufficient number of Congressmen were never reached by this campaign. One Congressman said:

> Bolling's best hope was forces outside the House—labor and civil rights groups. But I received not one communication in his behalf from anybody. There was nobody campaigning for him. Nobody knew if he was serious or not. Where was the heat?

Another Congressman, from a heavily populated area, said:

> Our delegation was never put on the spot. Bolling never tried to wage a campaign in our delegation. Apparently he tried to get labor leaders to pressure Cautious [the state party leader] to put pressure on our Congressmen. This is OK, but you really have to put the

---

[48] See, for examples of this tradition, H. H. Wilson, *Congress: Corruption and Compromise* (New York: Rinehart, 1951) and Karl Schriftgiesser, *The Lobbyists* (Boston: Little, Brown, 1951).

[49] An excellent example of this mode of thinking is contained in Max Lerner, *America as a Civilization* (New York: Simon & Schuster, 1957), pp. 415 ff. and especially p. 424. More generally, see Arthur F. Bentley, *The Process of Government* (Evanston: Principia, 1949), Earl Latham, *The Group Basis of Politics* (Ithaca: Cornell University Press, 1952), Oliver Garceau, "Interest Group Theory in Political Research," *The Annals*, CCCXIX (September, 1958), and David B. Truman, *The Governmental Process* (New York: Knopf, 1955). Truman explicitly rejects the notion that Congressmen are wholly passive.

[50] Lewis A. Dexter, *op. cit.*, and Dexter, "The Representative and His District," *Human Organization*, XVI (Summer, 1947), 2–13; Dexter, "What Do Congressmen Hear: The Mail," *Public Opinion Quarterly*, XX (Spring, 1956), 16–26. See also Donald R. Matthews, *U.S. Senators and Their World* (Chapel Hill: University of North Carolina Press, 1960), esp. chaps. viii, ix.

pressure on because if you know Cautious, he won't ever move unless he's really in a box.

In other cases, Congressmen were able quite easily to *resist* pressure. "The word got around," one liberal Congressman said, "that this wasn't like the Rules Committee fight, where there was a legitimate issue. Rather, it was all in the family, and any outside interference, even from the White House, would be resented."

Harlem's Representative Adam Clayton Powell, announcing his support of Albert, charged that some organized labor representatives were putting pressure on some Democratic members of his committee. He added, "I can't understand why labor union leaders would do this. Frankly, this is Democratic party business, not labor business." [51]

On the other hand, Bolling's campaign from the outside made several converts. Representative Leonard Farbstein of New York City, for example, announced that he would vote for Mr. Bolling on the basis of Mr. Wechsler's column.[52]

Another Congressman, a conservative veteran, wrote Bolling and detailed the substantial political disagreements between them, concluding, "But Famous Farmer tells me he is supporting you, and if he is supporting you, I am supporting you."

A leader of another interest group, in another part of the country, wrote, "I have just been informed by Congressman Dean Delegation's home secretary that Dean will be supporting you for Majority Leader. If there are any particular targets in [this state], I'm still available to apply whatever other pressures I can."

In aggregate, however, the impact of this campaign was not sufficient to accomplish Mr. Bolling's major goal. Edward Morgan commented with some asperity on the failure of Mr. Bolling to consolidate his support on an ideological basis, and at the same time he renewed the plea that the battle be defined in ideological terms:

[51] Robert C. Albright, "Powell Backs Albert for House Post," *Washington Post*, December 1, 1961. Powell, unlike the Congressman just quoted, checked with the White House before he made his announcement, obviously taking the position that the President had a legitimate interest in the outcome.
[52] *New York Post*, December 21, 1961.

If they voted . . . in support of their constituencies' needs for protection on gas prices, housing, civil rights and the like, the big city and industrial area representatives would have to come down almost unanimously for Bolling over Albert on their voting records alone and the man from Missouri would have it cinched. But he doesn't have it cinched. . . . At least one Massachusetts Congressman has already committed himself to Albert in writing . . . Adam Clayton Powell is looking South . . . So are a couple of New Jersey Representatives. . . . Most surprisingly, perhaps, two leading California Congressmen, Holifield and Roosevelt, have not dashed to Bolling's aid. . . .[53]

Over the long New Year's weekend, Bolling, Thompson, and Andrew Biemiller of the AFL-CIO met and assessed Bolling's "hard" strength at between sixty-five and seventy votes. Perhaps fifty more would have joined them if Bolling were going to win, but otherwise, they faded. A Bolling lieutenant said, "Everybody wanted to know, 'What's his chances?' The typical response was, 'I'll lie low. I'm with you if you've got a chance; otherwise, nix.'"

By the most realistic calculations, however, Mr. Bolling fell short of the 130 or more votes that he needed. He decided to withdraw his candidacy rather than embarrass his supporters in their state delegations and possibly jeopardize their future effectiveness in Congress.

VI

It is possible to identify at least four reasons why Mr. Bolling's attempt to win from the outside failed. The first two have already been mentioned: Mr. Albert's extreme popularity and Bolling's

[53] "Edward P. Morgan and the News," American Broadcasting Company, December 29, 1961. This account may be contrasted with a column put out by William S. White, a former Capitol Hill reporter. White's explanation of what happened is: "Whatever chance [Bolling] might have had, however, was sunk without a trace by the ultra-liberals themselves. They rushed forward to gather him into their arms, through zealous indorsements by such too-gooder groups as Americans for Democratic Action. No man in a House which—like the country itself—is essentially moderate could possibly have survived such embarrassing public embraces. So Mr. Bolling had to withdraw his candidacy. . . ." *Washington Star*, January 5, 1962—and elsewhere. I could discover little evidence which would lend credibility to this analysis. Regrettably, Mr. White offers none.

relative isolation provided little incentive for individual members to seek outside excuses of their own accord to do what they could more conveniently do for inside reasons. Second, the hands-off policy of the White House deprived Mr. Bolling's campaign of what would have been a major outside weapon had the President chosen to come in on Mr. Bolling's side.

The third major obstacle to the success of the outside campaign was the fact that, through no fault of Mr. Bolling's, a few of his supporters unwittingly blunted one of his principal weapons, the ideological contrast between himself and Mr. Albert. Just before the opening of the second session of the 87th Congress, and at the same time the struggle over the Majority Leadership was going on, a group of liberal Congressmen proposed that a policy committee be created in the Democratic party to be elected by the members from each of the eighteen whip zones. This committee was to advise and counsel with the leadership, and it was contemplated that it would be "more representative" (and presumably more liberal) than the leadership, unaided, would be.

Congressmen favoring this proposal circulated it among their Democratic colleagues in an attempt to get the fifty signatures necessary to place it on the agenda of the caucus which was to elect a new Speaker. Several liberals favoring Mr. Albert promptly signed, thus furnishing themselves with an excellent alibi, if they were challenged on ideological grounds by constituents and interest groups. They could claim that the fight over the Majority Leadership was not really significant since Bolling and Albert were, in their voting records, so close. But on the basic issue, on the institutional structure of leadership in the House, they were, as always, for liberalization.

This proposal went through several stages. At one point, it was seriously proposed that Mr. Bolling accept the chairmanship of this committee as the price for withdrawing his candidacy for the Majority Leadership. This proposal implied that the new Speaker had accepted the policy committee in principle.[54] Mr. Bolling was

[54] The rate at which tentative proposals and counterproposals of this sort fly around Washington is perfectly phenomenal. Theodore H. White rhapsodizes about the kinds of people who often act in the capacity of carrier pigeon: "Wash-

143

himself dubious about the chances that such a committee could perform the tasks its supporters envisaged for it. Counterproposals and negotiations buzzed back and forth about the possibility of putting "teeth" into the committee and about prior agreements as to its membership. At another level, Mr. Bolling and Mr. Thompson had to avoid being mousetrapped by the petition to put the policy committee on the agenda. To have signed the petition might have looked to Albert-McCormack forces like a proposal of terms and an acknowledgment of defeat. The fact that supporters of the Bolling candidacy were leading the fight for the policy committee was compromising enough as it was.

In the end, the whole idea came to nothing.[55] The proposal never received enough signatures to gain a place on the agenda, and at John McCormack's first press conference upon his nomination for the Speakership, he said, "A policy committee is out." [56] But the policy committee plan served one significant purpose. It softened and blurred Bolling's attempt to define the issue between himself and Mr. Albert in such a way as to embarrass liberals who were not supporting him.

ington holds perhaps fifty or a hundred . . . men, lawyers all, successful all, who in their dark-paneled law chambers nurse an amateur's love for politics and dabble in it whenever their practices permit. Where, in the regions, cities and states of the country, provincial lawyers love to counsel local politicians, promote names for the local judiciary, arrange the candidacies of lesser men, in Washington lawyers dabble in national politics, in appointments to places of high political destiny. Their influence, collectively, can never be ignored, because, collectively, they possess a larger fund of wisdom, experience, contacts, memories running back over thirty years of national politics, than most candidates on the national scene can ever hope to acquire on their own. . . ." *The Making of the President*, 1960 (New York: Atheneum, 1961), p. 33.

Newspaper people also quite often undertake this sort of activity, and occasionally lobbyists do, too.

Fortuitously, much of the activity described in this paper took place during the Christmas-Debutante-New Year's social season in Washington. As a result, many of the participants in these events kept running into each other at parties. Political science may some day catch up with the slick magazines and novels in comprehending the true significance of Washington parties. In this case, it appears that much of the negotiating on whether or not Mr. Bolling would join the leadership group as head of the policy committeee took place on an informal basis, through intermediaries and without any soul-stirring confrontation of rivals such as are found in Allen Drury's *Advise and Consent*.

The fourth reason for the failure of the outside campaign is probably the most important. It has to do with the conditions under which the actual choice was going to be made. Normally, a Congressman has considerable leeway in the casting of his vote because the issues are complex and technical, because the ways in which they are framed sometimes inspire no sharp cleavages of opinion, because interest groups are often uninterested and inattentive. But when an issue heats up and reaches the final stages of the legislative process, leeway dissipates. Interest groups become active. The mail begins to pour in.[57] Newsmen appear on the scene. Congressmen stick close to the Floor, listen to debate, mill around, stand ready to answer quorum calls or to vote on amendments.

There are four procedures for voting in the House: voices, standing, tellers, and roll call, in the order in which they expose members to public view. In the Committee on the Whole House, only the first three types of votes are taken. A diligent reporter or lobbyist can, however, even without benefit of a roll call, usually find out how a given member votes. The procedure is not foolproof, but, from the gallery, an outsider can always keep his eye fixed on one or a few Congressmen whose votes are of interest to

[55] That is, it came to almost nothing. In mid-March, 1962, three months after the events described here took place, the Democrats reactivated a "steering" committee along the lines of the "policy" committee proposed at the opening of the session. Mr. Bolling did not become a member. A leading Democrat in the House observed to me that the members of this committee, including James Davis of Georgia, William Colmer of Mississippi, Paul Kitchin of North Carolina, Clarence Cannon of Missouri, were likely, if anything, to be *less* liberal than the leadership they were supposed to advise. This was an outcome exactly opposite to the one envisaged by proponents of the policy committee idea.

[56] For the story at various stages, see: Robert C. Albright, "Drive Is Begun for Democratic Steering Group," *Washington Post*, December 30, 1961; Mary McGrory, "McCormack Silent on Liberals' Plan," *Washington Star*, December 31, 1961; Robert K. Walsh, "Party Harmony Setup Seen by House Liberals," *Washington Star*, January 5, 1962; Richard L. Lyons, "Liberal Democrats Defer Demands," *Washington Post*, January 9, 1962; Rowland Evans, Jr., "Democrats Unanimous," *New York Herald Tribune*, January 10, 1962.

[57] Lewis Dexter makes the point that the mail usually comes too late to affect the substance of legislation. However, mail is used here only as an index of attentiveness to issues on the part of publics. See Dexter, "What Do Congressmen Hear . . ."

him. Corroboration, if any is needed, can be obtained by asking around among other Congressmen.

The caucus at which voting for Majority Leader was to have taken place provided no such opportunities for outside surveillance. No spectators were admitted. Congressmen were even protected from the scrutiny of their colleagues; Representative Francis Walter, chairman of the caucus, sent word that the balloting for Majority Leader, when the time came, would be secret. The rules of the caucus say nothing about a secret ballot; rather, general parliamentary law governs the caucus meetings, and there is a special provision that "the yeas and nays on any question shall, at the desire of one fifth of those present, be entered on the journal"—all of which did not alter the fact that the balloting would be secret.

In spite of the interest which Mr. Bolling had stirred up among outside groups, these groups were operating under an insuperable handicap. The voting procedure maximized the chances that a Congressman cross-pressured between the demands of "local agency" and his own personal feelings could vote his private preferences with impunity.

VII

What does this case suggest about the general relations between inside and outside influences in the decision-making processes of the House? [58] Several things. First, it shows the extent to which inside and outside strategies tend to encourage different modes of communication among members and to evoke different definitions of the decision-making situation. The inside strategy is likely to define situations as "family matters," and to feature face-to-face interaction among members. The outside strategy is likely to

---

[58] Obviously, no real-world case will fit a typology perfectly. It may be well to remind the reader that the predominant strategies of the major actors were as I have indicated, but that Mr. Albert had some support from outside the House (such as from Senators Kerr and Monroney and Governor Edmondson of Oklahoma), and many of Bolling's supporters within the House backed him for reasons other than outside "pressures" which he might have been able to bring to bear on them. These included some members from the South whose position on civil rights was more accurately reflected by Mr. Albert.

evoke a more ideological, issue-oriented definition of the situation. Interaction among members is more likely to take place through third persons, lobbyists, and the press. Second, this case suggests conditions tending to promote the success of each strategy of influence. Inside strategies are favored when: (1) the matter to be decided can be rationalized as in some sense procedural rather than substantive; (2) there are great differences in the inside strengths of the two sides, but their outside strengths approach equality; (3) members are protected from surveillance by outsiders. Outside strategies are favored, presumably, when these conditions are reversed.

Additional conditions bearing on the effectiveness of inside and outside strategies may be imagined. Presumably, the autonomy of a representative from constituent pressures diminishes as his constituency approaches unanimity in its preferences *or* as the intensity of preference for a given alternative by any substantial portion of his constituency increases. We know that few decisions before Congress are likely to unite constituencies in this way or to inflame their passions to such a great extent. In addition, Congress takes routine steps to insulate its decision-making from certain kinds of outside influences.

One such device is the consideration of business in the Committee of the Whole, where substantial revisions of legislation can be made on the Floor without binding Congressmen to a record vote. The committees—whose composition and behavior sometimes reflect outside interests [59] and sometimes inside distributions of influence [60]—until quite recently marked up bills and voted on them in executive sessions only. A third device favoring inside distributions of influence in the House is the Rules Committee. One of the prerequisites for appointment to service on this

---

[59] As for example, the Agriculture Committee. See Charles O. Jones, "Representation in Congress: The Case of the House Agriculture Committee," *American Political Science Review*, LV (June, 1961), 358–67.
[60] There are numerous examples of this—e.g., the operation of the seniority system. See George Goodwin,"The Seniority System in Congress," *American Political Science Review*, LIII (June, 1959), 412–36. On the influence of state delegations on committee assignments and the force of tradition in determining the allocation of seats, see in general, Nicholas Master, "Committee Assignments in the House of Representatives," *American Political Science Review*, LV (June, 1961), 345–57.

committee is ability to "take the heat" and resist constituency pressures to report out bills which the House leadership wants killed.[61]

The enumeration of these devices hints at some of the problems facing two significant groups of outsiders: Presidents of the United States and political scientists. The President has a never-ending battle of converting decisions in the House from inside choices to outside ones. Most of his attempts to influence decisions are direct, but his efforts to dramatize issues before relevant publics may also be interpreted as attempts to activate interest groups and unify constituencies so as to make the employment of inside strategies of influence in the House difficult.

For political scientists, the lesson is clear. In order to understand the context within which decisions in the House are being made sufficiently well so that we can identify the goals in terms of which outcomes may be seen as "rational," it will be necessary to study the House at close range. On the whole, political scientists have taken a somewhat Olympian view of Congressional behavior. We have tended to organize our conceptions of rationality and legitimacy around Presidential goals and Presidential party platforms.[62] This has operated to obscure the constraints on the behavior of those in the House who share the policy preferences these political theories imply. It has also, I think, bred a kind of impatience with the study of strategies and tactics of House decision-making, which study, I believe, is a necessary step in understanding why the House operates as it does.

---

[61] On the Rules Committee, see Robert L. Peabody, "The Enlarged Rules Committee" in Peabody and Polsby (eds.), *New Perspectives on the House*, and the following articles by James A. Robinson, "Organizational and Constituency Background of the House Rules Committee" in Joseph R. Fiszman (ed.), *The American Political Arena* (Boston: Little, Brown, 1962); "The Role of the Rules Committee in Regulating Debate in the U.S. House of Representatives," *Midwest Journal of Political Science*, V (February, 1961), 59–69; "Decision Making in the House Rules Committee," *Administrative Science Quarterly*, III (June, 1958), 73–86; "The Role of the Rules Committee in Arranging the Program of the U.S. House of Representatives," *Western Political Quarterly*, XII (September, 1959), 653–69.

[62] This comment may be anachronistic, judging from much of the recent work on the House. It agrees with Ralph K. Huitt's similar judgment in "Democratic Party Leadership in the Senate," *American Political Science Review*, LV (June, 1961), 333f.

5
Leaders and Followers

The essays of this chapter are cast in a ruminative and on the whole pessimistic mode. They explore somewhat more directly than other parts of this book the dilemmas of leadership in a mass democracy, and especially the cruel disparities between appearance and reality that measure the distance between what large numbers of voters can possibly know about their leaders and what the few who interact with or closely watch leaders in the course of business know about them.

The chapter opens with a glum reflection upon the clear need for some device by which candidates for public office can be screened for characterological fitness, and the equally clear fact that Americans are increasingly contriving for themselves selection processes (and especially at the Presidential level where the need is greatest) that are less and less likely to meet this need.

The second selection was inspired by the unhappy experiences in 1968 of Vice-President Humphrey but is equally applicable to any Vice-President. The illusion here is of political power; the reality is, of course, powerlessness. To preserve the illusion, the Vice-President accepts responsibility for acts of an administration in which he has little or no influence. To refuse to foster the illusion is to hazard an isolation from the knowledge of events that in turn prevents him from fulfilling his one genuine and real function, which is, of course, to be prepared to step in and handle a complex job at a moment's notice.

In the third essay my jaundiced eye shifts to the problem of the reform of the Electoral College. The essential argument here is that things aren't that bad the way they are and most assuredly wouldn't be that much better if direct popular election were substituted for the eighteenth-century clockwork that presently elects our Presidents.

Is it merely a Hamiltonian disdain for the populace that prompts such sour thoughts about the prospects for democratizing American electoral processes? I don't think so. The difficulty is that there is so seldom a reasonable relationship between what proponents of electoral reform claim is going to happen and what a more gimlet-eyed analysis of the consequences of reform discloses. The gap cannot (or at least should not) be plugged with mere promises. The Electoral College, by counterbalancing the conservative tilt that Congress brings to the political system, has a democratizing part to play in American politics, and this fact should not be obscured by the majoritarian rhetoric of those who want to abolish the Electoral College while speaking in the name of people who most benefit from its persistence. The hard fact is that we live in a complex world, and twice round the barn is sometimes the quickest way home. I do despair, sometimes, of persuading many people that it is better to choose complex strategies that make use of the peculiarities of existing institutions, than to choose straightforward strategies that are wasteful of institutional leverage. But that, to me, is what debate over the fate of the Electoral College comes down to.

Presidential election times in America are times when image and reality get farthest out of synchronization. And 1968 was one of the worst years on record for that sort of thing. In the fourth essay, I belabor this point by taking some swipes at a book that manages to embody most of the things I hate about political journalism. Who says winners write the history of their time? Nonsense. It is more accurate to say that the political history of our times so far is being written by Kennedys—win or lose—and their idolators. This is unhealthy on many grounds. It is bad history, for one thing, that populates the world with heroes (Kennedys and their friends) and bums (everybody else). It is bad politics for a major political party to become so enthralled by the charisma that this sort of history writing conjures up that it is unable to choose its leaders by criteria other than those of surface popularity.

No doubt I am exaggerating the reality both of history-writing and of politics. The final selection in this chapter, in fact, illustrates that it is possible to write a book about a Kennedy that is both favorable and fair-minded. It is an account of mixed successes and failures—a pattern ingratiatingly human in its scale—and it is predicated on an assumption rarely found in books about American politics. This assumption is simply that governing and not publicity-seeking is the chief activity of government—a refreshing insight, and one that affords a good way of approaching the appreciation of politics.

SCREENING FOR CHARACTER

The aftermath of Watergate is producing as many by-products as the soybean. Along with such concerns as the proper sources of campaign financing, the limits of executive privilege, the legal and moral bases of domestic intelligence operations, one by-product has been a renewed concern at a more general level by many Americans about the characters of their public officials.

What do we mean by character? One definition, as good as any, might refer to a self-generated inclination to adhere to principles of decent conduct, to play by established customs and rules of the game, whether the tape recorder is on or off. People of character are mindful of the constraints as well as of the opportunities imposed by their enjoyment of the advantages of a social or political system. Presumably they are capable of entertaining a calculus which weighs private gain less heavily than long run public good.

There is little question that for a complex political system to operate successfully, it must be richly endowed with such people. It is a tribute to the success of the American system that our government agencies contain so few self-aggrandizing bureaucrats, and so very few corrupt ones, that Congress so seldom harbors a Joseph McCarthy. For there is little doubt that, while we are a government of laws, the conduct of the men and women who make and execute and adjudicate these laws powerfully influences the kind of government, and the kind of society, we are going to have.

Moreover the people who run the government, elected and appointed officials alike, must learn to work together, to develop rules of interaction, permissible bounds for conflict and competition, and areas of unquestioned mutual trust. It is the revelation of repeated and flagrant violation of these norms of behavior, and in some cases the outright defense on nation-wide television of such violations, which has as much as anything stimulated thoughtful people to consider the issue of character in our public servants, and to face the fact that the higher the official the more urgent the concern.

For the good of our country, we must have in charge of our government persons of honor, probity, and self-restraint—and the intelligence to grasp what these norms mean in an ongoing political context. Some commentators suggest that these qualities can best be stimulated by running for public office in this country, that much of the Nixon administration's problems would never have arisen if the President had surrounded himself with people who in this fashion had put themselves closer to the nuts and bolts of the political process.

Attractive as this notion is, it is almost certainly wrong. G. Gordon Liddy did run for public office; the experience does not appear to have done him a world of good. Likewise, there are too many honorable persons of sense and sobriety, such as Arthur Burns, Bryce Harlow, or Lawrence O'Brien, who have never run for public office yet have no trouble grasping what the rules of the game are and why observing them is important for the health of the political system.

How, then, can we do better at selecting our public officials so that they will meet high standards of character? Perfection is obviously not attainable. In the case of appointed officials, however, the problem seems at least partially soluble. So long as the news media and public opinion demand it, the elected officials who appoint, nominate, and confirm appointed officials can be encouraged to make a considerable effort to pay attention to the issue of character, and to inform themselves through private investigation of the characters of candidates for public service.

Elected officials present a more difficult problem, however. How can the voters in mass electorates possibly know if the candidates they see on a television screen are in real life stupid, dishonest in petty ways, incompetent, corrupt, or narrow-minded? Other politicians generally know, of course, but when it is directly in their interest to raise the matter publicly, the fact that it is in their interest makes their testimony suspect, and when it is not in their interest, there is no incentive to raise the matter at all.

Newsmen, contrary to the popular stereotype, generally as a matter of professsional objectivity lean over backward in their toleration of the various types of politicians with whom they come in contact, unless they can establish that actual laws have been broken. So the public is likely to remain substantially in ignorance of the kinds of people candidates for public office actually are.

Paradoxically, it is politicians themselves who are best equipped to screen nominees for public office according to the criteria I have suggested, because politicians are most likely to know one another well enough to make these judgments, and are most alert to the consequences of having to live with the results of the choice.

Politicians—and especially those in smoke-filled rooms—may themselves be corrupt, of course, or may not wish to screen on this basis. It was a smoke-filled room that gave us Warren Harding, after all. Nevertheless, selection by peers includes a capacity to screen for fitness of character, and alternative methods involving selection by strangers apparently do not. It is undoubtedly a good thing that smoke-filled rooms only operate in conjunction with appeals to electorates, so that there is an ever-present check upon the alternatives entertained there. Nevertheless, mass electorates cannot know all they—and we—need to know in order to make wise decisions. An additional safeguard is necessary. This is the underlying rationale for a mixed nomination process that includes appeals to both mass and elite criteria.

In recent years, however, selection by politicians as a method for nominating candidates has fallen into disfavor. More and more our selection processes for positions of national leadership rely heavily upon the popularity, "charisma," name recognition, or ideological identifications of candidates, and on their appeal to mass electorates, e.g., in Presidential primaries, in public opinion polls, and over television.

It is the fashionable thing right now to favor mass appeals and primary elections, presumably because they are "open" to widespread participation. This increased reliance upon a single mechanism for candidate selection, responsive to masses rather than to elites, comes at a cost, however. One of the indirect lessons of

Watergate ought to be that mass participation in the electoral process can take place largely in ignorance of important facts about nominees and what they really stand for as measured by their deeds rather than by their speeches.

DILEMMAS OF THE
VICE-PRESIDENCY

Thomas Riley Marshall, the genial Hoosier who was Woodrow Wilson's Vice-President, once observed that the office he had in the U.S. Capitol was so little protected from tourists that they used to come by and stare at him like a monkey in the zoo. "Only," he complained, "they never offer me any peanuts."

This is the way Vice-Presidents have viewed their constitutional office, not just its physical setting, for a long time. "Not worth a pitcher of warm spit" was John Nance Garner's rueful conclusion in the mid-'30s. "A mere mechanical tool to wind up the clock" was the way the first Vice-President, John Adams, described himself. "My country has in its wisdom contrived for me the most insignificant office that was the invention of man."

The main Constitutional function of the Vice-President is to wait. Clearly this is not much of a job for a major political leader, used to active leadership. Yet suppose a sudden tragedy should befall the President. Can we afford in the inevitable days of uncertainty and national bereavement that follow upon such an event to replace him with anything less than a major political leader who can step into the breach immediately, do the President's job and do it well?

Problem Is Not New

This is the first and fundamental dilemma of the Vice-Presidency, and as the quotation from John Adams amply testifies, it has been with us since the founding of the Republic. From this dilemma flow the problems characteristic of the modern Vice-Presidency.

We can date the modern Vice-Presidency from April 12, 1945, the day Franklin Roosevelt died. The next day his successor remarked to some newspapermen, "Boys, if you ever pray, pray for me now. I don't know whether you fellows ever had a load of

156

hay fall on you, but when they told me yesterday what had happened, I felt like the moon, the stars and all the planets had fallen on me."

Harry S Truman had been a respected but not a leading Senator before he assumed the Vice-Presidency. In his three months in that office Vice-President Truman saw President Roosevelt for only a few short times. As Vice-President he had not been told of the Manhattan Project to build the atomic bomb. Sticking closely to the duties prescribed under the Constitution, Mr. Truman spent the vast bulk of his time on Capitol Hill, presiding over the Senate.

His knowledge of the affairs of the executive branch and of foreign and military operations was the knowledge of an experienced legislator and not the inside information routinely available to top policy-makers in the Roosevelt administration. Mr. Truman wrote later, "It is a mighty leap from the Vice-Presidency to the Presidency when one is forced to make it without warning."

Since Harry Truman made the leap in the waning days of World War II the world has grown more complicated, and so has the Presidency. Efforts have accordingly been made to update the Vice-Presidency to meet modern conditions. The Vice-President now sits with the National Security Council as a matter of right. Under President Eisenhower, the Vice-President attended all meetings of the cabinet at the President's invitation and presided in the President's absence. Now in addition to his Capitol Hill quarters the Vice-President has a suite of offices in the Executive Office Building adjacent to the White House.

Moreover, since 1945, Presidents have made greater efforts to involve Vice-Presidents in various administrative activities: goodwill tours abroad, occasional attempts to promote legislation on Capitol Hill, honorific jobs "co-ordinating" programs to which the President wants to give a little extra publicity, and, especially, political missionary work around the country—speeches and appearances in behalf of Presidential programs.

These are the tasks of the modern Vice-President. In return for continuous briefing on the entire range of problems confronting the government, vastly improved access to the ear of the President and a closer view of the burdens of the Presidency, the modern Vice-President must carry some of these burdens himself.

Which burdens he carries, how many, and how far, are up to the President. Naturally a Vice-President may withhold his co-operation; but if he does, he impairs his relationship with the President. This is bound to affect adversely his capacity to fulfill the Constitutional obligation of the Vice-Presidency, to be genuinely prepared in case of dire need.

The Vice-President is in no sense the second in command in a President's administration. In truth, he is entirely removed from any chain of command at all in the government. This guranteed the independence of the Vice-President in the days of Aaron Burr, John C. Calhoun, Charles Dawes, and other free spirits who have occupied the office.

Today, the situation is quite different: it is much easier for high members of a President's administration to maintain independence from the Presidency. Top administrative officials can constitute a loyal opposition on governmental policy within the executive branch because their obligations run in at least three directions; upward to the President, downward to the agencies whose programs they supervise within the administration, and outward to the clientele their agencies serve.

Political executives serve the President best who serve their clients with devotion and promote the interests of their agencies with vigor. They know, moreover, that if in the process they conflict too much with Presidential plans or priorities the President can always fire them. If the President fails them in some serious way, they can resign.

The Vice-President can hardly fulfill his Constitutional responsibilities by resigning, nor, in mid-term, can he be dismissed. He has no anchor in the bureaucracy, no interest group constituency. Thus, uniquely in the executive branch, the modern Vice-President must discipline himself to loyalty to the President.

This sometimes has painful consequences for Vice-Presidents, especially when they attempt to emerge from the shadow of the President and run for the Presidency on their own. It is scarcely necessary to note Vice-President Humphrey's difficulty in persuading opponents of the Vietnam war that he and President Johnson are not Siamese twins.

Voters with longer memories may recall Vice-President Richard Nixon's similar problem in 1960, when Senator Kennedy wanted to get the country "moving again." Mr. Nixon somehow had to offer a new program of his own while defending the eight Eisenhower years, wrapping himself in the mantle of his popular predecessor, but taking no notice of the occasional pot-shots the General peevishly took at him. Neither Vice-President was fully able to run independently on his own record.

No Way To Escape

There seems, in short, to be no way for a Vice-President to avoid the dilemmas built into the office: unless he is scrupulously loyal to the President, he cannot get the access to the President that he needs to discharge his Constitutional function; when he is loyal to the President, he is saddled, at least in the short run, with whatever characteristics of the President or his program the President's enemies or his own care to fasten on him. He sits there in the limelight, visible, vulnerable, and for the most part, powerless.

Nevertheless, as long as Vice-Presidents have some chance eventually to run for the Presidency, as they presently do, and are not arbitrarily excluded from further consideration as independent political leaders in their own right, there will be plenty of takers for the Vice-Presidential nominations. This contributes to the strength of political parties.

Vice-Presidential nominees can balance tickets, help to unite a warring party, and campaign effectively with party workers and before the public—as, for example Senator Lyndon Johnson did with conspicuous success in the election of 1960. Thus, Vice-Presidential nominees can help a great deal to elect a President. It is after the campaign is over that the Vice-President's problems begin.

Unless, of course, by a stroke of good fortune, he and his running-mate lose.

THE ELECTORAL COLLEGE

All during the 1968 Presidential campaign political commentators frightened themselves by announcing that America was teetering on the brink of a Constitutional crisis. This may well have been true, but not for the reason generally given.

"What if nobody wins a majority in the Electoral College?" they asked, "What then?" Three major candidates instead of the usual two were on the ballot in all fifty states, they pointed out, and since each of the three could be expected to win in some states, there were grounds for apprehension. As it turned out, Richard Nixon did gain a majority in the Electoral College. But even if the Electoral College had provided no majority, there would have been no Constitutional crisis.

The Constitution gives clear instructions on how to resolve the problem when it arises: under the 12th Amendment, the matter is settled in the House of Representatives. Each state is given one vote for the purposes of this election, any of the three leading candidates in the Electoral College may be chosen, and a simple majority of state votes determines the outcome.

No Improvement

Although it was not necessary to resort to this procedure in 1968, the threat of the Wallace candidacy has given an important political impetus to abolition of the Electoral College. A Constitutional amendment has recently passed the House by an overwhelming majority, replacing the Electoral College with a direct election of the President and Vice-President. If two-thirds of the Senate concurs and the legislatures of three-fourths of the states ratify this amendment within seven years, the Electoral College will disappear.

In its place every four years will be a direct election. The winner would be the candidate with the most votes who receives at least 40 per cent of all popular votes cast; provision is made for a run-off if no candidate receives as many as 40 per cent.

Oddly enough, this new system would seem to encourage splinter candidates like the Wallace phenomenon. The temptation under a direct election system would be strong for all manner of demagogues and statesmen—whoever can raise the money—to run, whether sectional candidates or movie idols with widely scattered followings to appeal directly to the people. So there would be a high probability that under the House-passed plan as a matter of course the run-off would be the true election, and the initial election would look a bit like the start of the Boston Marathon, with its motley crowd of contestants.

Other Democratic Ways

Direct election would also confer an unusual distinction upon American Presidents. In most parts of the globe, there is no meaningful popular participation in the choice of chief executives. The heads of government in "people's democracies" and military dictatorships are selected by a variety of methods—coups, selection by elites of single parties, and so on. The rituals of selection in these nations sometimes include a facsimile of popular electoral participation, but the alternatives are usually restricted to "yes" or voting a blank ballot.

In parliamentary democracies like England, the Scandinavian countries, the Low Countries, West Germany, Italy, and Japan, a two-step process selects governmental chiefs: first the people elect members from districts to parliament; these members belong to parliamentary party caucuses, whose leaders become candidates for the top executive positions in government. The leaders that succeed are usually those having the backing of the largest party in parliament; lesser posts are sometimes filled by leaders from smaller parliamentary parties who are particularly agile in making alliances.

The Electoral College, as it was originally conceived, was intended to play a significant part in a similar two-step process. It was invented in an era before the emergence of organized, legitimate, political parties as vehicles for the orderly expression of opposition and for the transfer of power between elite groups. The college was to be a council of wise men, elected (as it still is today) from the states in proportion to state entitlements to representatives in Congress. The wise men were expected to sift through the qualifications of Presidential candidates and select the person best suited to the job.

Of course, nothing of the sort has happened in practice. Electors' names rarely even appear on ballots. Whether they are wise or not, no one will ever know. Except for a few isolated eccentrics who occasionally violate their promise to the voters to act as electors "for" the Presidential candidate on whose slate they were victorious, electors perform their task automatically.

They meet after the election in the several state capitols more or less ceremoniously and dispose of the business of casting their ballots quickly. The real work of winnowing and sifting candidates goes on elsewhere in our political system. Knowledgeable, experienced, and powerful people do ask such questions as "Which candidates are smart enough to do the job? Which are honest enough?" But they are located not in the Electoral College, but in the political parties.

These are the sorts of questions that get bandied about in smoke-filled rooms by party professionals who must anticipate the trials of actually governing as well as the joys of electoral victory. Naturally, they also ask which candidates are popular and presentable, but the answers to these sorts of questions are increasingly given by the electorates in primary elections.

In any case, the work that the Electoral College was cut out to do in fact gets done—not by the College but by a party nominating process that was never anticipated by the founding fathers. The Electoral College itself has no functions. It does have consequences, however. These consequences come about because of the way the college operates to aggregate votes.

The rule by which this is accomplished is simple enough: within each state, winner takes all. This means that the candidate who wins New York by one vote gets all 43 New York electoral votes; the winner of Delaware by 15,000 votes gets all three Delaware electoral votes. It is easy to see what manner of political strategies this leads to: since winning the big states by even the narrowest margin leads to such a huge boost in the Electoral

College, and losing by a hair could lead so easily to disaster, the Presidential contest in most years is fought out primarily in the large states, where the electoral votes are.

Over the long run this has made for more liberal "Presidential" wings of both major parties, since large state electorates typically include more immigrants, laborers, black voters, and others who have, for one reason or another, favored an active, service-providing government.

Doing away with the Electoral College is bound to make some difference in the influence of these groups, though how much difference is hard to say. There are many more voters in large cities than in rural areas, and neither of the major political parties is likely to forget that simple fact for very long. So they will still spend a lot of their resources trying to woo urban voters.

Shift in Power

Elsewhere in the political system, other changes are taking place. State legislatures and Congressional districts, under decisions of the Supreme Court, have been made more even in their populations. This has tended over time to undermine some of the power of rural and one-party areas in Congress, which traditionally balanced off the more liberal Presidential parties with more conservative Congressional activity.

The ultimate effect of all these reforms taken together would be to move both Presidential and Congressional elements closer together in the see-saw of national power. But these elements would not necessarily move at precisely equal rates of speed.

It is impossible to predict who would gain the upper hand over the short run. It is clear, however, that direct election of the President would, over the short run, not further the interests of urban minorities. This is one of the major reasons that Washington lobbyists for such groups as the National Association for the Advancement of Colored People have been unenthusiastic about the proposed amendment.

If, despite their efforts, the amendment passes the Senate and proceeds on its way to the state legislatures, urban minority groups and their allies can be expected to place much greater emphasis upon attempts to change voting registration laws so as to make it a good deal easier than it presently is in most states for qualified citizens to vote for the President, since it would only be by increasing their participation that they could protect their power.

No Panacea

Direct election of Presidents, it is clear, will not solve all the problems of American politics. It will undoubtedly encourage splinter parties, and might well lead to minority Presidents even more frequently than occurs at present. Over the short run it could disadvantage many Americans already among the most disadvantaged.

It is, on the other hand, a simple, straightforward, clear, and workable substitute for the Electoral College. These virtues are by no means trivial, since citizen understanding and approbation of the processes by which they are governed are greatly to be desired in political systems such as ours, in which government depends so heavily upon the good will of the people.

But it is no simple matter to decide upon the substitution of this seemingly tidy system for the more complex but in some ways more effective Electoral College.

OUR QUADRENNIAL DRAMA *

In his latest collection of essays, Alistair Cooke writes: "Very soon after Lyndon Johnson took over the Presidency, I had a cable from an English editor saying, 'WOULD APPRECIATE ARTICLE ON TEXAS AS BACKGROUNDER JOHNSON STOP COWBOYS COMMA OIL COMMA MILLIONARIES COMMA HUGE RANCHES COMMA GENERAL CRASSNESS BAD MANNERS ETC.' " Cooke, evidently a man who knows·general crassness bad manners etc. when he sees them, declined the assignment, and he does not say whether anyone else took it up. But the impulses that inspired the cable will, no doubt, be richly gratified if the editor reads *An American Melodrama*, the English entry in the 1968 election retrospective sweepstakes, by three members of the London *Sunday Times* "Insight" team.

As though the events of 1968 were not appalling enough, we now have an appalling eight-hundred-odd page book to remember them by. Inching glacially along in the accepted you-are-there style, it deposits a midden of itty-bitty details, half-digested sociological studies, sloppy deep-think, news bulletins, gossip, and ransackings from hither and yon. What gives the production coherence, aside from the helpful linearity of last year's calendar, is a barely suppressed tone of lip-smacking *Schadenfreude*, suitable, one supposes, for festivities celebrating the dissolution of empires, and other events confirming the natural superiority of observers over participants.

We are given to understand early in the book that America in 1968 has a lot to atone for, such as its hubris, as revealed in the plight of its urban poor, its inability to extricate troops from Vietnam, its optimism, its faith in progress, and its hyperbolic advertisements, including some patriotic doggerel that a Washington,

* Review of Lewis Chester, Godfrey Hodgson, and Bruce Page, *An American Melodrama: The Presidential Campaign of* 1968 (New York: Viking, 1969).

165

D.C., men's clothing store seems to have placed in a newspaper on what Americans incomprehensibly refer to as "Independence Day." Other symptoms of America's underlying sickness in 1968 are also ticked off: a "naïve" Secretary of Defense, Robert Mc-Namara, who "revealingly" sponsored the use of jargon like "inputs" and "outputs" in the Pentagon; "unskeptical" Lyndon Johnson, whose misfortune it was to escape the heady learning experience of the Bay of Pigs, thus arriving at the end of his third decade of service in Washington unaware that a government bureaucracy might mislead him; an inadequate Presidency, whose institutional structure had been weakened "since Eisenhower's time"; a lack of subtlety and courage in social thinking that kept the White House from self-evident truths at home and abroad. ". . . Johnson's aide Joseph Califano was a great one for producing lists showing how many fewer poor people there were this year than at some earlier time. . . ." "As poverty is relative," Messrs. Chester, Hodgson, and Page helpfully explain, "so there can be no useful 'attack' on it that does not involve the effective redistribution of goods, services, and wealth." No doubt the well-fed look that all three authors have mustered up for the group picture on the book jacket was, under the instruction of this dictum, accomplished not by their own exertions at table but by putting a squadron of Rockefellers on a diet.

After thus setting the scene, the authors commence their recitation of who said what to whom in various hotel ballrooms, restaurants, and airplanes, pausing occasionally to launch into digressions as the main dramatis personae stumble on stage. In due course, we meet mysterious Eugene McCarthy, he of the gnarled psyche and gnomic utterance; lovable, boyish Robert Kennedy, torn between practical politics and ambitious idealism; malevolent, hulking Lyndon Johnson; Hubert Humphrey with his putty nose and floppy shoes; and a raft of other vaudeville favorites in cameo roles. Only one character momentarily eludes stereotyping: Richard J. Daley, who turns out to be only partly ogre. A lovable, boyish side comes out when he bargains in the back room as a semi-ally of the Kennedys.

In the little set piece on Richard Nixon, the retailing of clichés gives way to the wholesaling of *déjà vu*. Here is a passage from the sympathetic biography, *Nixon: A Political Portrait*, by Earl Mazo and Stephen Hess, describing Nixon's Senatorial campaign of 1950:

> After Smathers' primary victory in May, Nixon carefully studied it and adapted what he could to his own campaign. (Thus, "Red Pepper," a slogan in Florida, became "Pink Lady" in California) . . . Nixon's greatest windfall, of course, was the mass of accusations her fellow Democrats had hurled at Mrs. Douglas in the Spring. Chotiner and his associates gathered them all, added an embellishment here and a nuance there, and played it back in the fall campaign.

Adding an embellishment here and a nuance there (but without mentioning the Mazo and Hess book), the authors of *An American Melodrama* write:

> The first "red smears" against Mrs. Douglas came not from Nixon but from her party colleague Manchester Boddy during the campaign for the Democratic nomination . . . Boddy's smears against Mrs. Douglas were sufficiently comprehensive that Nixon did not need to add too many of his own. Some of the techniques he did borrow came from another Democrat, George Smathers of Florida. . . . As Smathers' opponent was called the Red Pepper, so Nixon and his manager, Murray Chotiner, nicknamed Mrs. Douglas the Pink Lady. Smathers swamped his state with a booklet entitled *The Red Record of Senator Claude Pepper*. It was effective, and Nixon, who studied the Smathers campaign with great care, followed suit.

Mazo and Hess write of Nixon's oratorical style:

> It was what seemed to be said that paid off, not the intricate lawyerlike interweaving of facts and qualifications. Nixon did not exactly call Secretary of State Acheson a "pink" for instance. But he did refer to "Acheson's color blindness—a form of pink eye toward the Communist threat in the U. S." . . . In 1954 he charged that "real Democrats are outraged by the Truman-Acheson-Stevenson gang's defense of communism in high places"; and Truman, Stevenson and Acheson were "traitors to the high principles in which many of the nation's Democrats believed."

In *An American Melodrama*, a passage reads:

Nixon's style therefore appears as a mixture of fury, caution and legalism. This is to be found in all those famous phrases which attempt to link Democrats, and especially liberal Democrats, with Communism; Dean Acheson suffered "color blindness—a form of pink eye toward the Communist threat." "Real Democrats" were "outraged by the Truman-Acheson-Stevenson gang's defense of Communism in high places." He went close to the edge with his claim that Truman, Acheson and Stevenson were "traitors to the high principles in which many of the nation's Democrats believed."

The point of exhibiting these funny coincidences is, of course, not to suggest that *An American Melodrama* is literally plagiarism. Rather, it is pastiche, pulled together from a variety of unacknowledged sources and informed by a point of view that owes little to the inductive comparison of insight with observation and much to the bombastic repetition of received press corps opinion, some of it rather stale and thoughtless.

The fact that the authors are foreign observers makes this weakness of the book especially poignant. American readers have been spoiled by visitors like Henry Fairlie and Alistair Cooke, whose prose gives evidence of having been composed in order to express the thoughts of orderly, lucid and skeptical minds. We have come routinely to expect of foreign journalists a freshness of perspective permitting glimpses of inward truths about our political men and institutions that those of us who have grown up with them might easily have missed. But nothing of the sort is visible in *An American Melodrama*.

Perhaps the most signal failure of the book is in its portrait of Hubert Humphrey—and to a lesser extent also in that of Edmund Muskie. Muskie's quiet and effective work in the Senate for over a decade is dismissed as though he had all that time been engaged in basket weaving in the House of Lords. For Humphrey, all too predictably, the authors reserve their ripest scorn. The work of a political career in behalf of civil rights, welfare, disarmament, federal aid to education, and so on, barely attracts the notice of these authors, who think to put it in perspective by summoning Lyndon Johnson to praise Humphrey's ephemeral deeds. "Friends and apologists," they note, were unaccountably eager to defend Humphrey, and kept irrelevantly pointing to the record. "Humphrey's friends," they pout, "lay heavy stress on his practicality, his effectiveness."

> Humphrey himself is proud of his ability to get things done. "People say to me," he says, "whatever happened to that liberal program you stood for?" "I say to them, 'we passed it. Does that upset you?'" . . . There it all is in two dozen words; bragging, defensiveness, and crass incomprehension both of the nature of political dissent and of the mood of America.

Whence all this crass incomprehension?

> To bask in the acceptance of [the Senate]. . . . These are heady delights for any man, and for the country boy from Huron, South Dakota, who loved all his life to be loved, they were intoxicating. For this, surely, is the key to Humphrey. . . .

And the key to McCarthy?

> . . . a bored, proud man, contemptuously aloof from the masonic bonhomie and the routines of the life of the Senate around him. . . . There is something about McCarthy, some mark of an enviable inner self-confidence. . . . You would start with a sense of security if you grew up in Watkins, Minnesota.

We may term insights such as these examples of the emerging science of geo-psychiatry. Clearly they betoken an attempt on the part of the authors to probe beneath the surface of events. But it is a puerile attempt. Swift visits to childhood home towns cannot substitute for detailed knowledge of what adults have made of themselves, or (and this is the deficiency I see as most glaring in *An American Melodrama*) the institutional constraints and opportunities within which they must currently live. Although the authors learned enough about the electoral process to be properly skeptical of Robert Kennedy's chances of victory if he had lived, their understanding of our governing process is too weak to sustain a hardheaded assessment of Kennedy's chances of delivering on his promises if he had somehow won the nomination and the election.

They seem to understand something of the reasons behind Nixon's Southern strategy, although they never resolve the partial contradiction between their assertion that Spiro Agnew had been Nixon's secret choice for the Vice-Presidency all along and the strong implication that he was yielded up as a means of placating Strom Thurmond when Ronald Reagan became a threat at the convention itself. Liberal Republicans—especially Nelson Rockefeller—receive sympathetic portraits, but the authors do not second guess their maladroitness—as they do practically everyone else's maneuvers—at the Republican convention, although it seems plausible to suggest that liberal Republican inability or unwillingness to bargain with Nixon may have thrown Nixon into the arms of the South.

They are able to see the complexity of relationships among party insurgents but not among party regulars. One little set-piece describes Robert Kennedy's entourage as a feudal retinue. Another describes it as a sect-like group held together by "charisma," a concept that is given its full Weberian exposition. Still another interlude describes in detail an inner dialogue between young New Left and old John Kennedy holdover factions, later reproduced in what seem to be alternate sentences in a Robert Kennedy speech.

If Robert Kennedy occupies both the traditional and charismatic boxes in their rather odd paraphrase of Weber, perforce the regular Democratic coalition must occupy the bureaucratic box. Labor "automatically" transfers its allegiance from Johnson to Humphrey. Congressmen, Senators, assorted state party leaders, the staff men of the "bureaucratic" candidate are "faithful" "retainers" and "admirers," men of no independent judgment, having no discernible justification for their preferences beyond loyalty to the "machine." The emergent description owes less to Max Weber than to W. S. Gilbert.

The book illustrates that it is hardly possible to write with discernment about American elections without an understanding of American government. This curiously non-obvious truth makes Presidential elections, of all the political institutions of contemporary America, singularly difficult to capture. It is not merely the confusion of events, or the multiplication of actors and supernumeraries rushing to and fro, the impossibility of being everywhere at once, or of knowing in advance which meeting out of a hundred will matter a few weeks later. These present problems of technique and logistics, and they are formidable. It is, for example, a serious methodological flaw that inner struggles and dilemmas of the Kennedy camp are painted in this book in such beautiful and elaborate and flattering detail, whereas the equally great complexities of the Humphrey and Nixon groups on the Vietnam issue, say, or on the choice of a Vice-Presidential candidate, are sketched with perfunctory haste.

But the heart of the difficulty lies elsewhere, in the fact that American mass politics as played out in an election year is not the whole of American politics. To understand the characters as they pop up in the quadrennial drama it is necessary to see them also in the light of a longer view, encompassing knowledge of their participation in the ongoing, everyday context of our other political institutions and against a background of detailed information about the fundamental commitments of their careers as revealed in their actions in the more mundane encounters of day-to-day life. Unlike dramas that are written for the stage, the encounters of a Presidential year cannot be counted upon to serve as perfect illustrations of the lives and characters of the men involved. A fortunate few politicians may have the gift of so contriving their images, or of having such images thrust upon them. But such matters are fortuitous. It is, needless to say, in the interests of journalists who give accounts of Presidential election dramaturgy to portray these events as deeply symbolic of our national life and as importantly emblematic of the true inner beings and ultimate worth of the persons who are enmeshed in them. It takes great integrity in an author, great sophistication, and rare devotion to hard work to resist forcing American politics, American society and American culture into the mold our spectacular Presidential elections provide.

I do not see that integrity, that sophistication or that devotion in *An American Melodrama*. I do see evidences of desultory homework, of casual learning, but in the end no commitment to the pursuit of the truth or to its illumination in this frivolous and lumpish book.

KENNEDY JUSTICE *

It is difficult for the reader of the daily newspapers to get a sense of the fact that Presidencies are actually about the politics of capturing—or learning to be captured by—the routines of government, and then making the government run. It is doubly difficult for the student of the Kennedy Presidency to get this sense, for reasons that are well enough known. We can be grateful to Victor Navasky for not being so beguiled by the Kennedy glamor as to have produced yet another misleading and redundant tribute to Camelot. Instead he has given us a detailed chronicle and serious assessment of the way in which Robert Kennedy operated the Justice Department—the best discussion I know of that deals with national politics from the perspective of a cabinet officer.

Navasky's study is generally instructive precisely because, as he points out, the Kennedy Attorney Generalship must constitute a limiting case; surely no head of a department has ever enjoyed better or more assured access to and support from a President than Robert Kennedy did from his brother. Thus Kennedy was, as Navasky says, the maximum Attorney General, at least so far as constraints and difficulties from above are concerned.

Yet, as we rapidly discover, this is by no means enough to assure maximum performance on all fronts. Rather than a clear-cut hierarchical Justice Department, in which the maximum Attorney General automatically gets the outcomes he wants, Navasky (courtesy of Max Weber) proposes the metaphor of a Justice Department which embodies an interaction among three giant forces: the code of the Kennedys, legitimized by charisma, activist, result-oriented, red-tape cutting, and loyal to persons; the code of the Ivy League Gentleman, embodied in Kennedy's top appointees (Burke Marshall, Nicholas Katzenbach, Byron White, Louis Oberdorfer, et al.), legitimized by tradition, proceduralist, oriented to civil liberties, limited government, due process, fed-

---

* Review of Victor S. Navasky, *Kennedy Justice* (New York: Atheneum, 1971).

eralism, and letting the chips fall; and the code of the FBI, legitimized by the existence of files, secretive, routine-oriented, self-
protective, and loyal to habit.

The first and in some respects the most significant part of the
book describes the way in which Robert Kennedy came to terms
with J. Edgar Hoover, the maximum Bureau Chief. Since the
FBI employs almost half of the people in the Justice Department,
the nature of this bargain was bound to have enormous impact
upon what Kennedy and his appointees could do in their time in
office. Navasky concludes that the FBI imposed considerable con-
straint upon Kennedy Justice, especially in the field of civil
rights, where the Bureau was not quick to adapt its priorities to
those of the Attorney General. Navasky suggests one highly plausible reason for Bureau-Department tension in this area. Increasingly in the early 1960's, the Department came to view the civil
rights problem as entailing a need to ride herd on local law en-
forcement agencies throughout the South in order to provide minimal levels of protection to civil rights workers. Navasky surmises
that part of the FBI's reluctance to participate in this effort arose
from long-standing ties between the Bureau and local law enforce-
ment agencies. To disrupt these ties in order to meet an extraordinary situation might have jeopardized the ongoing routines in
which the Bureau was productively enmeshed with locals.

The identification, examination, and diagnosis of dilemmas
such as these are central to at least one branch of political science.
Navasky shows how and why Attorney General Kennedy
challenged, circumvented, and gave hostages to the FBI and to J.
Edgar Hoover. This contributes helpfully to our understanding,
otherwise seriously deficient, of the politics of running the great
departments of our national government.

Other sections of *Kennedy Justice* take up other facets of the Attorney General's world. Herewith, a small sample: A long section
on federalism, slightly marred by an excess of second-guessing by
Navasky, explores the roles of the Justice Department in the in-
tegration of Southern universities. Here, Navasky argues that the
code of the Ivy League Gentleman, and the theory of federalism
to which it gave rise, hemmed Kennedy in too much. Another

173

chapter argues that the eagerness of the American Bar Association to legitimize its participation in the selection of federal judges coupled with serious lapses in the attentiveness of the Justice Department to the credentials of nominees produced some very bad judicial appointments in the South. However, Navasky only takes up in detail the handful of notorious cases. His legal training (though a practicing journalist, Navasky is a graduate of Yale Law School) might have led him to a more ambitious, and more enlightening task, that of examining the performance of a larger sample of Kennedy judicial appointees in order to see if the imputed pattern of semi-indifference in the Department of Justice to the quality of the bench was sustained in areas other than the South and for issues other than segregation of public facilities.

Where Attorney General Kennedy's light touch with his bureaus is held to have been relatively ineffective in dealing with J. Edgar Hoover, with Archibald Cox, the distinguished and independent Solicitor General, Navasky thinks Kennedy struck just the right note. Navasky gives a detailed and intriguing account of the complex negotiations in and around the Solicitor General's office surrounding the decision to file an amicus brief for the government in one of the reapportionment cases. My view is that he is a little too sure that the outcome was the right one.

The *pièce de résistance* of the book is the last chapter, on the campaign to get James Hoffa, showing Kennedy Justice at its least inhibited, as the early chapters show it at its most inhibited. Navasky raises some proper questions about this project, and I think quite eloquently puts the case for a constrained Attorney General to counterpoise the case he makes earlier, in regard to civil rights, for a less constrained one.

This is not a flawless book. It is a bit repetitious, and once in a while a bit smug. I found a few small inaccuracies in it. On the whole, however, I think *Kennedy Justice* is thoughtfully, artfully, and carefully done. There are a good many lessons in it for students of the craft of governing. Some of these are hard lessons, since they force us to consider what we can reasonably expect from leaders of government less advantageously placed than the maximum Attorney General.

6
The Press

On the whole, I suppose that pound for pound there is no more avid consumer of the press and broadcast news outside the press corps itself than the average political scientist. So it should come as no surprise that from time to time the news media themselves should be at the focus of a political scientist's attention.

Conversation about the news media in this country is a fairly narrow-gauge affair, concentrating mostly on two themes. The "Fourth Branch of Government" theme argues the proposition that, far from being the neutral recorders they sometimes claim to be, the news media themselves have an autonomous influence upon the course of politics.

By far the best statement of this theme in print is, of course, Douglass Cater's book, *The Fourth Branch of Government*. Discussions of the influence of news media people upon public affairs generally run heavily to anecdotage and moralizing. The anecdotes record instances where news people have had political influence, e.g., when James Reston (at least it is usually James Reston in the stories I have heard) persuaded Arthur Vandenberg to vote for the pre-World War II peacetime draft, which, of course, won by one vote. Or when James Reston withheld from *New York*

Times publication advance information on the Bay of Pigs. Poor James Reston is apparently to the political influence of newspaper people what Dorothy Parker was to their collective reputation for witty remarks.

The moralizing consists mostly of regretting the inevitable entanglement of news people with their "sources," and upholds the sacredness of the obligation of the news media to remain independent of political manipulation. At this point in the discussion there are usually a few harsh words spoken about attempts at "news management" by the incumbent Presidential administration.

A second theme in the literature has to do with bias in the press. This conversation is usually conducted by people who are for one reason or another disappointed or aggrieved by news coverage and who want to show that it is unfair. Out of this genre spring studies of the "one-party press," and quite often the culprit is monopolistic publishers who exercise thought control over large chunks of the citizenry by owning the newspapers in one-newspaper towns. A right-wing version of this complaint has come into vogue ever since the rise in some sectors of the "new journalism," in which reporters are supposed to let their preferences and opinions all hang out in their news stories. Since new journalists are apparently mostly New Left in their sympathies (whereas plutocratic publishers were all allegedly mastadons of the Neanderthal Right), the rise of this art form has vastly increased the number of people who could give essentially conspiratorial reasons for the appearance of news coverage they did not like.

I do happen to think that there are serious and substantial problems associated with news coverage in this country, but that the reasons commonly given for the existence of these problems do insufficient justice to the intelligence, dedication, integrity, and professionalism of news media people. It is the fact that so many problems remain in spite of the demonstrable abundance of these qualities that makes for an interesting set of intellectual puzzles.

It is no easy matter to say what, precisely, is wrong with news coverage, and when it is inadequate. The plain fact is that much of the time it is excellent. At other times it is inadequate because of fortuitous failures of dedication, skill, luck, or intelligence. And sometimes there is indeed bias introduced either by hippie newsmen or cigar-chomping publishers. All of these causes for failures of performance are uninteresting. What is more intriguing is to ask whether any sources of persistent error remain that are related in some habitual way to characteristics of the news-gathering system itself, and to the constraints this system places upon its members.

Evidently, the answer is yes, and it therefore becomes part of our responsibility to understand the craft norms, training experiences, economizing devices, time-binds, managerial demands, and subcultural definitions of the situation that create the political theories that news people live by. A few scholars have risen to this bait, and gaps in our information are beginning to fill in. My own contributions to this line of inquiry are rather sparse, in part because so far I have permitted myself to concentrate for too long on attempts to devise a reasonably convincing argument on the prior question: that in fact there are special performance characteristics of the news media that differ from the conventional descriptions news people give of what they do, and which therefore need explaining.

The first selection in this chapter essentially restates this theme, while lamenting a lost opportunity to raise these issues in a serious way owing to the questionable intellectual standards of a well-publicized book on bias in network news coverage. The second selection discusses some opportunity costs of one of the worst sins of network news—convergence. And the third selection describes and attempts to account for news coverage in a particular case in which systemic characteristics were apparently intermingled with the political biases of reporters and columnists. As I have suggested, these selections only begin to address the central problem of accounting for the political theories of news people.

TRUTH AND/OR FAIRNESS
IN THE NEWS*

There have been a lot of complaints about the news media lately, and not only from Vice-President Agnew and other presumed soreheads in the Nixon administration. Like most of our institutions, newspapers and the networks have been a target of a general upsurge of mistrust and anger in recent years. Indeed, it has become almost fashionable to argue that perhaps the Vice-President was on the right track in accusing media managers of insularity, inaccuracy, elitism, squishy softness, or whatever it was.

Into this promising atmosphere comes Edith Efron's reassuringly titled *The News Twisters* (initials TNT, get it?). As the first full-length book on the subject to appear since the Vice-President issued his official hunting license to media critics, it is likely to receive unusual notice from people who are concerned about the difficulties of getting fair, coherent, timely, and informative news to citizens, as well as from people who simply think this is a hot issue.

The message of Miss Efron's book is that during the election campaign of 1968, TV news coverage was "severely biased" in a left/liberal direction. The basis for this claim is a study of the three main 7:00 p.m. national network news programs that Miss Efron, a reporter for *TV Guide*, conducted under the auspices of an organization called the Historical Research Foundation. For eight weeks during the fall of 1968, these programs were tape-recorded and their contents typed up. Miss Efron and, one gathers, an assistant went through this material and coded passages as being "for" and "against" each of the three Presidential candidates, U.S. policy on the bombing halt, U.S. policy toward

* Review of Edith Efron, *The News Twisters* (Los Angeles: Nash Publishing, 1969).

the Vietnam war, demonstrators, violent radicals, and six other very closely related subjects.

A series of bar graphs shows that, according to Miss Efron's criteria, disproportionate numbers of words were spoken on each network on one "side" of some of these subjects. When this was not the case, other suspicious goings-on are alleged. Vice-President Humphrey, for example (8,458 words pro, 8,307 words con), was, according to Miss Efron, portrayed by the networks as "a quasi-saint," whereas Mr. Nixon (1,620 words pro, 17,027 words con), was portrayed "as corruption incarnate." Seven hundred six words were spoken against liberals to 178 words for them. Six hundred two words were spoken against conservatives to 96 words for. The number of words spoken against demonstrators was 4,218; the number for was 3,715. The number of words for violent radicals was 0; the number against was 281.

What is the explanation for these alleged disproportions? Miss Efron assures us that we can rule out the possibility that the data are not as she gives them, because she describes her findings as overwhelming. It is hard to know whether to believe this. Some of her results do not in fact look overwhelming at all. The figures on "quasi-saint" Humphrey, for instance, seem to show him only half-saint, half-quasi.

With respect to some of the other figures, she appears to have been cooking her data. Take the use of the term "demonstrator" on a network news show. Of this Miss Efron says:

> By omitting the correct legal and moral nomenclature, the network reporter omits the critical opinion of organized society itself on such actions and tacitly communicates his sympathy for them.

It seems to me that someone less certain of "correct moral nomen-clature" might well score as neutral a report that Miss Efron ap-parently has no difficulty in interpreting as sympathetic to dem-onstrators. This is a serious matter. It suggests that any or all of the figures on which she bases her charges of bias may be utterly contaminated by the prejudices she brought to the study.

There is an even more basic problem, that of truthfulness.

Consider, for example, the words in Miss Efron's book itself. They are unsparingly hostile to the television networks. Nearly every word could, by her own scoring procedures, be classified as "anti-network news." Virtually no words would be scored as "pro-network news." Thus, by Miss Efron's own standard, she has written a book so filled with bias as to be unworthy of serious consideration.

Still, one assumes she attempted to write a truthful book and would not want it dismissed on the basis of one of her own bar graphs. In her behalf one might argue that good reporting entails a capacity to make judgments and distinctions, so that unlike things are not treated alike because of some copy-book conception of symmetry. Do all subjects, after all, resolve themselves neatly into two sides? Does each side have identical contours?

Consider, as an example of this problem, Miss Efron's reference to a "one-sided editorial assault on Nixon as an evader of issues, while Mr. Humphrey, whose ambiguities merited a similar charge, is spared." Can reasonable people maintain that the Nixon campaign of 1968 was in fact more evasive than Humphrey's? If so, then some of the "one-sidedness" that occurred in the network news coverage of Nixon occurred because Nixon—not the networks—put it there. Or, to take a less difficult case, consider "U.S. policy on the Vietnam war" (700 words for, 3,144 words con). This policy was, at the time of the campaign, ambiguous, changing, and, according to contemporary opinion surveys, unpopular. It was, moreover, in varying degrees under attack within both major parties. Is it surprising that fewer words during the campaign were spent in praise than in disparagement of it? What seems to me at issue here is a question as to the underlying shape of reality. If reality is in some meaningful sense asymmetrical, then truthful reporting entails a faithful rendering of the asymmetry.

Miss Efron cuts this knot unhesitatingly. She regards what goes on the airwaves not as aimed at truth but rather as wholly arbitrary, the product of a sequence of choices made by reporters and network news producers. This, of course, is not her original discovery. She goes on to argue, however, that these choices are governed by strong political biases that in various places she characterizes as "anti-anti-communism," "liberal," "radical chic." Network executives and newsmen deny these biases, she says, but hiring and professional rewards are severely restricted to those who follow the party line, and all others are systematically excluded. This, she argues, violates the "fairness doctrine" of the FCC, which provides that representative opinions in the community on all controversial matters shall be given equal time and be presented with equal force. Thus, on any controversial issue the matter of truthfulness or of the underlying contours of reality need not arise. What is required of the networks is equal time (which can be measured), not truthfulness (which cannot be). Miss Efron does not conceal her belief that in fact the networks are untruthful about many matters, although her claims to superior knowledge of reality are asserted baldly, rather than presented with any skill or persuasiveness. But I believe that pessimism—perhaps cynicism—about the intentions of the networks and network reporters to be truthful underlies her recommendation that "fairness," which can be legally enforced, substitute for the professional journalist's standard of "objectivity," which she argues is merely a Trojan horse for radical chic.

Thus, what Miss Efron's argument comes down to is this: liberals have been dominating network news with their propaganda for too long. They should be made to move over and give the other side a chance.

People in the news business are likely to take offense at this, citing, as they customarily do, the First Amendment, which says in part, that "Congress shall make no law . . . abridging the freedom of speech or of the press . . ." Miss Efron claims that as a matter of fact Congress has already enacted such a law, the Communications Act of 1934, under which the FCC has promulgated its "fairness doctrine." She paraphrases this doctrine as follows:

> Broadcast news is explicitly denied the First Amendment right to be biased.

181

Although this statement accords perfectly with the context in which it is found, it might equally well have been copied off a wall in *Animal Farm*.

Her argument is bound to make the legions of sanctimonious defenders of the media even more nervous than usual. I have a journalist friend who claims that as a matter of course all members of his profession get the First Amendment tattooed on their kneecaps. When confronted with criticism from outsiders, he says, kneecaps all over the industry begin to twitch. Consequently, news people fail often enough to draw a distinction between ugly diatribes of the Efron-Agnew ilk and more responsible commentary by outsiders on the performance of the media, such as that of Bernard Cohen, or Paul Weaver, or recent essays by George Lichtheim, Irving Kristol, and Daniel Patrick Moynihan.

The distinguishing feature of criticisms that media people need to take seriously is the willingness to entertain the idea of professional standards. To these critics, as to professional newsmen generally, there is such a thing as a world that has to be reported on and that exists outside the prejudices or preferences of newsmen. In short, truthfulness continues to be an issue to serious critics of the media, as it is to serious newsmen. Neither bother much with blanket definitions of "objectivity." Rather, they are concerned with what it takes to discover and deliver coherent, meaningful, and truthful information about civic life to citizens.

To my mind, the performance of the American news media does leave something to be desired. And their worst sins are these: *incoherence*, stemming from a style of news coverage and reporting that is highly mechanical and tailored more to the techniques of presentation than to the needs of citizens or the contours of events; *sparseness*, a characteristic that is mostly a consequence of the pressures on reporters to converge and concentrate on a narrow range of phenomena; and *inexpertise*, a quality that has its roots in journalistic craft norms that value amateurism, the general ability to turn out an undifferentiated product (the "story"), and egalitarianism ("we write for the man in the street"). I think these sins are increasingly the enemy of truthfulness, and certainly of an informed citizenry.

In the past, the favored explanation for all shortcomings of the news media was concentration of ownership. This may still explain some of the faults of bad newspapers, as Ben Bagdikian's recent study of Wilmington in the *Columbia Journalism Review* intimates. But how does one account for the vast recent improvement in the *Los Angeles Times*, as it edged closer to monopoly? Surely not by citing the anemic and short-lived *New York Times* West Coast experiment. Or, on the other hand, how did one explain the incredibly low quality for all those years of the hotly competitive and numerous Boston newspapers?

The currently fashionable explanation—radical reporters—proposed by Miss Efron and the Vice-President is equally simpleminded. Some reporters, to be sure, meet the description, and some of these are willfully untruthful and biased. But most are not. In the vast preponderance of journalistic situations, honest and, not uncommonly, intelligent people go about their jobs in ways that are, as far as I can see, scrupulously within the canons of the ethic of "objectivity." In these situations, too, the end product is often incoherent, sparse, and amateurish, conceivably "unfair" by Miss Efron's standards, or otherwise deficient. Why?

I think the way to answer this question is to do what Bernard Cohen did in his important and unjustly neglected book, *The Press and Foreign Policy*. That is, watch reporters make their appointed rounds, see them in the act of defining their daily agendas, capture them in their routines of creating the news. From seeing the constraints of time, the demands of middle management, the glut of information, it is possible to discover how certain economizing devices grow up and to understand how some of them are sanctioned by common usage. These are the operational codes by which all of us—each in his own walk of life—live. Because in democracies newsmen have so much to say about how the rest of us dispose of our political power, it is especially important to understand the codes that guide their work, for in that way we can get a clearer sense of how ordinary people come to view the choices they have and how the business of choosing can be made to work better.

And so, while I am prepared to entertain the proposition that network news programs are in some ways deficient, Edith Efron's criticisms seem to me wide of the mark as well as questionably supported by evidence. More importantly, I suspect that the simple-mindedness and crudity of her address to this complex issue, by coddling the paranoia of hard-hats and eliciting self-righteous responses from the networks, will make it much more difficult to conduct sensible conversation about causes and cures for deficiences in the presentation of the news.

ELECTION NIGHT TELEVISION

As the television coverage of election night gets more expensive and elaborate, it gets much more boring. One scarcely knows whether to thank Parkinson or McLuhan for it, but the much-advertised competition for ratings among the networks is producing not three distinctive styles of coverage but rather a dull gray similarity spread evenly across all channels. All three networks share the same strengths and the same weaknesses, and so the disgruntled viewer has not much incentive to go channel-hopping. His only real alternative is to turn the machinery off and get a good night's sleep. And unless there is some promise of more information per hour this time around, that is what eye-sore viewers ought to do.

Without doubt the networks have improved over the years in several ways. Everyone remembers what happened when they first introduced the computer. News announcers used to bat their eyelashes helplessly at it and wonder out loud if it could "really think." But by the 1964 election, people who knew what they were doing were loading the computers on each of the networks with useful information about past performances of intelligently chosen places around the country. As a result, the networks were able to forecast the outcome of the Presidential race on a state-by-state basis with reasonable speed. It would be ungracious to mention in passing that the election of 1964 just happened to have been very easy to call in most states. Even so, the computers and the men who ran them did creditably in getting out of these oversized adding machines what there was to get out of them—fast comparisons of 1964's results with the results of other years on a state by state and social group by group basis, and quick estimates of results to come based on a comparative reading of early returns.

The use of the computer so far this year has not been uniformly good. Efforts at making the primary elections intelligible deteriorated before pressure to pick a winner first on election night. At least once in 1968 this pressure led to some notably sharp practice.

In reporting the results of the California primary before the assassination of Senator Robert Kennedy, CBS news picked Senator Kennedy as a big winner. Two hours before their nearest competitor, CBS had Kennedy winning by a 14-point margin. CBS newsmen aggressively went out after reaction stories and elicited a number of comments based on the 52 per cent win they had predicted for Kennedy.

Since the principal effect of a primary is not the allocation of delegates in a single state but the impressions it creates in the minds of political leaders nation-wide, the CBS news reaction stories could have had a sizable influence on subsequent events, had tragedy not intervened.

Yet these stories, indeed most CBS election night coverage of the California primary, were based upon a CBS manufactured non-event. Senator Kennedy's margin of victory was actually a far less impressive 4.5 per cent. CBS went wrong because they introduced at least two last-minute modifications into the sampling procedures upon which they claimed to be basing their prediction. According to a CBS official's interview with the Los Angeles *Times*, the projection was based on results from only thirty of the eighty-nine precincts in the CBS sample; and in half of the thirty, the reports were based not on actual election statistics but on a poll CBS took on election day of voters emerging from polling places.

Had these short-cuts been reported fully and candidly on the air, the CBS projection could have been taken with the grain of salt it deserved. But there is still a tendency at all three networks to cultivate illusions of prescience at the expense of straight-forwardness when dealing with computers.

A big improvement over the years in network coverage has been the gain in the general readability of the signs, charts, tote boards, and maps that the newscasters have been using as visual aids. The network election service which collects the results and transmits them to the networks is fast and fancy, but it would not matter very much if we had to wait a few more hours for the relevant numbers to trickle in. More impressive than the method of data collection is the ease with which the networks make it possible for the casual viewer to take in the main facts at a glance.

But the networks are being done in by the very clarity and efficiency of their visual aids. Like sports announcers in the early days of TV, election night newsmen spend entirely too much time tediously reading off the popular vote totals in the Presidential race when these are continuously visible to the naked eye. Early in the evening, when only 3 per cent or 4 per cent or 6 per cent of the vote is counted, it is maddening to have to return constantly to the Presidential scoreboard for an oral recital celebrating each and every twitch of the tabulating machine.

The networks have also fallen too much in love with remote pick-ups as an end in themselves. Itchy fingers in the control room is the only conceivable explanation for early evening jumps around the circuit for two deadly minutes with each of the special correspondents in an endless succession of nearly empty hotel ballrooms, awaiting the appearance of a candidate, or at least a few inebriated camp-followers. Later on at the remote locations, the screen fills up with exciting shots of blinking lights, deep shadows, the backs of heads, and the breathless news that somebody's bubble-top car is somewhere out there.

Of course, every last movement of the major candidates or members of their families unto the fourth generation on election night comes under the heading of top priority "human interest." But surely until a reporter can get his quarry actually talking into a microphone, the whole thing is a waste of time. It is also embarrassing to have to watch newspeople repeatedly harassing politicians into saying a few words—any few words—into the camera when it is obvious that if they would just let the candidates get where they are going, they might be able to make the news that the reporters are supposed to be covering.

It is probably futile to expect moderation from the networks in the use of remote pick-ups—but one cannot help thinking that the coast-to-coast national network time spent in chasing important people through crowds, around hallways, and up the stairs with what must add up to tons of television equipment is mostly sheer waste.

Network producers may feel that, on the whole, they have nothing much better to do anyway with the hours and hours of the election night. But if this is their problem, then one would think there would be time for a little more depth and continuity in the analysis of what is happening—and, in particular, more time to discuss in detail results other than Presidential. The bare bones of the Gubernatorial and Senatorial results are broadcast with some regularity and with a minimum of bumbling, it is true, but the coverage of Congressional results on a national basis on all three networks is on the whole nothing short of a disgrace.

The election of 1964, for example, was an important one for the House of Representatives. A large number of incumbent Congressmen were defeated, including ranking Republicans on the two most important committees of Congress. Republicans for the first time since Reconstruction elected Congressmen in Mississippi and Georgia and no less than five Congressmen in Alabama. This called for explanation and full reporting. Representatives in Congress are national, not local officials. Year after year, the House is the arena in which Presidential programs are made and broken. And yet not one of the networks made even a half-hearted attempt to cover the Congressional story as it unfolded. About all I heard on the subject was Chet Huntley mispronouncing the names of two or three Congressmen, and mixing up the name of an incumbent with a challenger. It would have been excusable, if this clutch of mistakes were not practically the only attention to specific Congressional races I heard NBC attempt all night long. CBS was no better. The only complete rundown of state-by-state totals on the Congressional races that I caught on CBS all evening was hopelessly garbled by the normally suave and convincing Robert Trout. In state after state, he read the totals for 1962 as 1964's results, and vice-versa.

The first specific mention of any House race on CBS, so far as I am able to tell, took place at 11:20 p.m., Eastern Standard Time, 4 hours and 20 minutes after election coverage began. They announced (big surprise) that Speaker McCormack had won re-election. Trout even ignored the election of the Mississippi Republican Congressman in order to make a breathless joke out of the fact that Senator Stennis, who was running unopposed, had been re-elected.

Although I tried to give ABC equal time on my television set, I was unable to catch them in a single mistake. One factor which contributed to their spotless record was the fact that they never mentioned the House of Representatives within my hearing at all.

Is it too much to ask that the networks provide minimally decent coverage of the House races? Perhaps all it would take is asking one of the many able and intelligent people who work for the networks (and I fear I have been too harsh with the men in front of the camera) to devote a little time before election day to learning the names of the candidates, and perhaps one or two things about some of the more interesting Congressional races. In a burst of big spending, one network might even go so far as to grant the House a kind of parity in keeping with its Constitutional role, and establish a House desk that could follow and report trends and important developments on election night with a modicum of discernment and intelligence. If a network had had a House desk in 1964, they could, for example, have predicted on election night the passage of Medicare legislation in the 89th Congress by noting not only what was happening to the House races in general, but to the Ways and Means Committee in particular.

The purpose of this suggestion is to make election coverage more informative and perhaps more meaningful. In the three-network race to attract the largest election night audience this may be beside the point. On the other hand, if the networks intend to talk all election night, they may as well find something interesting to talk about.

POLITICAL SCIENCE AND
THE PRESS

Allegations of bias about the press are not rare. But it is unusual that an opportunity arises to conduct an empirical examination of press coverage where it is possible to do more than compare one newspaper story against another. This is a report on one such opportunity. It concerns press coverage of a poll on American public opinion toward the Vietnam war, which was designed and conducted by a group of social scientists in Stanford, California, in cooperation with the National Opinion Research Center of the University of Chicago.[1] The text of their report on the poll's results constitutes the "event" to which the press responded. Thus, unlike instances when the event is recorded only through the varied reports of first-hand observers, here it was possible to compare alternative accounts directly with the document on which they were based. This adds a useful dimension to the study of press coverage, since we could study not only variation among news accounts, but also differences between each news account and the document itself.

In the aftermath of the American decision to resume bombing in North Vietnam during the last week of January 1966, it seemed apparent to academic observers that a new level of tension was being reached in domestic debate on the Vietnam issue. This debate had, as we all know, in the previous year and a half included the full panoply of public demonstrations: debates, teach-

---

[1] The authors of the study were Richard A. Brody and Sidney Verba, both of the Stanford University Political Science Department, Paul Ekman, a research associate of the Stanford Institute of Political Studies and associate professor of psychology at San Francisco State College, Edwin B. Parker of the Stanford Communication Department, Gordon Black and Norman H. Nie, graduate students in political science at Stanford, and the present writer, then a Fellow at the Center for Advanced Study in the Behavioral Sciences, located in Stanford, California. In addition to this Stanford group, two officers of the National Opinion Research Center were listed as authors: Peter Rossi and Paul Sheatsley.

ins, protest rallies, Congressional speeches and hearings, and so on. Yet our knowledge of public opinion on the Vietnam issue was confined to reports of two or three item responses to the commercial national opinion polls and to White House interpretations of responses to small numbers of questions that had been planted in the sample surveys of market researchers.[2] The time was clearly ripe for a more elaborate attempt to investigate the structure of public attitudes on this issue in greater detail. During late February and early March of 1966, the Stanford group devised a questionnaire of some 30 items, pretested the questionnaire on over 200 respondents in Northern California, engaged the cooperation of the N.O.R.C., which provided part of the money for the use of its nation-wide survey facility, and raised additional money to pay for the study by private subscription from over 200 individuals in the San Francisco Bay Area.

A detailed account of the substantive results of the survey is reported elsewhere.[3] For present purposes, what will concern us is the initial report of the study, and the press reception it received. The report was issued as a press release on Tuesday, March 15, from the Stanford University News Service. It consisted of five parts. The top two pages were a conventional press release, under a Stanford University News Service letterhead, written by a University press officer, summarizing compactly the major findings. Next came the report proper: a six-page essay discussing the findings in an organized way. Following that were three appendices: a page identifying the authors; eight pages of tables, giving exact percentages, verbatim questions from the interview instrument and the full cross-tabulations for all findings reported in the

[2] William Chapman, " 'Piggy-back' Polls Guide LBJ on Public Opinion," *Washington Post*, February 19, 1966; James Reston, "Washington: Where Did We Go Wrong?" *New York Times*, November 21, 1965; C. L. Sulzberger, "Foreign Affairs: A Prevalence of Hawks," *New York Times*, March 6, 1966; "Johnson Finds Polls Ask Harder Vietnam War," *New York Times*, March 10, 1966.
[3] Most of the initial report of the study is reprinted in Sheldon Appleton, *United States Foreign Policy: An Introduction With Cases* (Boston: Little, Brown, 1968), pp. 336–46. See also, for an extended analysis of the poll's findings, Sidney Verba, Richard A. Brody, Edwin B. Parker, Norman H. Nie, Nelson W. Polsby, Paul Ekman, and Gordon S. Black, "Public Opinion and the War in Vietnam," *American Political Science Review* 61 (June 1967), 317–33.

report proper; and, finally, a two-page comparison of the results of the Stanford poll with other polls on Vietnam that had appeared in the press. This document was the stimulus to which the press reacted.

The Prestige Papers

Since the poll concerned public opinion on a foreign policy question, the response of the "prestige papers" that have been found to be most influential to foreign policy makers was of particular interest.[4] In two of the seven "prestige" papers—the *Christian Science Monitor* and the *Wall Street Journal*—there was no coverage of the poll. The *New York Times* gave the poll front page news coverage on March 15, in addition ran a news analysis on the poll, and later in the week referred to the poll in an editorial. The *Baltimore Sun* gave the poll an extended news analysis.[5] The *Washington Post* and the *Washington Evening Star* printed fairly long reports on the poll on inside pages; later—on April 7—the *Post* ran an attack on the poll by the syndicated columnists Rowland Evans and Robert Novak and later still an extended defense by the Stanford group. The *New York Herald Tribune* printed no news coverage of the poll, but did print the Evans and Novak column and the reply.

Apparently the poll fell into a middle range of "events" for these newspapers. It was not so insignificant as to be universally ignored; on the other hand, it was not regarded as of such an importance as to evoke the strongly convergent coverage which

---

[4] In his valuable study, *The Press and Foreign Policy* (Princeton: Princeton U. Press, 1963), Bernard C. Cohen says: "There can be no question that the *New York Times* is of prime importance; but it has distinguished company on the desks of foreign policy-making officials, very few of whom limit their consumption to one or even two newspapers: the *Washington Post*, the *New York Herald Tribune*, the *Wall Street Journal*, the *Christian Science Monitor*, the *Baltimore Sun*, the *Washington Evening Star*. Collectively these papers, with extensive foreign affairs coverage and in many cases independent sources of news via their own staffs of foreign correspondents and foreign affairs reporters and analysts, form the prestige press in the foreign policy field." Pp. 136–37.

[5] In addition, the *Baltimore Evening Sun*, not a prestige paper, but operated by the same ownership as the *Sun*, ran a sympathetic editorial on the poll: "Opinions on the War," March 15, 1966.

Cohen suggests is the hallmark of the major foreign policy news story.[6]

The prestige papers provided widely differentiated coverage of the poll: in two cases a "straight" news story, which preserved the organization of the original document; one news story which reported the contents of the poll in such a way that many of its findings were ignored or somewhat distorted; two "reinterpretations" which described the major findings of the poll much differently from the report; an all-out attack, and one friendly commentary.

Straight News Stories

Both "straight" stories in the prestige press appeared in the two Washington papers.[7] They preserved the original report's emphasis upon what the authors regarded as their most newsworthy set of findings: That majorities of those polled approved of a number of steps to de-escalate the Vietnam war, even though a 61 per cent majority also approved of President Johnson's handling of the conflict. In the original report, de-escalation sentiment was indicated by many separate findings which the authors assembled into a coherent line of exposition: First, four specific de-escalation steps were approved by majorities: 88 per cent were willing to negotiate with the Viet Cong; 70 per cent would approve a U.N. negotiated truce; 54 per cent favored holding free elections in Vietnam, even if the Viet Cong might win; 52 per cent were willing to see the Viet Cong in a coalition government. Second: Four out of six corresponding escalation alternatives were rejected by majorities and one of the remaining alternatives produced a tie vote.[8] Third: All four de-escalation alternatives were favored by

[6] *Op. cit.*, chapter III.
[7] John Maffre, "Poll Backs Bringing Viet Cong into Talks," *Washington Post*, March 15, 1966, p. A12; "Poll Finds Public For Easing of War, Viet Cong in Talks," the *Evening Star*, March 15, 1966, p. A6.
[8] A majority (55%) *favored* fighting the Chinese within the borders of Vietnam if necessary to continue the war. The population split 45% for and 46% against an increase of U.S. troops to 500,000. Majorities *rejected* bombing the cities of North Vietnam (55% against), a ground war in China (60% against), an atomic war with China (63% against), atomic war with Russia (71% against) if necessary to continue the fighting in Vietnam.

majorities of the President's supporters. Fourth: Increased domestic costs—a number of items were involved here—to continue the war were disapproved of by majorities.[9] And fifth: Large numbers of respondents who agreed to support escalation alternatives supported de-escalation alternatives as well.

Not all of these facts and figures found their way into the *Post* and *Star* stories, but some did—especially the figures on de-escalation steps. The *Washington Post* went beyond de-escalation figures and figures on domestic costs only to indicate that these did not agree with previously published polls by both the Louis Harris and George Gallup organizations, whose findings regularly appear in the *Post*.

The *Star* continued on, however, to report a second major cluster of findings from the original document—that, contrary to published reports,[10] opposition to the President was coming from those favoring de-escalation of the war, and those favoring de-escalation of the war—the Vietnam "doves"—nevertheless overwhelmingly approved of firm policies toward communism elsewhere in the world.

A third major cluster of findings noted briefly by the *Star* showed rejection by majorities of extreme alternatives—of policies amounting to unilateral withdrawal from Vietnam or, at the other extreme, of various alternatives involving vastly increased military involvement.[11]

[9] The items involved were: approve or disapprove of doing the following in order to continue fighting: (a) reducing aid to education (78% disapprove) (b) increasing taxes at home (67% disapprove) (c) reducing the Medicare program (66% disapprove) (d) putting government controls over wages and prices (53% disapprove) (e) spending less money for the War on Poverty (50% disapprove).

[10] See, e.g., "Johnson Finds Polls Ask Harder Vietnam War," *loc. cit.*, Robert E. Thompson, "President Sees Gain by Hawks," *Washington Post*, March 30, 1966.

[11] Associated Press and United Press International stories were not used by any of the "prestige" papers, but were, of course, widely printed. Both stories preserved the emphasis of the Stanford report, noting support for President Johnson qualified by support for what UPI called "a more flexible attitude" and the AP "a more flexible U.S. policy" in Vietnam. The word "flexible" appears in the first sentence of the Stanford press release. The AP, as is their custom, attributed the findings to "a Stanford University political science professor" rather than to an impersonal (though signed) report. One sentence in the AP story began: "He said the survey was conducted by himself and six other social scientists. . . ."

"Confusion"

The *New York Times* front page news story bore less resemblance than the *Post* and *Star* stories to the original Stanford report.[12] The lead sentence said that the Stanford poll showed majorities of Americans ready to negotiate to end the war. But the second sentence, in which the first actual figure was cited, was somewhat misleading. It said, "The poll also showed that, confronted with the choice of withdrawal or all-out war in Vietnam, 60 per cent of those questioned favored all-out war." This figure was one of 16 percentage figures reported in Table 12 of the appendix to the report. It was based—unlike the negotiation figures that the *Times* lead alluded to but did not give—on slightly less than half of the sample of respondents, and was arrived at in the following way.

It is often asserted that the frustrations of limited war lead American public opinion to prefer extreme alternatives to patiently waiting it out.[13] And so the authors of the poll devised a test of this proposition. They asked a hypothetical forced-choice question: "Suppose you had to choose among continuing the present situation indefinitely, fighting a major war with hundreds of thousands of casualties, or a withdrawal of American troops leading to an eventual communist takeover. Which would you choose?" The responses rejected the "frustration" hypothesis. Forty-nine per cent preferred the present situation, 23 per cent the major war and 19 per cent withdrawal. When the 49 per cent *who preferred the present situation* were asked to choose between the extreme alternatives, 60 per cent chose the major war.

The Stanford press release was not clear on this point—but the point was not beyond hope of clarification. In succeeding paragraphs, the *Times* story quoted one of the poll's authors directly; an interview had in fact taken place which could have dispelled any lingering doubts in the mind of the *Times* reporter

[12] Wallace Turner, "Public Backs Negotiation with Viet Cong, Poll Says," *New York Times*, March 15, 1966.
[13] See e.g., Talcott Parsons, "Social Strains in America," Daniel Bell (ed.), *The New American Right* (New York: Criterion, 1955), pp. 91–166. Samuel Lubell, *The Future of American Politics* (2nd ed.; New York: Garden City, Doubleday, 1956), p. 164; *The Revolt of the Moderates*, New York: Harper, 1956, 268 ff.

who inserted the qualification "of those questioned" to the finding of 60 per cent.

In the last half of the *Times* story, for nine column inches, a large number of exact percentage findings from the poll were reported, under the stupefying rubric, "Following are examples of questions and answers in the survey." What followed were the figures on the four de-escalation alternatives. "However," the *Times* went on, "other answers showed the public opposed to abandoning the defense of Southeast Asia." After this unilateral withdrawal rejection figures were given and the "frustration hypothesis" figures introduced once again, in greater detail. Corresponding figures rejecting escalation alternatives were not given. The *Times* story closed with a number of figures on domestic costs of the war.

In essence, the *Times* news story neutralized the analysis offered in the Stanford report. It omitted many of the Stanford poll's findings, and selected among the remainder in such a way as to suggest that for every majority backing one set of policies, there was another majority backing a set of incompatible policies.[14]

This interpretation was made explicit in the accompanying "news analysis" by the *Times* Washington bureau chief, Tom Wicker. Wicker's analysis, headlined "confusion on Vietnam," made use almost exclusively of the "frustration hypothesis" question.[15] Three times Wicker referred to this question: once to support the proposition that Americans "don't want more appeasement" because "60 per cent would favor fighting a major war . . ."; once to show that "the Administration's stated objective—defending South Vietnam from a communist takeover—was overwhelmingly supported—most significantly by the 60 per cent who said they preferred a major war . . ."; and once to show that "there appears to be considerable unrest about the indecisive ap-

[14] Notable among the findings omitted by the *Times* were those showing that persons disagreeing with President Johnson on Vietnam policy were predominantly "doves" rather than "hawks." On March 6 and March 10, the *Times* had printed stories based upon White House statements claiming the opposite. See note 2.
[15] Tom Wicker, "Confusion on Vietnam: Public Backs a Limited War, but Not at Expense of Communist Take-Over," *New York Times*, March 15, 1966.

pearance of the war [because] 42 per cent would favor either a major war or a withdrawal. . . ." This last percentage appeared nowhere in the Stanford report. It is arrived at by simply adding together the 23 per cent whose first choice was a major war and the 19 per cent who chose unilateral withdrawal rather than continuing a limited war indefinitely—an ingenious way of forming a coalition between two highly unlikely allies. One wonders whether in fact "dissatisfaction" is a homogeneous, aggregate phenomenon: whether those 19 per cent who voted to get out, being "dissatisfied," would, as their *second* choice, have voted for the major war; and whether the 23 per cent who preferred the major war would rather get out of Vietnam than prolong the fighting indefinitely. No concrete evidence that would confirm or reject this interpretation was presented; but it is most implausible. Certainly few of the activists taking either extreme position in public debate on the issue gave much approval to the other extreme. Furthermore, Wicker's interpretation suggested that these two responses indicated unrest about the *present* state of the war. A less daring assessment might have noted that the middle alternative was the present situation projected into an indefinitely lengthy future. A much better figure to use for the purpose of determining present attitudes toward the war would, of course have been the very first finding reported in the text of the Stanford report: "In general, do you approve or disapprove of the way the Johnson Administration is handling the situation in Vietnam?" (Disapprove: 29 per cent.)

Wicker's other two allusions to the "frustration hypothesis" figures also involved questionable interpretations. Wicker gave the impression that the 60 per cent choosing the major war represented "overwhelming" sentiment—when, in fact, it represented a fall-back position for 60 per cent of 49 per cent of the sample—or, put another way, a second choice for 30 per cent of the respondents.

"A study of [the poll's] seeming contradictions," Wicker concluded, "and of its findings as a whole suggests . . . that a confused and worried public backs President Johnson but shies from casualty lists and paying the bill; it prefers a settlement to a war but it is determined to defend South Vietnam from the Communists."

In a letter to the editor of the *Times*, the authors offered an alternative to Wicker's "confusion" interpretation.[16] Instead of regarding as contradictory the majorities that (1) approved of the President, (2) supported de-escalation steps and (3), rejected unilateral withdrawal, the authors found these positions compatible with a position of reasoned moderation—especially when the rejection of most escalation alternatives, which Wicker ignored, was juxtaposed with the rejection of unilateral withdrawal. They said: ". . . attitudes favoring moderate steps in either direction but no extreme moves do not appear confused. And unwillingness to bear domestic costs . . . is by no means inconsistent with desires for a negotiated settlement or opposition to major escalation."

The "confusion" analysis had something of a vogue. T.R.B. in the *New Republic* said, "There is a ring of authenticity about [the poll] because it is so confused. As N.Y. Timesman Tom Wicker observed, 'The public seems to be more certain of what it won't do than of what it ought to do.' " [17] Ignored in this conclusion were the majorities *for* various de-escalation alternatives reported in the *Times*—and in the *New Republic*.[18]

An ingenious demonstration of "confusion" was offered by *Time* Magazine.[19] *Time* said: "Oddly enough the Stanford Poll . . . showed that 88 per cent would favor negotiations with the Viet Cong. . . . In fact, only 29· per cent of those interviewed could correctly define the Viet Cong as South Vietnamese Communists: the rest thought they were North Vietnamese (41%), Red Chinese (10%), or an arm of the 'government we are supporting' (4%), or else had no notion who the Viet Cong were (16%)." [20]

Consider the plight of the poor reader of *Time*, who, on March 25, learned that to identify the Viet Cong as North Vietnamese

[16] "Attitudes Toward War," *New York Times*, March 30, 1966.
[17] T.R.B. from Washington, *New Republic*, March 26, 1966.
[18] "New Poll on Vietnam," *New Republic*, March 26, 1966.
[19] *Time*, March 25, 1966. "The War—Deflating the Dragon," p. 16.
[20] These figures did not appear in the report, but were supplied to *Time* by one of the authors.

was incorrect. On January 14, *Time* had said, "A more important issue is Hanoi's insistence that the National Liberation Front, the political arm of the Viet Cong, be seated. . . . This the U.S. has rejected because it considers the Front the pawn of North Vietnam. . . . Some critics of U.S. policy disagree, asserting that the Liberation Front is, in large measure, a genuine nationalist movement. . . . While the Front certainly includes many non-Communists and nationalists, every reasonably well-informed source agrees it is an integral part of Hanoi's Communist apparatus. . . ." [21] Thus, in a scant two months what formerly might have been a "well-informed" response could safely be disregarded. Confusion indeed! [22]

Hawk and Dove Interpretations

A second re-analysis of the Stanford poll in the prestige press by Philip Potter of the *Baltimore Sun* carries the same line of argument a bit farther. Under the headline, "Poll Shows Strong Vietnam War Support," Potter identified as "some of the most inter-

[21] *Time* essay, January 14, 1966, p. 33. For further identification of the Viet Cong, see the article by U.S. intelligence official George A. Carver, Jr., "The Faceless Viet Cong," *Foreign Affairs* 44 (April 1966), 347–72. " 'Viet Cong' is a contraction of the phrase 'Vietnam Cong-San' which means, simply, 'Vietnamese communists.' . . . It is a useful, precise and . . . accurate generic label for the individuals leading the present insurgent movement, at all levels, and for the organizational structure through which that insurgency is controlled and directed. . . . As an organization . . . the N.L.F. is a contrived political mechanism with no political roots, subject to the ultimate control of the Lao Dong Party in Hanoi. . . . It is essentially the relationship between a field command and its parent headquarters."

[22] In a letter to the *New York Times*, April 6, 1966, Professor Herman Finer of the University of Chicago defended the Wicker "confusion" analysis by citing the figures from *Time*. A reply to Finer, by Professor Eugene Feingold of the University of Michigan, was carried in a letter to the *Times* on April 23, 1966. It is probably not irrelevant to observe that *Time's* version of "confusion" could have been used to lend support to an argument that negotiations or a coalition would not have been preferred by a majority of Americans if they had "correctly" identified the Viet Cong. Thus, the argument would go, Americans who believed the Viet Cong were (e.g.) Red Chinese (10 per cent) would be *less* likely to approve of negotiations if they knew that in reality the Viet Cong were South Vietnamese communists. Readers may wonder, as the authors of the poll wondered, why *Time* insisted upon their classification of "correct" and "incorrect" responses if it was not to lend support to some such implausible argument.

esting findings" of the poll two findings showing opposition to unilateral withdrawal from Southeast Asia, and the "frustration hypothesis" results.[23] The two paragraphs following this lead were devoted to an identification of the poll's auspices, with particular attention to the fact that it was partially financed by private subscription from residents of the San Francisco Bay Area, including faculty members of the University of California at Berkeley, "a hotbed of anti-war demonstrations."

Ten column inches down in the story, Potter mentioned some of the Stanford poll's findings about majorities favoring de-escalation, but, these findings, unlike the "interesting" findings which he reported in his lead, were given not unequivocally as facts, but as "claims," e.g., "In their own analysis . . . claimed to be a fuller exploration . . . than commercial pollsters have made to date, the Stanford men accented . . . what they claim to be 'widespread support' for de-escalation. . . ." Potter claims: "It also was said that the new study . . . showed that adults critical of the President are mainly 'doves,' not 'hawks.' On the other hand the Stanford faculty men found that most Americans are not 'real hawks' or 'real doves.' . . . Only 6 per cent were put in the former category, and consistent 'doves' were found to be only double that number." Actually, the figure was not "only" double 6 per cent, but rather more than twice 6 per cent—14 per cent. The "real hawks" were respondents who rejected all de-escalation alternatives and accepted most escalation alternatives. "Real doves" rejected all escalation alternatives and accepted most de-escalation alternatives. There is, of course, no inconsistency between these findings and the finding that most of the 29 per cent who disapproved of President Johnson's handling of the Vietnam war are "doves" rather than "hawks." Thus Potter's use of the transition phrase "on the other hand" is puzzling. The *Sun* story gave the poll's figures showing overwhelming support for "firm" policies toward China, Russia and Cuba, and went on: " 'In this respect, those who favor dealing with the Viet Cong are as firm on communism elsewhere as are those who oppose dealing with

[23] Philip L. Potter, "Poll Shows Strong Vietnam War Support," the *Baltimore Sun*, March 15, 1966.

the Viet Cong,' it was said. The Stanford men did not draw the obvious inference that having to prove firmness in the field is unlikely to be as popular as 'firmness' expressed only in words."

It would be difficult to infer from a survey of public opinion much of anything about behavior "in the field." But Potter's remarks suggest another inference: that the interpretation of the poll proffered by its authors was regarded with suspicion in at least some quarters. Moreover, it appears that the poll was regarded as a "dove" document that had somehow to be made to yield a more "hawkish" interpretation. Both Wicker and Potter seem to have undertaken to perform this task, the former more cautiously than the latter.

On March 17 a *Times* editorial said, "There is little support in the country—as a recent Stanford University poll showed—for the extreme alternatives of withdrawal or all-out war. But there is substantial support for a policy of holding military operations at their present level while taking new initiatives to seek peace. The Stanford poll demonstrated that the country is far ahead of the Administration in its willingness to take such initiatives, even if they should entail serious risks." [24]

This interpretation was in sharp disagreement with the *Times'* own news story and analysis, and was in almost complete harmony with the original Stanford report. What accounts for the discrepancy? Can there have been "hawk" and "dove" factions within the *Times* itself? Only speculation is possible. Newsmen are entitled to write stories as they see fit; and it is not easy to reconstruct the reasons why they may "see" a story in a particular context. Still, the fact that Wicker's news analysis was considerably more supportive of the Johnson administration than the *Times* editorial may have had something to do with Wicker's location in Washington. The Stanford poll's exploration of public attitudes could legitimately have been read—as it was by the *Times* editorial writer—as an indication that public opinion was ready to approve alternatives that had been rejected for the time being by the Johnson administration. Furthermore, in the light of news

[24] *The New York Times*, "The Vietnam Debate," March 17, 1966.

stories emanating from the White House asserting that public opinion disagreement with the President was predominantly from the "hawk" side of the controversy,[25] this reading of the Stanford poll's findings was definitely news. Yet the Wicker and Potter analyses suggested counterinterpretations which played down this aspect of the poll's findings. Clearly it will not do to characterize the Washington news-gathering community as "a hotbed" of support for the administration. Many Washington newsmen, including the *Times'* own James Reston, have been critical of the administration's Vietnam policy. Yet we know that in many instances proximity does breed sympathy. And it is perfectly proper to wonder to what extent these counterinterpretations were produced for the comfort of policy-makers as well as for the instruction of the newspapers' lay readers. The symbiosis of newsmen and political leaders on the Washington scene has often been observed.[26] The amount of criticism that the Johnson administration has had to absorb on the Vietnam issue—especially from academic precincts like those from which this poll came, could not have been far from the minds of Washington correspondents as they read the initial report of the Stanford poll. Under the circumstances, it seems plausible to expect a posture of skepticism toward this academic production on the part of Washington reporters—especially those reasonably close to the Johnson administration—as Philip Potter in particular certainly has been.[27]

[25] See note 10.

[26] See, e.g., Douglass Cater, *The Fourth Branch of Government* (Boston: Houghton Mifflin, 1954); Cohen, *op. cit.*, pp. 28 ff. and *passim*.

[27] One indication of Potter's closeness to the President was his ability to elicit an exclusive story, told from Mr. Johnson's point of view, of his original nomination as Vice-President. See Philip L. Potter, "How LBJ Was Nominated," *The Reporter*, June 18, 1964, pp. 16–20. Pierre Salinger says: "Like JFK, President Johnson had personal favorites in the press corps, among them Phil Potter of the *Baltimore Sun*. . . ." *With Kennedy* (Garden City: Doubleday, 1966), p. 338. See also Gay Talese "The Kingdoms, the Powers, and the Glories of the *New York Times*," *Esquire* (November 1966). On p. 201 Talese describes criticism by *Times* New York editors in early 1966 of the Washington Bureau under Tom Wicker. "There was . . . the recurring theme that the Washington Bureau was overly protective of its friends in government. . . ." This tension between headquarters and the Washington bureau of the *Times* apparently continued through 1968. See Paul H.

A further indication that the Stanford poll had become embroiled in the politics of the Vietnam debate came on April 7, when the columnists Rowland Evans and Robert Novak, whose column is syndicated to 119 newspapers—including the Washington *Post* and the *New York Herald Tribune* among the foreign policy prestige press—launched an all-out attack on the poll as a "scandalous job of rigging." [28] "The Stanford poll," they wrote, ". . . has become a prime document for the peace block on Capitol Hill. . . .[P]eace Senators use the poll as ammunition for anti-war arguments." [29]

Invoking the opinions of unnamed "non-ideological professional pollsters" Evans and Novak said, "The Stanford group knew what answers it wanted before it asked any questions." The Stanford group was also charged with stretching its data, sweeping to a broad conclusion, and slanting questions. The number of professionals sharing this opinion would be difficult to determine from the column itself. At one point, Evans and Novak mentioned "two highly reputable private pollsters who constantly probe opinion on Vietnam for political clients." At another point, they referred to the conclusion of "every professional pollster."

Inflammatory language aside, Evans and Novak's bill of particulars could be boiled down to the following argument: The Stanford group rigged its findings by slanting its questions. This could be shown, first, by the fact that they got results that disagreed with results other pollsters were getting, according to what some of these pollsters told Evans and Novak, and second, because they resisted the "confusion" analysis.

The columnists made a special issue of the following Stanford poll question: "Would you approve or disapprove of the following

Weaver, "The New Face of the *New York Times*" *New York*, 1 (June 24, 1968), 22–28. Wicker himself by 1968 was arguing that the "loss of consensus" over Vietnam policy constituted the fatal flaw in the Johnson Presidency. See Tom Wicker, *JFK and LBJ: The Influence of Personality upon Politics* (New York: William Morrow, 1968).

[28] Rowland Evans and Robert Novak, "Rigging the Polls," *Washington Post, New York Herald Tribune*, April 7, 1966.

[29] Evans and Novak could have mentioned, but did not, that the poll was also being used by journalists to demonstrate that the public was "confused" on Vietnam, and that the public was strongly opposed to unilateral withdrawal.

action to end the fighting: forming a new government in which the Viet Cong took some part?" This, of course, was the least popular (52 per cent approve) of four de-escalation alternatives accepted by majorities. Evans and Novak charged that the question assumed "an incredibly high level of sophistication" and that other phrasings of the same question by other pollsters received "resounding no" answers.

If by sophistication Evans and Novak meant political information, they could have noted in the report the high level of correct response (70 per cent) to the identification of the Viet Cong, and that those who correctly identified the Viet Cong were about as willing to see them in a coalition as those who could not. If by sophistication Evans and Novak meant an ability to make discriminations among policy arenas, they could have noted that those favoring this de-escalation alternative generally did not favor soft policies toward Russia, China, or Cuba. If by sophistication they meant internal consistency, they could have inquired and ascertained how many persons favoring this alternative also favored other de-escalation alternatives.

Three days before the Evans and Novak attack appeared, a Louis Harris poll reported, "In no case is the desire for a peaceful settlement more decisively demonstrated than in a recent Harris survey . . ."—hardly a "resounding no" to de-escalation.[30]

The set of findings in which respondents rejected increased domestic costs to continue fighting the war, according to Evans and Novak, showed "slanting of the questions . . . sure to get a 'no' answer." But, as the report said, this has not always been true: an almost identically worded question by George Gallup about increasing income taxes "in order to build up our military strength here and abroad" received the approval of a 63 per cent majority in January 1958, soon after Sputnik was launched.[31]

The final substantive charge was that the Stanford group had rejected the Wicker "confusion" theory—"the conclusion of every professional pollster"—and thus "gave away its intent" by equat-

[30] *Washington Post*, April 4, 1966.
[31] See Gabriel A. Almond, "Public Opinion and the Development of Space Technology," *Public Opinion Quarterly* (Winter 1960), pp. 553–72.

ing "snap opinions of a puzzled public" with sophisticated political doctrines, such as had been expounded at hearings of the Fulbright Committee.

Not every professional pollster, however, in published work, took the view that public attitudes on the Vietnam issue were so puzzled or confused as to be entirely unintelligible. Louis Harris, for example, three days before the Evans and Novak attack, attributed the following, fairly sophisticated, line of reasoning to American public opinion: "The reasoning of the public in support of U.N. arbitration stems from two widely held beliefs: (1) such peace-making is precisely what the U.N. was set up for in the first place; (2) any reasonable solution for settling the war is better than expending more lives and money." [32] And Oliver Quayle, in a poll cited by Stewart Alsop classified 81 per cent of the American people into meaningful policy positions, and left only 19 per cent as "bewildered." [33]

In a larger sense, Evans and Novak were raising in an indirect and fragmentary way two problems of interpretation. First, a problem of standards of adequacy. The "confusion" theory is tenable on the general principle that public opinion polls mean little anyway—that, in the lapidary phrase of Lindsay Rogers, far from feeling the pulse of America, they are listening to its baby talk.[34] This can be developed into a legitimate and meaningful argument. Enough is known about public opinion generally to suggest that the cognitive maps that members of the general public construct on complicated issues of public policy are simple and unstable. The use of public opinion polls in order to justify the pursuit of any particular policy—which typically entails complicated calculations of risks, probabilities, resources and demands—

[32] Louis Harris, "Viet Arbitration by UN Backed 2–1," *Washington Post*, April 4, 1966.
[33] Stewart Alsop, "What the People Really Think," *Saturday Evening Post*, October 23, 1965, pp. 27–31. Ironically, three years later, the Stanford poll was cited by one prominent commercial poll executive to lend the authority and prestige of the social scientists who conducted it to the argument that the normal sampling procedures of poll-takers are scientifically acceptable. See the letter from Paul K. Perry, Associate Director, American Institute of Public Opinion (Gallup Poll) "Opinion Sampling," *New York Times*, February 11, 1966.
[34] Lindsay Rogers, *The Pollsters* (New York: Knopf, 1949), p. 17.

is for this reason normally highly questionable. Nevertheless, assertions about public opinion are made in the course of political debate. And when they are made, they can be subjected to tests to determine their accuracy and completeness. Thus, accepting the limitations of the sample survey method, there still may be valid reasons to attempt to make sense of public opinion polls. Furthermore, it is possible to think of standards of adequacy by which alternative interpretations of the same data can be compared. Two obvious such standards would be fidelity to facts and inclusiveness. The confusion hypothesis suffers by the former standard on account of Wicker's reckless use of the hypothetical forced choice on future alternatives, and by the latter standard because he ignored the data rejecting escalation alternatives. The analysis provided by the authors of the Stanford poll took many more findings into account in their analysis than did any of the interpretations in the prestige press.

The second larger issue to which the Evans and Novak column is indirectly addressed concerns the extent to which findings about distributions of public attitudes should govern the policy choices of political leaders. In a sense, the identification both implicitly and explicitly in the prestige press of the Stanford poll as a "dove" document implied that this report of opinions constituted a set of demands for certain policy choices. To those who disagreed with these policies, it may well have made sense to try to neutralize the poll's interpretation, or to discredit its findings.

But no such demands were explicitly a part of the report of the Stanford poll. The most its authors were willing to say on the subject appeared in their published reply to Evans and Novak: "So far as public opinion is concerned, it appears that a considerable leeway exists for American policy makers"; and "we do not believe that public opinion on any particular issue should necessarily determine what policy makers do." [35]

Nevertheless, by dealing with a "hot" issue, and owing to its wide and prompt diffusion, the poll was used as a political instrument. Apparently it was unequally useful to parties to the

[35] "A Communication," *Washington Post*, April 16, 1966.

continuing debate on Vietnam policy. It would be a mistake, however, to follow the ancient custom of beheading the bearer of bad tidings and attack the scientific adequacy of the poll because of the asymmetry of its usefulness. The laboratories at Oak Ridge are not equally available to the nation-states of the world, yet it is hard to deny that their operation entails scientific skills and theories. This was also true of the Stanford poll; the fact that its results contributed meaningfully though unevenly to policy discussion is not sufficient to impeach its scientific adequacy.

Conclusions

The coverage of the Stanford poll in the prestige press illustrates a number of things. First, perhaps owing to the sharply hierarchical classification of news events by editors, the coverage of items of intermediate importance is widely divergent from newspaper to newspaper and hence entirely different from the highly convergent coverage of items at the peak of the hierarchy.

Second, the tendency to regard newspapers as monoliths—which is an impulse natural in viewing all institutions from the outside—might well receive a salutary reproof based upon the schizoid coverage of the Stanford poll in the *New York Times*. It may be that, like many organizations in American society, the prestige press, in the process of bureaucratizing and impersonalizing its internal management, and dividing labor among increasingly professionalized personnel, has also sown the seeds of diversity in its approach to individual stories.[36]

[36] Here is a further illustration of this process. Charles Mohr, a *Times* correspondent in Vietnam, was asked: "Do you keep in touch with the *Times* editorial board?" He replied: "No. Not directly. I mean, I'm sure that the stories from the *Times* staff here influence the *Times* editorial board. But in American journalism—I don't think it's ever been true at the *Times*—but just generally, the day of the policy story is over. Very few stories ever have to be written to conform in any paper with editorials. And in responsible papers, it doesn't happen at all. My own opinions about the Vietnam conflict are complex. But they're not in definite accord with the editorial page, which is fine. The whole essence of intellectual freedom in the U.S. is that persons who have the responsibility must say what he believes and the editorial board of *The New York Times* has done that in a lucid, distinguished way, I believe. My responsibility is to report out here, and I must do it the way I see it." *At Issue 69: The Information War*, National Educational Television, August 1, 1966, transcript p. 21.

Third, prestige press coverage of the Stanford poll made, overall, exceedingly little use of the carefully prepared report and analysis supplied by the poll's authors. Two substitutes for employment of the report were, first, the telephone interview, in which one of the authors was asked either to assure reporters of the Stanford group's scholarly motives or to repeat in imprecise language thoughts which had been more effectively committed to paper in the reporter's hands; and second, the attempt to produce an original analysis of the tables. Some of these interpretations were indeed original; but they were also overhasty, careless, and amateur performances. The small use of the authors' report on the Stanford poll cannot be attributed wholly to a craftsman-like disinclination of reporters to rely upon press releases. Two other factors were also involved. The report contained many more findings than could be comfortably assimilated to a news story of even the most generous length. And second, because of the report's political "relevance," the interpretation of the poll's findings by the authors of the report was not acceptable to some reporters.

Perhaps the major contribution to political debate of the initial report of the Stanford poll was to shift the discussion of public opinion in connection with Vietnam temporarily out of the limelight. Far from focusing upon what public opinion forbade the President to do—as Tom Wicker's analysis mistakenly said—the poll's impact seems to have had the opposite effect. As Richard Rovere put it in the *New Yorker:*

> . . . [I]t is hard to imagine a political atmosphere in this country more favorable to statesmen trying to make their hard choices soberly and responsibly. The pressures under which Presidents always work are in this case distributed in such a way as almost to liberate Lyndon Johnson from any pressures at all. The polls continue to show that the country supports the administration in its present conduct of the war. . . . "Decisive majorities," according to the researchers who made the widely discussed survey sponsored by Stanford University, "reject unilateral withdrawal as they reject extreme escalation." The proponents of withdrawal and of escalation are about equal in numbers and thus cancel each other out in terms of pressure. But the polls also show that the majority that supports the

President as a war leader would also follow him in almost any effort he might make toward negotiation, going so far as to approve, the Stanford survey reported, "forming a new government in which the Vietcong took some part." It added: "So far as public opinion is concerned, it appears that a considerable leeway exists for American policy makers." That is the general view here. . . .[37]

This was, of course, a radical reversal from the earlier conventional wisdom about alleged pressure on the administration to escalate the war.[38]

Soon after the initial report of the Stanford poll was publicized, commercial surveys began to turn up confirmatory evidence of a large body of public opinion willing to support moves to de-escalate the conflict.[39] But response from the White House had diminished: "James Deakin of the St. Louis *Post-Dispatch* recently noted that White House correspondents have observed that Mr. Johnson 'is not mentioning the polls as much as he once did. White House officials confirmed this impression.' "[40]

Public opinion polls, it is clear, could no longer be invoked in support of at least some policy alternatives: in order to justify these alternatives, more compelling reasons of state had to be given. Since it is doubtful that a momentary distribution of public opinion could ever have been regarded as more than a very insignificant factor in the actual determination of policy, the subtraction of public opinion from the rhetoric of justification surrounding the Vietnam war must be counted as an important contribution to the clarification of the premises upon which choices were being made.

But this clarification was not achieved without cost. Academic social scientists often hear the complaint that their work does not have sufficient practical use, and that it should be, as the saying goes, "relevant." Sometimes such complaints are themselves fool-

---

[37] Richard H. Rovere, "Letter from Washington," *New Yorker*, April 23, 1966, p. 185.
[38] See note 10.
[39] Harris, *op. cit.*; the Gallup Poll, "Viet War Appears Big Issue in Two Parties," *ibid.* Louis Harris, "Support of Viet Commitment Still 62%," *Washington Post*, May 9, 1966.
[40] "Notes in the News," *The Progressive*, May 1966.

ish and impractical, when they come from persons unwilling to formulate a question to which social science could conceivably speak. Often, too, the urge toward "relevance" translates into a temptation for the academic to exploit the prestige of the academy in behalf of his policy preferences directly, without doing relevant scholarly work. Yet the complaint is an important one, and it does assert one—if only one—legitimate demand upon the resources which society devotes to self-knowledge. Compliance with this demand may, however, force social scientists to face the same dilemma that has in the last twenty years so dramatically seized hold of hard scientists: "Policy relevance" means that research is capable of being used by political actors, for political purposes, and not necessarily for everyone's political purposes equally. Neither actors nor purposes may be easily controlled by the researcher; indeed he may in fact heartily disapprove of both. To what extent may he nevertheless be held responsible for the uses to which his work is put? There is, one suspects, no formula to cover all cases, other than the fortune-cookie wisdom: "He who would be relevant had better also be prudent."

7
Political Extremism

Understanding extremism in America is one of the great unmet challenges to political scholarship. Considering the magnitude of its impact on people's lives, the state of our knowledge about extremism is especially disappointing. We know little more than that the influence of political extremism comes and goes, and when it comes it taps a level of emotion among the politically aware that makes it comparable to the tulip mania, the witch-burning craze, and other historic instances of mass hysteria. The laws of social interaction governing extreme forms of collective behavior are not at all well formulated. The best-known theoretical works mostly give generalized descriptions of the natural histories of instances of extremism, without really explaining why these sequences of events occur when they do or as they do.

We can probably say one other thing with a reasonable degree of confidence about political extremism, and that is that the causes assigned to their own behavior by extremists are not adequate to explain what is going on. Various forms of injustice had been prevalent in America for a long time before the campuses exploded in the late 1960's; communism as an influence on domestic politics was distinctly on the wane by the beginning of the

McCarthy era in 1950. So it will not do to point to domestic communism as the cause of pro-McCarthy hysteria, or to the alleged rottenness of American society as the cause of student unrest or the resurgence of radical politics.

Many people have expressed annoyance at my readiness to bracket McCarthyism with student radicalism. I do so for two reasons. One of them is entirely subjective, and in a way accidental. During the 1950's I lived in Washington, D.C., where McCarthy did most of his damage. During the 1960's I was teaching and could see a good bit of campus turmoil close at hand. On a day-to-day basis, both episodes seemed much alike to me, featuring high emotions, unexpected damage to settled lives, and a state of general, severe, apprehensiveness among innocent, nearby bystanders. I never did arrive at a satisfactory understanding of the sources of either phenomenon, and more and more have become fascinated with the response rather than with the stimulus side of the problem. That is, I have been willing to take as a mysterious given the outbreak of extremist craziness. The question for me then becomes, how is this craziness responded to by the society and its institutions? Why do people give in to it so easily? What accounts for the institutional incorporation of irrationality, the routinization of extremism?

Underlying this conception of the problem there undoubtedly lurks a quasi-medical analogy: extremism is like a virus in the body politic that to a certain extent is there all the time. When for one reason or other the resistance of the host organism drops below a certain point, the host gets sick. Thus the proximate cause of extremist outbreaks in American history is not the existence of extremists, who are always around, but rather their peculiar, episodic ability to gain support in the populace at large and among political leaders.

This is the concern that informs all three of the essays printed in this chapter. The first essay, a review of Roy Cohn's book, lays out the general argument. The second, a review of books by Nathan Glazer and Sidney Hook, attempts to portray the varieties of faculty response to campus turmoil, and to describe those characteristics of faculty groups that predispose them to resistance to or acquiescence in extremist behavior. The third, and most substantial article, constitutes my main attempt to come to an understanding of the social sources of support for Joseph McCarthy. The article is fairly well known and has caused some momentary and I believe unnecessary discomfort among scholars holding different views of the matter.

The central finding is, of course, that an extremely powerful source of support for McCarthy came from his fellow Republicans. Other explanations, when matched against party affiliation, appear weak. Republicans supported McCarthy, and this was the main source of his strength. Contrary to common belief at the time there is no good evidence that McCarthy had a significant independent impact on various Senatorial election campaigns where he is held to have defeated incumbent Senators who opposed him.

One little-remarked feature of this article is its failure to reject alternative hypotheses about support for McCarthy. Much socially interesting human behavior has the characteristic of being overdetermined, that is, it can be adequately accounted for by more than one explanation. There is no reason to believe that support for Joseph McCarthy was caused only by partisan sentiment simply because partisan sentiment was clearly and heavily involved for many people. I took some pains not to treat the hypotheses already in the field dismissively when I offered my political alternative. My view at the time I wrote the article (in the late 1950's) was that there was simply not enough evidence available to do justice to the various explanations that students of McCarthy had cooked up. Now, over a dozen years later, with revisionist historians busily trying to pin responsibility for McCarthy on Harry Truman, of all people, the situation is much the same. Only the indefatigable Seymour Martin Lipset seems to have retained any interest in gathering empirical evidence on the sources of support for Joseph McCarthy; these he interprets so as to lend some comfort to the "status anxiety" hypothesis that he and his colleagues popularized in the 1950's. Lipset also acknowledges, as did Richard Hofstadter, that the political interpretation first developed in the article printed below is probably here to stay.

It is easy enough, at least in retrospect, to see why. Many of the groups into which social scientists divide people for the purposes of analysis have no reality to the people themselves. This is notoriously true in America, for example, in relation to social classes. For a very large part of the population, membership in a social class is meaningless. They do not think of themselves as having class interests, as over against the interests of some other class. On the other hand, many Americans really belong to political parties in the sense that party membership makes an explicit claim on their feelings of loyalty. Political parties are organizations which to a greater or lesser extent actually work at gaining the allegiance of people. No doubt more Americans would show class loyalties if every once in a while leaders of each class went about the country asking for support in state-wide elections, if members of each class met in a week-long conclave under the scrutiny of national television to fight over a platform, and if each of the classes spent millions of dollars to advertise themselves and to activate their "members." But, of course, social classes do not do any of these things; political parties do, and no wonder ordinary citizens respond by organizing their feelings and perceptions of the political world around party loyalties.

This is even true, I suggest, when they must respond to the extraordinary stimulus offered by politically extreme sentiments. How they respond is therefore very much in the hands of the political leaders to whom they normally attend. If for strategic reasons of their own political leaders attempt to make partisan use of the strong currents of popular feeling that extremist movements evoke, the political system undergoes extremely disagreeable times. For political leaders by their self-restraint and moderation can damp down raging currents of popular feeling—if they choose to do so. Radical critics of American politics quite correctly point to the McCarthy era as one period when many leaders failed to perform this moderating function. From this they have leapt to the quite erroneous conclusion that American political elites are no more solicitous of due process, civil liberties, and political decency than the ordinary citizen. This, alas, is not so. Political elites in America are by any reasonable standard much more attached to the civic decencies than any randomly selected population of citizens. This means that when elites fail to observe these decencies, as they sometimes do, there is nobody else to uphold them.

This is what makes the periodic episodes of extremism that grip the American political system so dangerous, and so compelling as an object of speculation and observation.

JOSEPH McCARTHY REMEMBERED *

Some American philosopher—perhaps W. C. Fields—once said that inability to handle a pool cue was a sure sign of a misspent youth. In these turbulent days, university people are becoming intimately acquainted with other, more obtrusive symptoms of the same malady. But, lest we forget, there is still in our midst a contender for the all-time record on this continent for pubescent waywardness. In this, his first book, Roy Cohn, now in his early forties, recalls the grand old days from 1950 to 1955 when he and his playmates, G. David Schine and Senator Joseph R. McCarthy, cavorted upon the public stage while incidentally crippling portions of the U.S. State Department and the U.S. Department of the Army, smearing the reputations of a few, or a few score, people in and out of government, and causing something very like mass hysteria in the community of official Washington. Cohn repents of none of this; thus, this book bears witness not only to a notably reprehensible adolescence, but one of extraordinary duration. Cohn seems determined to cultivate into middle life and beyond what was once America's most famous case of acne of the superego.

Persons who were old enough to read the newspapers in the 1950's are probably not going to be very interested in this book, and persons who were not reading the newspapers in those years will probably not even be curious about it. It is written in dreary boilerplate style, and consists mostly of heavy-handed, new-minted ripostes for conversations that ended fifteen years ago. There are, however, a few moments of hilarity that we can only assume were not intentional.

Return with us now to those thrilling days of yesteryear. Roy Cohn, boy committee counsel, puts suspect Annie Lee Moss on the stand before the McCarthy subcommittee investigating Communist subversion in the Department of the Army. It shortly

---

* Review of Roy Cohn, *McCarthy* (New York: New American Library, 1968).

becomes painfully apparent that if he has got the goods on a Communist subversive named Annie Lee Moss, it is not this Annie Lee Moss, who turns out to be a puzzled, grandmotherly Negro lady who seems to have been employed as a Pentagon messenger. Cohn denies all in his current, garbled account, defends his actions, claims everybody else made a mistake, not Roy Cohn. Perhaps he is talking about some other Roy Cohn, some other hearing when he says:

> I called Mrs. Moss to the stand during the public hearing. As I started to question her, I noticed that Senator McClellan was presiding. I knew Senator McCarthy was unable to attend because of illness, but I had not realized until that moment that all of the Republican members of the subcommittee were also absent, leaving the chair to McClellan as the senior Democrat.

One of the *sotto voce* themes in the book is, of course, Cohn's persecution at the hands of various and sundry persons, such as misguided Democratic liberals, who wanted to stop his daring and resourceful exposés of Communist subversion.

But for the particular day of which he writes, March 11, 1954, the day Annie Lee Moss was called to the stand in open hearing, there is, aside from the official committee print, still another record, since the occasion was televised by a cameraman from CBS News, and the transcript of the CBS program that resulted is printed in Edward R. Murrow's and Fred W. Friendly's (editors) *See it Now* (Simon and Schuster, 1955). The accompanying pictures clearly show two Republican Senators, McCarthy himself and Karl Mundt, in the room. And the text shows that McCarthy and Cohn conducted a long, bumbling, hostile examination of the uncomprehending, docile witness.

The purpose of this small digression is to reassure: the new, up-to-date, 1968 Roy Cohn is not about to disappoint by an excess of late-blooming truthfulness the legion of admirers he won in his salad days. These included, according to his book, such luminaries as Louis B. Mayer and a woman who, as a result of his testimony at the Army-McCarthy hearings, "no longer believed that all Jews were Communists."

Perhaps the only new revelation the book provides (other than the characterization of G. David Schine as "an able young businessman") is some background information on the famous episode during the Army-McCarthy hearings when McCarthy viciously and irrelevantly attacked Fred Fisher, an associate in the firm of Joseph Welch, the Army's counsel, and Welch eloquently demolished the Senator. Cohn reveals that there had been an explicit agreement between the two sides: If Welch would not cross-examine Cohn on his embarrassing service record, McCarthy and Cohn would not smear Fred Fisher. Cohn seems to think that this little tidbit proves that Welch could not have been sincere in castigating McCarthy when McCarthy went ahead and smeared Fisher anyway, rather than drawing the obvious conclusion that this shows McCarthy was just a mite undependable along with his other sterling qualities of character.

Since, as this book makes quite clear, it is unpleasant to do so, why think about Joseph McCarthy anymore? The answer is, because we let him happen to this country, and therefore a consideration of what he wrought is really an occasion to ask ourselves by what flaws in our body politic he came to have such a powerful influence.

My judgment at the time, since then fortified by a few years more of experience and contemplation, was that no society can hope definitively to purge itself of political desperadoes, lunatics, publicity-seekers, frauds, cynics, or nihilists. McCarthy's nonnegotiable demands to remove distasteful books from U.S. Information Agency libraries, to hire and fire persons he designated, were not the first such demands this country has ever seen, and I daresay will not be the last. Persons will arise from time to time and proclaim that the urgency of the social or political problem that they have the honor uniquely to descry demands that mere due process, academic freedom, free speech, or what have you be swept under the rug.

What is crucial, it seems to me, in preserving a decent and civilized political order lies not in the rooting out of these people, or preventing them from stating their demands. It lies, rather, in not acquiescing to them, which is a responsibility more widely spread in the community, in maintaining the principles—and the practices—of due process, academic freedom, free speech, and so on in the face of demands, disruptions, or threats uttered in the name of allegedly "overriding" emergencies. Yet there are occasions when "moderate" Americans weaken. The McCarthy era was such a period. It was not McCarthy but John Foster Dulles who dismissed John Paton Davies. It was C. D. Jackson speaking for the Eisenhower White House that forbade the top management of the Voice of America to resist McCarthy's demands. Thus "moderates" found themselves doing McCarthy's work for him, with other moderates as the chief victims.

Michael Rogin has shown in his new book, *The Intellectuals and McCarthy*, that, on the whole, the mass of voters regarded McCarthy as just another Republican. Republicans voted for him, Democrats did not. As Samuel Stouffer's surveys documented at the time, McCarthy's real threat to American democracy took place much less in the minds and attitudes of ordinary citizens than in Washington itself, where elite decision-makers had to deal with him.

How did they manage? Many, especially Republicans, including some who were professedly "moderate," were eager to fellow-travel. The moderate incorporation of McCarthy took many forms. It became popular to distinguish between his "methods" (character assassination, careless use of innuendo, and so on) and his "ends" (presumably ridding the government of Communist spies). Misguided idealism was attributed to him. Persons who attacked him could be considered "soft on Communism" unless their own "ends" could be shown to be conspicuously anti-Communist as well.

The analogy with contemporary turmoil from the left on many campuses is striking. An undoubted emergency is proclaimed (the war in Vietnam, the alleged complicity of the university in the "military-industrial complex," the inequality of treatment accorded black persons in American society) that somehow becomes the exclusive property of the group proclaiming it (S.D.S., Black Student Union, Third World Liberation Front, etc.). Because the emergency is so urgent, it is announced, certain steps must be taken at once ("non-negotiable demands"). These may or may not be within the university administration's power to grant, and may or may not entail the abrogation of professors' rights to teach, students to attend classes, or the maintenance of the university premises as a place where orderly persons such as, say, Dow Chemical recruiters and prospective employees in the student body may communicate under the law. If these demands, whatever they are, are not met with lightning speed, extreme behavior follows, analogous to McCarthy's hearings and press releases attacking named persons, and his private threats. Recently on university campuses, buildings have been burned and bombs have been placed in them. Other buildings have been occupied, windows broken, walls smeared with slogans, private files rifled, deans manhandled. Professors' manuscripts have been destroyed, students threatened, classes disrupted by outside intruders. All, as in McCarthy's case, in the name of overriding emergencies of one kind or another.

As in McCarthy's case, there has been a strong impulse on the part of "moderates" to sympathize, to incorporate "non-negotiable" demands, violently demanded, into presumably "rational" discourse. Ends and means are laboriously distinguished. The nobility of the ends espoused is given much consideration in extenuation of the means employed. Persons in the community who are disposed to view due-process-destroying means as the overriding issue risk the charge of being "soft" on "relevant" education, black studies, chemical warfare, the military-industrial complex, or possibly even secretly hawkish on the Vietnam war. And when moderate administrations or faculties acquiesce in the demands of extremists, as often as not the chief victims are themselves moderate: students who did not strike, occupy buildings, or smash windows, but who now see the administration making deals with radical leaders over the disposition of university resources; black students who will find it increasingly difficult to major in economics or engineering or biology in the face of various forms of suasion from militant, organized black groups to whom the universities are busily ceding academic control over "black studies" programs. To those who lived in Washington in the 1950's, conversation on the campus of a major university today would sound quite familiar.

What do episodes such as these teach us about ourselves? Perhaps only that we are not wholly exempt from the reach of Samuel Johnson's rather grisly pleasantry: "Mutual cowardice keeps us in peace. . . . Being all cowards, we go on very well." Sometimes, as the examples of McCarthy and his idealistic young contemporary emulators may suggest, we do not seem to have quite enough cowardice in our political system; or, as the response of the rest of us then and now may show, we have rather too much.

TWO VIEWS OF CAMPUS TURMOIL *

I

Very few members of university faculties have been able to insulate themselves effectively from the turmoil that has overrun campuses as disparate as Wesleyan and Kent State, as distinguished as Berkeley, Columbia, and Harvard, as geographically distant as San Jose and Brandeis. What has caused this turmoil? Those who point to the presumed pathologies of impersonal mass education have to account for the difficulties at some of the nation's smallest, least impersonal schools. Those who blame American involvement in the war in Vietnam must explain the appearance of severe campus disruptions in nations unengaged in this conflict, such as Japan, Germany, France, Great Britian, and Holland. In some places, campus disruption has been associated with traditions of student radicalism, in others with racial tensions, in still others with administrative ineptitude or some shocking incident. But no explanation will cover all cases, and for most explanations many counterexamples can be marshalled. Not even the assertion, which I think of as Ginsberg's theorem,[1] that disturbances on the campuses are in some sense the logical outcome of disaffection from society by the "best minds" of the younger generation, is free from probable error.[2] So in spite of the proximity of campus turmoil to trained students of social phenomena, much of it remains mysterious.

* Review of *Academic Freedom and Academic Anarchy* by Sidney Hook. (New York: Cowles Book Co., 1970); and *Remembering the Answers* by Nathan Glazer. (New York: Basic Books, 1970).
[1] See Allen Ginsberg, *Howl, and Other Poems* (1956), the first line of which is, "I saw the best minds of my generation destroyed by madness, starving hysterical naked." Empirical studies attempting to make the same point include: Richard Flacks, "Who Protests: The Social Bases of the Student Movement," in *Protest: Student Activism in America* (J. Foster and D. Long, eds., 1970); Kenneth Keniston, *Young Radicals* (1968).
[2] A comprehensive review and criticism of findings on this point are contained in Travis Hirschi and Joseph Zelan, *Student Activism: A Critical Review* (Survey Research Center, University of California, 1970, mimeo).

With all this data staring university faculties in the face, it is a wonder that more books and articles have not emerged about campus disturbances. In part, the dereliction—if that is the right word—can be explained by the fact that the uproar has distracted scholars from writing books, which some of them know how to do, and sidetracked them into political action, at which most of them are at best fair to middling.

It never fails to amaze people outside the academy that presumably highly intelligent professors are collectively only semi-competent at the politics of managing their own affairs. Yet a moment's thought will yield some reasons why this is so. Professors are selected, after all, for certain abilities, notably knowledge of highly specialized kinds and the capacity to communicate it. Knowledge, however, is not wisdom. The smartest people are not necessarily the best people. They may or may not have sturdiness of character, impulses to decency and fairness, good humor, common sense, dignity or restraint. These are gifts as much honored by university faculties as by others, and as rare among professors as in the population at large.

Professors, more nearly than any occupational group of which I am aware, are selected on the basis of merit alone; merit, however, not as whole human beings but as producers and processors of certain kinds of information. Professors are judged less by qualities that inhere in their personalities than in their work, by strict, sometimes harsh, but invariably technical criteria. Thus when university faculties find themselves face to face with severe problems such as those which have arisen these last few years, they are not particularly well equipped to deal sensibly with them. Institutional difficulties aside—when, for example, there is no custom of faculties meeting together even when they want to—it has turned out that they have been only normally endowed with wisdom, political skill, decency or altruism. They are, however, phenomenally verbose, a product of the skills and gifts for which they were originally selected.

Faculty people also set rather more store by abstract principle than most outsiders would think possible. In part this is once again a reflection of the merit system, since they are selected in part for abilities to think abstractly. It also reflects the nature of academic work, in which material rewards are hard to strive for directly and more often appear only as secondary effects of having made meaningful contributions to scholarship. To contribute to scholarship means originality on one hand—sometimes vulgarized into one-upmanship (verbal skill again)—and academic integrity on the other. That is, the contributor of scholarly work warrants that his work is properly attributable to him. Ideas, formulae, words, and sentences not original must be properly credited. Just as a retail merchant lives by the line of credit at his local bank, the academic lives by his scholarly rectitude. This fundamental condition of his life, together with the merit system which he administers as well as inhabits, encourages him to think of his professional acts as justified by the relevant application of principle.

Academic men are, therefore, principled men and wordy men. This is a well-nigh intolerable combination when the political heat is on. The capacity to speak and write fluently creates symbolic issues, justifications, heroes, villains, rationalizations, anathemas, that in the mouths of less articulate men would never come into being. Principles, once uttered, are terribly difficult to compromise. They do not lend themselves to logrolling, splitting the difference or other tactics for antagonistic cooperation that are possible when men are fighting over relatively tractable things like, for instance, money.

Thus, the positions that academic men hold with respect to campus turmoil are, by and large, principled positions, intensely felt. No book, and certainly no review, can possibly do justice to the richness and variety of these positions. Indeed, they lend themselves to caricature by friend and foe alike, most notoriously by meddling politicians who hope to activate anti-elitist prejudices in the general population by stigmatizing academics as "effete snobs," "nattering nabobs" and so on, or by opportunists who see an occasion for short-run personal gain in the misfortunes of educational institutions.

It is, in fact, not always easy to distinguish the opportunist from the true believer in times of crisis, since motives are hard enough to fathom at a distance in the best of circumstances. Crises, moreover, act as gigantic projective tests, which people use to validate their pre-existing views of human behavior. The educational reformer John Holt, for example, saw in some skirmishes at Berkeley in the winter of 1968, data which freshly and unequivocally supported his well-known ideas on the reorganization of higher education.[3] Others, it is safe to say, drew rather different conclusions.

II

The fact that a variety of views exist within the university as well as outside, and that academic crises seem to evoke them, suggests that a brief overview of the main types of faculty thinking on campus turmoil might help people outside the cloisters to keep track of what may otherwise be incomprehensible patterns of alliance and animosity.

Allowing for the usual exceptions, hybrids and fence-straddlers, there seem to me to be at least six discernible positions on campus unrest. Starting on the far left, we have what I would call University-Haters. These are people who think of universities as handmaidens of a society that is "a vast processing plant which converts human lives into trash for consumption and weapons for destruction."[4] Although attacks on the university from the right wing, from politicians or from the outside, are sometimes condemned by University-Haters as "repressive," assaults on the same institutions from the left, from students or from within, are more likely to be hailed as "creativity in the political realm."[5] Violence, likewise, is a message that for University-Haters depends upon the medium. Thus Wolin and Schaar contend that "when students assault police, the physical contact becomes a way of asserting that there is a human reality to the world."[6] University-

[3] John Holt, *Letter from Berkeley*, 33 *Yale Alumni Magazine* (Nov. 1969) 30–37. Holt says: "Nothing worth saving, or worth having, in the university is seriously threatened by the demands of even the most radical students." *Ibid.*, 35.
[4] Sheldon S. Wolin and John H. Schaar attribute this view admiringly to the young. Wolin and Schaar, *The Berkeley Rebellion and Beyond* (1970) 14.
[5] *Ibid.*, 140.
[6] *Ibid.*, 142.

Haters are typically far from pessimistic about human nature or about the possibilities of reconstructing communities for learning. They are, rather, optimistic, idealistic and soured because of what universities have become—"a bewilderingly complex collection of special institutes, centers, bureaus and schools" [7] (rather than a somewhat more comprehensible collection of libraries, art galleries, laboratories, classrooms, meeting halls, lounges, dormitories, gymnasiums, playing fields and dining facilities). University-Haters have more or less written off contemporary American universities as they presently exist. These present-day institutions have been corrupted by vocational demands. They "socialize" students for jobs in a technologically advanced but morally reprehensible society. Therefore, they must be cleansed.

It is not too much to say that in consequence of this analysis University-Haters have welcomed the spread of campus disturbances. It has provided them with what they believe to be a vindication of their view that universities as presently constituted are evil (since otherwise why would small and not-so-small groups of students and/or others perpetrate extreme acts against them?). Second, the disturbances give some hypothetical promise of providing the not-at-all hypothetical ashes from which newly reconstituted, better universities might arise. To paraphrase Marianne Moore, University-Haters roast imaginary marshmallows over real fires.

Some of the most effective faculty meeting orators can be found in this group. Faculties, as I have said, set a great store by principle; University-Haters are rather more seized by the absolute than most and are far less confused by lack of information or by occasional temptations to temporize, compromise or seek short-run political accommodations. They generally can discern, or improvise, a policy that on any given occasion will give them at least a little of what they fervently want, *i.e.*, disruption. Thus, although I would not put the numbers of University-Haters at more than one-sixth to one-fifth of most major university facul-

[7] *Ibid.*, 112.

ties, some members of this group are invariably people about whom those outside the university hear.

Quite often University-Haters find themselves allied in faculty politics with a group whose manners and motives strike me as quite different, whom I refer to as Permissives. These are professors disturbed by the generation gap, uncomfortable with authority—sometimes including even their own authority to act as arbiters of the quality of students' performance in academic matters—vaguely guilt-ridden about what they keenly perceive to be injustice in the world and in the larger society and disturbed about the possible complicity of universities in things that are going wrong. These are the people who worry about "the kids," about "institutional racism," about the unfairness of life and the difficulties that the young have in reconciling themselves to it. They sometimes convince themselves that the young have developed new forms of understanding and even consciousness which in some mysterious way avoid the corruption entailed by the compromises with reality that they themselves have made.[8]

Perhaps the most emblematic Permissive statement yet uttered came early in the years of campus turmoil, when, following the victory of the students in the Berkeley Free Speech episode, campus rules were established at the University of California respecting the time, place, and manner, but not the content, of public utterances on the Berkeley campus. Extremists launched a short-lived "Filthy Speech" movement, consisting mostly of the public display of signs containing obscenities and the organized chanting about the campus of such pleasantries as "Fuck you." At an Academic Senate meeting called to deal with this problem, one Permissive is alleged to have argued, "These young people are trying to *tell* us something." Thus, as I see it, on many campuses the faculty party of the left consists of a coalition between the purposeful and the anxious, between accusers and self-accusers, between inciters and condoners.

Immediately to the right of the Permissive sixth stretches a

[8] This I take to be one of the several garbled messages in Charles Reich, *The Greening of America* (1970).

metaphorical but perfectly real barricade separating faculties, in some cases merely into caucuses but increasingly into different friendship groups and cliques. On the right side of the line are four groups, also in uneasy alliance. Furthest on the right are what I would call Student-Haters. These are members of the faculty who take the view that universities are for them and not for students. They denounce student activism because it is distracting and annoying, and they make little distinction between one sort of student demand and another. Student-Haters undoubtedly contribute a disproportionate share to the legitimate grievances which students have about faculty neglect.

A second group, much like Student-Haters in their basic preoccupations and stakes in the university are Apathetics. If they could be mobilized to vote, they would vote *No* on initiatives of all kinds taken in response to campus upheaval, except for those involving police protection of campus property and campus routines. More characteristically, however, Apathetics do not participate in faculty politics. For some of them, the university is less a community for learning and teaching than a convenient base from which to do consulting work and to pursue outside interests. For others, the notion of participation in any sort of collective enterprise like a faculty senate is inconceivable. There is no place in the lives of these scholars—some of whom are devoted teachers—for the recognition of purely organizational needs of any description.

Closer to the center of the spectrum is a small group of what I would call Paternalistic Traditionalists. These are professors who are typically very much engaged with colleagues and with students but who, for one reason or another, cannot accept the notion of student participation in any form in the shaping of educational policy. Many distinguished faculty members having European upbringings take this position. Not a few of them see in student disturbances echoes of pre-World War II Germany. The memory does not make them comfortable, nor does the analogy dispose them to great flexibility in dealing with what they perceive as severe threats to academic freedom by means of threats to academic decorum.

Finally, there are what I would call Institutional Liberals—nearest to the Permissives in many of their impulses and ideas of academic life, yet separated from them because of the mutual unease which each feels about the alliances and compromises the other group is willing to make. On the whole, Institutional Liberals have been highly receptive to academic reform and to the decentralization of power in universities. Faced with the destructiveness of contemporary campus turmoil, however, they have refused to condone it and have adopted as their first priority the preservation of university routines, traditions, and activities. For Institutional Liberals, improvement of the university is not synonymous with its radical transfiguration, but in general it is unclear what actually differentiates them from Permissives in any programmatic sense. The difference may come down to nothing more substantial than the disposition of Permissives to credit the accusations of University-Haters and to condone the acts which presumably "follow" from their analysis and of Institutional Liberals to reject both.

III

The two books to be reviewed here are the work of Institutional Liberals, who agree about nearly everything having to do with campus upheaval but who nonetheless display great differences in intellectual styles. Sidney Hook, the philosopher, has written a polemical book which seeks to persuade by argument and debate; Nathan Glazer, the political sociologist, seems less intent upon persuasion than on description of what he conceives to be a sensible point of view, in part the product of reasoning from premises but more interestingly the product of his own shareable life history and the succeeding outlooks on the world that have emerged from his experiences. I have had very few life experiences like Glazer's, yet I found his description of them engaging, sensitive and pertinent to the opinions we currently share. I agree almost entirely with the message of Hook's book, yet I found it leaden, pedantic, and enervating to read. Thus I can recommend each book for different purposes: Glazer for the neutral, uninformed, or already right-minded, and Hook for the enemy.

I say this despite the fact that debaters on the left can dispose of Hook's main points without difficulty, since it is presently fashionable among them to scorn rational discourse as a hang-up better suited to earlier, less exalted states of consciousness. It will do them good nevertheless to travel down memory lane and hear some of the old tunes that Professor Hook bangs out on his calliope: the differences between *lehrfreiheit* and *lernfreiheit*,[9] the recounting of horrible episodes—the business at Berkeley,[10] at Cornell,[11] at Columbia,[12] at Harvard.[13] The refrain consists of a sorting out of who was right and who was wrong according to the principles stated in the beginning of the book.

Hook's basic principles are by my lights good ones. He believes that universities are, on the whole, places where academic freedom can and should be fostered. Academic freedom he defines as "the freedom of professionally qualified persons to inquire, discover, publish, and teach the truth as they see it in the field of their competence."[14] He is against anything that threatens this value, and, as he sees it, a large number of disjointed incidents in recent years have.

There is a sense in which a discussion of this sort is helpful, in that it tells people something they quite often want to know—*i.e.*, what side to be on. One infers also that the cause of the difficulty is lack of firmness in adherence to principle and that a little less spinelessness on the part of faculties and administrations will drive their troubles away. It is not too much to say that, in giving this impression, Hook radiates optimism.

Glazer radiates pessimism. He is convinced that the forces of reason and decency have been pretty much routed in the battle for the minds of the politically aware young. Why not give up, then? Principally, because Glazer believes that the prescriptions of the left are based on a self-contradictory and quite incompetent set of social analyses. In due course, even in a very affluent society, reality comes crashing in. When this happens, as it must

[9] Sidney Hook, *Academic Freedom and Academic Anarchy* (1970), pp. 32–76.
[10] *Ibid.*, 183–231.
[11] *Ibid.*, 100–05. *See also* 82–83, 90–91.
[12] *Ibid.*, 123–36. *See also* 86–88.
[13] *Ibid.*, 83, 99–100.
[14] *Ibid.*, 34.

sooner or later even to the comfortable middle-class white radicals of America's universities, the rather more hardheaded kind of social theorizing that Glazer espouses may conceivable carry the day after all.

The best example Glazer gives has to do with the implications of spreading the benefits of industrialized society to more and more people. Radicals claim to love equality and approve of high standards of living but also despise the complex economic and social organizations that make them possible. Glazer points out:

> The young radical guerrillas now engaged in the sabotage of social organization take it for granted that they will be provided with complex means of transportation and communication, with medical care, easy availability of food, clothing, and shelter. All this is based on a system they deride and which in their confusion they want to bring down, not realizing it would reduce themselves and all those they wish to help to misery. The arduous and necessary discipline of Cuba and China does not deter them from taking those countries as models, or perhaps really only as symbols, since they often know little about them. The mild discipline of free countries, which makes it possible for large numbers to withdraw to nonproductive styles of life, chafes them more.[15]

Glazer's contribution is to address some of the underlying problems identified by the new left and to show just enough of their complexity to expose the shallowness of new left discussions of them. Glazer himself had the unusual opportunity of living at close quarters through the troubles of two great institutions. He made the early show at Berkeley and then attended the nightcap at Harvard, as did a number of very distinguished Berkeley refugees. Two chapters in Glazer's book[16] give lucid and disheartening accounts of critical events in both places, complete, in the latter instance, with *déjà vu* effects.

IV

Is there an iron law that distributes faculty responses to campus disruption into the categories I have suggested? The descriptive material in both books, which allude to events from many cam-

---

[15] Nathan Glazer, *Remembering the Answers* (1970), pp. 27–28.
[16] Chapters 3 and 13.

puses, suggests that there probably is. Faculties everywhere, or at least at the first-rate places, are pretty much the same. Some are perhaps a shade readier than others to buy peace at any price—in the form, for example, of "symbolic" bongo drums for Cornell Afro-American students, the surrender of faculty authority over Black studies at Harvard—but if the strength of the factions and the nature of the specific issues vary slightly from time to time and place to place, the general deployment of the faculty does not. The ability of both Hook and Glazer to reach into experience on a number of different campuses in order to illustrate their argument also suggests that the effectiveness of faculty in the midst of campus turmoil does not vary much either.

If differences in faculty behavior cannot explain variations in the course and effects of campus turmoil, what can? I can think of three things. First, and probably foremost, the strength of external pressure on the institution, from both left and right. In this respect, it is plain, the public institutions of higher education in the state of California are in some ways unique, with their cadres of left wing militants in and around the student bodies of many of the state colleges and universities and the right wing impulses of some trustees and regents. The second external factor has to do with administrative management. It is clear that college administrators vary more than faculties do, and so do the institutional structures and traditions within which administrators must work. One reason the University of California campuses at Berkeley and San Diego, despite enormous outside pressures, held together through immense difficulties has been the fact that chancellors in both places, while they have made mistakes, have also been men of tremendous talent, energy, and wisdom. Further, the traditions of strong faculty governing bodies helped to provide appropriate legislative sanction for administrative activity. In contrast, places like Columbia, Harvard, and Wesleyan have not been so lucky, in spite of heroic efforts by extraordinary number two men. The recent experience of all three schools suggests that certain responsibilities devolve upon college presidents and must be legitimized by faculty action. Yet, in varying degrees, the appropriate mechanisms could not be activated when they were needed. All three suffered by comparison with Yale and the University of Chicago, where alert administrative leaders met their troubles more successfully while employing greatly varying mixtures of adroitness and firmness.

The third significant environmental factor can be stated only clumsily: whether or not a university is a community. It appears that universities that are in some meaningful sense communities—Chicago, Yale, and Cornell—tend to fall on either end of the spectrum. Either they hold together extraordinarily well or things fall very seriously apart when the center fails to hold. Universities that are very large or intermingled with the metropolitan areas in which they are situated fall somewhere in the middle; for them life can go on despite severe strains and disruptions.

Attempting to explain variations in the institutional effects of campus disorder is not, of course, the same thing as explaining where it all comes from. Indeed, there are many signs that the tide of campus disturbances is beginning to ebb all over the nation. The phenomenon is fading before we shall have had a chance to understand, much less to deal with it. Like the last great episode of national madness, the security mania of the McCarthy era, it is bound to leave enormous social debris—damaged institutions, blighted careers, and a sense five years afterward that too many of us were in the grip of attitudes that did us no credit.

Glazer and Hook are notable exceptions; they can be—and no doubt have been—faulted by some of their colleagues for a lack of responsiveness to the passions of the moment, although in Glazer's case even this seems to me unjust. What distinguishes both authors even more is their fidelity throughout to principles that so far have endured more than one season of irrationality. Both have written survival manuals for negotiating heavy seas. Hook relies rather heavily to my taste upon tying himself (and the rest of us) to the mast. Glazer distinguishes usefully between the sinking of the ship and the rising of the water. But neither writes from the perspective of the oceanographer or the meteorologist and attempts to explain why life on American campuses became so difficult in the late 1960's. Perhaps we shall never know.

TOWARD AN EXPLANATION
OF McCARTHYISM [1]

The recent appearance of an apparently definitive journalistic post-mortem on Senator Joseph McCarthy underscores the rather striking professional inattention of political scientists to one of the most spectacular political phenomena of our time.[2] For those of us who view political science as a potentially powerful weapon in the cause of rational political decision-making, this lost opportunity seems especially poignant.[3] If it is too late to assist politicians in determining the extent to which they should have allowed themselves to be imprisoned by the demands and the rhetoric of McCarthy and his followers, it is not too late to ask more academic questions about who McCarthy's followers really were, and about the sources and extent of his power.[4]

Three Hypotheses

This paper is by no means the first attempt to discuss the social sources and political pretensions of McCarthyism. In fact, nu-

[1] I have received an extraordinary amount of help and encouragement while pursuing the research reported here. I want to thank Eugene N. Feingold and F. L. Kilpatrick of the Brookings Institution, Robert A. Dentler of the University of Kansas, Aaron B. Wildavsky of Oberlin College, Duane Lockard of Connecticut College, and Malcolm C. Moos and Francis E. Rourke of the Johns Hopkins University, none of whom is responsible for anything second-rate, badly written, or libelous which may appear in this article.

[2] Richard Rovere, *Senator Joe McCarthy* (New York: Harcourt Brace, 1959).

[3] No political scientist can properly elaborate upon the subject of policy science without acknowledging a debt to Harold D. Lasswell. A recent contribution of Lasswell's is his Presidential Address to the American Political Science Association, appearing in the *American Political Science Review* (vol. 50, Dec. 1956) as "The Political Science of Science," pp. 961–79. See also Lasswell, "Strategies of Inquiry: The Rational Use of Observation," in Daniel Lerner, ed., *The Human Meaning of the Social Sciences* (New York: Meridian, 1959), pp. 89–113, and Lasswell, "The Intelligence Function: Built-in Errors," *PROD* 3 (Sept. 1959), pp. 3–7.

[4] The extent to which academic men, as well as men of power, failed to ask these questions when they were politically relevant is documented in Paul F. Lazarsfeld and Wagner Thielens, Jr., *The Academic Mind* (Glencoe: Free Press, 1958).

merous ingenious explanations of the McCarthy phenomenon have been proffered.[5] Furthermore, sophisticated students have seldom relied upon any single explanation. In reducing previous explanations to three hypotheses, then, I have no doubt greatly simplified the viewpoints of the writers who first suggested them.

One hypothesis which attempts to account for McCarthy's rise to prominence lays heavy stress on "atmospheric" conditions surrounding the position of the United States after the Second World War. Instead of being allowed to relax into their customary inter-war posture of "normalcy," Americans were faced with the necessity of continuing their foreign entanglements, owing to the hostility of the Russians and the debilitation of our overseas allies. This hypothesis suggests that many Americans were unhappy at this turn of events, and that many of them interpreted these events as the inexorable result of involvement in "foreign" wars. These citizens opposed large-scale spending for foreign economic aid, were progressively angered by the fall of China and the discovery of atomic spies both here and abroad, had always been skeptical of alliances with Great Britain, and became bitterly frustrated at the seemingly endless maneuvers of the Cold War and the Korean conflict. Senator McCarthy's approach to politics, so runs the argument, gave support to the nostalgia of isolationists, many of whom had ancestral ties with Germany, and was congenial to those who harbored populistic and anglophobic sentiments.[6]

From this hypothesis we should deduce that McCarthy would find support among people of German extraction, among isolationists, and among those who preferred dramatic activity to patience in the conduct of foreign affairs. Evidence on these points is not conclusive, but certainly suggests the plausibility of this hy-

[5] See an excellent review which extracts explanatory propositions from mostly hortatory literature on McCarthyism: Dennis H. Wrong, 'Theories of McCarthyism', *Dissent*, I (Autumn 1954), pp. 385–92.

[6] See, for expositions of this hypothesis, Samuel Lubell, *The Future of American Politics* (2nd ed., Garden City, N.Y.: Doubleday, 1956), p. 164; Samuel Lubell, "The Question is Why," review of *The New American Right* in the *New York Times Book Review*, 11 Dec. 1955; Peter Viereck, "The Revolt Against The Elite," in Daniel Bell, ed., *The New American Right* (New York: Criterion, 1955), pp. 91–116; Talcott Parsons, "Social Strains in America," *ibid.*, pp. 117–40.

pothetical description of McCarthy supporters. For example, Samuel Lubell has reported two chief sources of strength for Senator McCarthy:

> One was the frustrations that arose out of the Korean War, which often took the form of voters demanding "Why don't we clean up these Commies at home with our boys dying in Korea?". . . . The second main source of McCarthy strength came in areas which opposed our entry into the last war.[7]

Lubell also indicates that McCarthy ran better in those Wisconsin townships with high German populations than he did in the rest of the state.[8]

Hodges, Graham, and Anderson, in a study of Pierce County, Wisconsin, discovered that McCarthy supporters could be found disproportionately among those of German extraction, and among those who are "skeptical about foreign involvements on the part of the United States . . . [favoring] discontinuing both economic and military aid to Asiatic and European nations, and [feeling] that the Korean conflict was a mistake." [9]

Information from various Gallup surveys is also relevant. A study of New London County, Connecticut, indicated that one of the major reasons people gave for supporting McCarthy was that "They admire greatly his 'courage' and 'sincerity,' feeling that he is not afraid to 'get tough.' " [10] Gallup also reported a similar response among citizens of East Stroudsburg, Pennsylvania, where many citizens favored McCarthy because of his "fearlessness," and because he "gets a lot done the way he goes about things." [11]

It seems likely that the political atmosphere contributed in some general sense to McCarthy's rise, and supplied his followers

---

[7] Samuel Lubell, *Revolt of the Moderates* (New York: Harper, 1956), p. 268.
[8] *Ibid.*, p. 269.
[9] Harold M. Hodges, Jr., Charles Graham, and Philip Anderson, "A Sociological Analysis of McCarthy Supporters," a paper delivered at the Fifty-second Annual Meeting of the American Sociological Society, Washington, D.C., Aug. 1957.
[10] John M. Fenton, " 'Barometer' Area Divided on McCarthy," American Institute of Public Opinion news release, 22 Jan. 1954.
[11] George Gallup, "Two Pennsylvania 'Test-Tube' Towns Split Sharply in Views on McCarthy," American Institute of Public Opinion news release, 26 June 1954.

with rationalizations for supporting him. But presumably this atmosphere existed for everyone, and, save in the case of the relatively small German-American group, the hypothesis does not explain, for the purpose of assessing his political possibilities at any time, where in the population most of McCarthy's supporters could have been located.

Many people have been persuaded that McCarthy's potential was considerable, since for a great length of time Gallup surveys recorded that a substantial proportion of the population "approved of" McCarthy in some sense.[12] The atmospheric hypothesis differentiates only crudely between those favorable to McCarthy and those unfavorable, on the basis of generalized attitudes toward historical events, and identifies more exactly only a small portion of McCarthy's alleged followers.

A second hypothesis derives from the researches of Adorno and his associates [13] and identifies McCarthy as an authoritarian leader. Authoritarianism implies a host of rather misanthropic social attitudes including "toughness," superconformity, intolerance, generalized hostility, and an unusual concern with sexual "goings on."

---

[12] A trend line on Senator McCarthy's popularity was released on 12 Nov. 1954 by the American Institute of Public Opinion, showing the following results:

Date	Favorable %	Unfavorable %	No opinion %
June 1953.........	35	30	35
Aug.	34	42	24
Jan. 1954	50	29	21
Mar.	46	36	18
Apr.	38	46	16
May...............	35	49	16
June...............	34	45	21
Aug.	36	51	13
Nov.	35	46	19

McCarthy also ran fourth in the Gallup nation-wide survey of "most admired men in the world," in 1954. George Gallup, "Ike Tops Ten Most Admired Men," American Institute of Public Opinion news release, 26 Dec. 1954.

[13] T. W. Adorno, Else Frenkel-Brunswik, Daniel J. Levinson, and R. Nevitt Sanford, *The Authoritarian Personality* (New York: Harper, 1950).

Many observers, pointing out that Senator McCarthy exhibited more than his share of these hostile attitudes, deduced that throughout the population those individuals who were most authoritarian would be most likely to be McCarthyites.[14]

This hypothesis has gained some confirmation, but contrary evidence suggests the need for more precise specification of the personality characteristics which are supposed to have caused pro-McCarthy sentiments.

Hodges, Graham, and Anderson report that McCarthyites were "more conformistic, agreeing that there are too many 'oddballs' around, that the 'good' American doesn't stand out among his fellow Americans, and that children should not develop hobbies which are . . . unusual"; and more misanthropic, "concurring with statements that 'people are out to cheat you,' and that 'there is wickedness, cheating, and corruption all about us.' "[15]

However, some students have noticed that there were relatively intolerant groups in the population whose members nevertheless seemed markedly impervious to McCarthy's charismatic charm.[16] And, conversely, it has been established that members of other groups which were not notably intolerant have supported him to

[14] The "authoritarianism" hypothesis is advanced by Richard Hofstadter, "The Pseudo-Conservative Revolt," in Bell, *op. cit.*, pp. 33–35, and David Riesman and Nathan Glazer, "The Intellectuals and the Discontented Classes," *ibid.*, pp. 56–90. See also Immanuel Wallerstein, "McCarthyism and the Conservative," unpublished M.A. thesis, Columbia University, 1954; James A. Wechsler, "Where Proof of Innocence Becomes Damning Evidence of Guilt," *Washington Post*, 3 May 1953; Richard Rovere, *op. cit.*, *passim*; and Michael Straight, *Trial By Television* (Boston: Beacon, 1954), *passim*.

[15] Hodges, Graham, and Anderson, *op. cit.*

[16] This criticism is in effect a special application of more general strictures against the Authoritarian Personality study. See Richard Christie and Marie Jahoda, eds., *Studies in the Scope and Method of the Authoritarian Personality* (Glencoe: Free Press, 1954). For indications that non-followers of McCarthy may be at least as authoritarian as his followers see Samuel A. Stouffer, *Communism, Conformity and Civil Liberties* (Garden City, N.Y.: Doubleday, 1955), p. 129; Seymour Martin Lipset, "Democracy and Working Class Authoritarianism," *American Sociological Review*, 24 (Aug. 1959), p. 484. Hodges, Graham, and Anderson, *op. cit.*, found that Mc-Carthyites in Pierce County tended to be more anti-Semitic than non-McCarthyites, but were not more anti-Negro. This too suggests that a general "authoritarian" personality syndrome is not an adequate category for the analysis of McCarthyism.

a disproportionate degree.[17] A third hypothesis attempts to account for these findings by making reference to the needs and aspirations of certain groups within the population which were satisfied, it is suggested, through McCarthyite activity.

The authors of *The New American Right* have advanced this hypothesis in its most full-blown and persuasive form. This volume is a collection of essays by a distinguished group of social scientists, all attempting to explain the social sources and consequences of McCarthyism. The nature of American politics has changed, they say, so as to render the McCarthy movement unintelligible to conventional forms of political analysis. They call for a "new" type of analysis, one that recognizes the significance of the emergence of status groups as entities making important demands upon the rest of American society, through the political system.[18] In times of economic distress demands are made along class lines; economic "interests" divide the nation's wealth and income by putting pressures of various kinds upon one another and on the government, which acts as a mediating and legitimizing agent for society and as a forum for the expression of dissatisfactions and the promulgation of panaceas. In periods of prosperity the continuing adjustments of interests to each other and to the resources of the economy yield the center of political attention to the demands of status groups, which use the arena to insist on the improvement or maintenance of their status position in society. In times of economic well-being the "dynamic of dissent" resides in those status groups who wish to change the *status quo*—and of course consider themselves at a disadvantage in the status hierarchy. The McCarthy movement, the authors agree, expresses a non-economic form of protest which can only mean that those in society who supported McCarthy did so because of status dissatisfactions.[19]

---

[17] See Stouffer, *op. cit.*, p. 129; Martin Trow, "Small Businessmen, Political Tolerance, and Support for McCarthy," *American Journal of Sociology*, 64 (Nov. 1958), pp. 270–81.

[18] Daniel Bell, "Interpretations of American Politics," in Bell, ed., *op. cit.*, pp. 4 ff.

[19] *Ibid.* Hofstadter, pp. 33, 34, 43f.; Lipset, "The Sources of the 'Radical Right,' " pp. 167 ff. This hypothesis suggests a new application for the concept of "relative

The authors could have predicted from this hypothesis those groups which should be pro-McCarthy and those which should be anti-McCarthy. Secondly, they could have checked these predictions against the available evidence. In fact, they took only one of these steps, deducing who McCarthy's followers might be. It can easily be seen from an inspection of Table I that the "status politics" hypothesis is much too inclusive to have very much explanatory power. Although it may accurately estimate why specific members of each of the groups named may have found McCarthy an attractive political figure (i.e. because of their status anxieties) it neither differentiates successfully among groups, nor provides criteria by which some groups can be excluded from its purview.

TABLE I

Groups Comprising the New American Right
(i.e. McCarthyites)

I. *Named in six out of seven essays:* New rich.
II. *Named in five essays:* Texans, Irish, Germans.
III. *Named in four essays:* Middle class, Catholics, Midwesterners.
IV. *Named in three essays:* Lower middle class, up-mobile, less educated.
V. *Named in two essays:* "Cankered intellectuals," old family Protestant "shabby genteel," recent immigrants, down-mobile, minority ethnics, Old Guard G.O.P., ex-communists, Midwest isolationists.
VI. *Named in one essay:* Lower class, small town lawyers, auto dealers, oil wildcatters, real estate manipulators, small business men, manual workers, elderly and retired, rentier class, youth, Southern Californians, South Bostonians, fringe urbanites in middle-sized cities, transplants to city, Polish Catholics, hick Protestants, patriotic and historical group members (e.g. DAR), Scandinavians, Southern Protestant fundamentalists, soured patricians, small town residents, neo-fascists.

Source: *The New American Right*.

deprivation," which urges that disprivilege be considered not as an objective social position, but rather as a state of mind which occurs when the aspirations of a group exceed its current resources. See Alice S. Rossi and Robert K. Merton, "Contributions to the Theory of Reference Group Behavior," in Robert K. Merton, *Social Theory and Social Structure* (Glencoe: Free Press, 1957, revised ed.), pp. 225–80.

TABLE II

*Groups Comprising the New American Right,
According to Empirical Evidence*

The vertical axis ranks groups according to the number of essays out of
seven in which they are explicitly mentioned in *The New American Right*.
The horizontal axis lists sources of empirical data in support of (Yes) or
against (No) the listing of groups as nuclei of New American Right sentiment. See footnote 1 on pp. 242–43 for an evaluation of these sources.

Group	Gallup	Bean	Harris
5			
(1) Germans	—	No	—
(2) Irish..............................	—	—	No
4			
(3) Catholics	Yes	Yes	—
3			
(4) Less educated...................	Yes	Yes	—
2			
(5) Minority ethnics	Yes & No	Yes & No	Yes & No
(6) Republicans	Yes	—	—
(7) Recent immigrants.............	Yes & No	Yes & No	—
1			
(8) Lower class......................	Yes	Yes	—
(9) Manual workers	Yes	—	—
(10) Polish Catholics	—	Yes	—
(11) Elderly	Yes	—	—
(12) Youth............................	No	—	No
(13) Scandinavians...................	—	No	—
Groups not named in *The New American Right*			
(1) Farmers	Yes	Yes	—
(2) New Englanders	Yes	—	—

Sources: American Institute of Public Opinion (Gallup Poll), *Influences in the Mid-
Term Election*, 1954 (Bean), *Is There A Republican Majority?* (Harris).

A second step would have been to check deductions against
facts. Only Lipset, among *The New American Right* essayists, attempted to do so, and he presents only his conclusions from findings, rather than the findings themselves. At the time of publication of *The New American Right* there were several sources

available which might have confirmed at least partially some of the predictions made in these essays. I present the relevant conclusions of these sources in Table II.

As Table II indicates, the "status anxieties" hypothesis yields rather indifferent results, since it apparently fails to account for two groups in the populace found to have been disproportionately pro-McCarthy, yet on the other hand evidence indicates that some groups named as McCarthyite in fact were not. Although there is no reason to be enthusiastic about the quality of the sources on which these conclusions are based, they are very much better than mere surmises about McCarthy's grass roots followers.[20] Given the speculative nature of most writing on McCarthy, attention should be paid to these empirical findings, despite their limitations.

[20] A tremendous number of Gallup quota control surveys in which questions about Senator McCarthy were included have been taken. These surveys followed two patterns: first, interviewers would enter a given locale and ask why respondents did or did not support McCarthy (e.g. the New London county survey reported 22 Jan. 1954, or the Pennsylvania "test-tube" towns reported 26 June 1954). The reports of these surveys do not include demographic breakdowns of respondents, and did not contribute to Table II. The second kind of survey was the nation-wide poll, in which respondents were asked questions such as those appearing in Tables III–XI. In these surveys respondents were broken into various demographic categories: e.g. occupational, religious, and geographical. The percentages for and against McCarthy in each category were reported. Reports of surveys such as this appeared, among other dates, on 15 and 16 Jan., 14 Mar., and 23 May 1954. The 15 Jan. survey, for example, yielded the following results in the geographical category:

	Response		
Location	*Pro-McCarthy* %	*Anti-McCarthy* %	*No opinion* %
East.............	55	27	18
Midwest	48	27	25
South...........	47	30	23
West............	46	36	18

Now these categories are obviously not precise enough to furnish intelligible data on the location of McCarthy supporters within the population. Nevertheless, the relationships among various segments of the population with respect to their sen-

Other criticisms can be made of *The New American Right*. The assertion that "status groups" are at the heart of the McCarthy movement is essentially trivial. The task was to determine *which* status groups were peculiarly situated so as to be especially favorable to McCarthy. And the identification of some of the groups named as McCarthyite is simply implausible. This should weigh heavily in the case of the book under discussion, where the basic argument depends on plausibility rather than more "scientific" demonstrations of truth. For example, it is unclear why members of the DAR should release status anxieties by joining in an attack on the very social groups whose history their organization celebrates. That status anxieties can drive people to attack others—especially the weak—is a reasonable enough argument, but if it is in principle possible to negate *The New American Right*

timents towards McCarthy remained stable over a great many polls, and give us a basis on which we can rank these groups for McCarthyite sympathies. It is in this sense that Gallup data is used in Table II. When Gallup data show consistently that a high proportion of Easterners (let us say) favor McCarthy, over those who oppose him, as compared with a similar ratio among other people from other parts of the country, I felt justified in giving a 'Yes' in the appropriate box in Table II. I gave a 'No' when any groups registered consistently anti-McCarthy, ranked behind half of those groups in a similar category (i.e. geographical) in support of McCarthy.

Louis Bean's monograph *Influences in the* 1954 *Mid-Term Elections* (Washington: Public Affairs Institute, 1954) provides the second source of data. Bean analyzed election returns in races where McCarthy ran for office, in 1946 and 1952. He also discusses the impact of the issue of Communists in government by making inferences from 1950 and 1952 election returns in selected states and counties throughout the country. Bean's major findings are (1) that McCarthy seems to have enjoyed greater support in rural than in urban areas in his home state, (2) that pro-McCarthy results seem to have occurred in those areas where the 'Catholic index' was relatively high. This Catholic index is apparently the 1936 census of religious bodies, brought up to 1954 on the assumption that changes in the intervening years were proportional in all areas. This assumption weakens Bean's case considerably, but alternative sources of data about the geographical distribution of religious groups within states were not available. Bean also presents data in an appendix relating 1950 census data on the ethnic composition of Wisconsin counties to their support of McCarthy.

Louis Harris presents an analysis of the 1952 Roper election surveys in *Is There a Republican Majority?* (New York: Harper, 1954). He says that people of Irish descent were split about evenly on McCarthy (p. 90), and that young people broke with Eisenhower in 1952 because of his appeasement of McCarthy and the right wing of the Republican party generally (p. 168). Harris does not concern himself directly with McCarthy, except briefly, and he presents little in the way of hard data on the subject; hence his book is of limited value.

thesis in any way, surely the cases of white Protestant "shabby genteel" McCarthyites succeed in doing so. Finally, it should be noted that the introduction of ethnic and status considerations into political analysis can hardly be said to have originated with the authors of *The New American Right*, as they themselves, aware of the practices of "ticket balancing," the folklore of political "availability," and long-standing academic interest in the group conflict theory of politics, no doubt realize.

Since the publication of *The New American Right*, Martin Trow has come forward with new data bearing on the "status anxieties" hypothesis.[21] He concludes from his study of Bennington, Vermont, that: (1) Supporters of McCarthy were not more politically intolerant than non-supporters of McCarthy when formal education was held constant. McCarthy received a disproportionate share of his support from the less educated members of the community, who are always less tolerant.[22] (2) McCarthy received much greater support from those members of the middle class who were *economically* at a disadvantage (e.g. small business men) and who expressed hostility towards modern forms of political and economic organization.

These findings support all three hypotheses in so far as they identify McCarthyites as members of a movement of generalized protest. But they also indicate that economic and political factors may have been as important as status anxieties in explaining the social sources of McCarthyism.

[21] Martin Trow, *op. cit.*
[22] See Stouffer, *op. cit.*, and Lipset, "Democracy and Working-Class Authoritarianism," *loc. cit.* Herbert McClosky has some findings which indicate that greater degrees of intolerance, hostility, and misanthropy also characterize those persons subscribing to "conservative" ideology. Herbert McClosky, "Conservatism and Personality," *American Political Science Review*, 52 (March 1958), pp. 27–45. This presents an interesting puzzle for the student of McCarthyism. It is generally well recognized that the content of McCarthy's political "program"— such as it was—was destructive and profoundly anti-conservative, as well as politically intolerant, hostile, and misanthropic. It is entirely possible that McCarthy's followers were either conservatives responding favorably to the tone of his approach, or radicals responding to its manifest content—or both. Regrettably, McClosky's data do not relate personality characteristics and ideological predispositions to current political sympathies or activities, hence this puzzle must go unsolved.

A Political Interpretation

I want to turn now to a fourth hypothesis, one which attempts to explain McCarthyism as a political phenomenon. It is a surprising fact that analysts have discounted so heavily the purely political aspect of his success. Therefore I want to review now the rather heavy evidence supporting the hypothesis that McCarthy succeeded at the grass roots primarily among Republicans.

For example, I present immediately below in Table III the results of a re-analysis of a Gallup survey.[23] In this re-analysis I have attempted to differentiate between those who were for and those against McCarthy. Pro- and anti-McCarthy populations were selected by tabulating responses to the following question: "In general, would you say you have a favorable or unfavorable opinion of Senator Joseph McCarthy?"

TABLE III

Popularity of Senator Joseph McCarthy

In general, would you say you have a favorable or unfavorable opinion of Senator Joseph R. McCarthy?

	N	%
Favorable	456	31
Unfavorable	693	46
No opinion	287	19
Don't know him	41	3
	1,477	99

Source: Gallup Survey 529 K, 6 April 1954.

The data at hand were limited; none the less they provided an opportunity to test in some approximate way the predictions of

[23] This work was computed for me by the Roper Public Opinion Research Center at Williams College, on a grant made available by the Political Science Department of Yale University I am grateful to Philip K. Hastings and Robert A. Dahl, of Williams and Yale, respectively, for supporting this part of my research. The Gallup Survey whose results appear here was number 529 K, 6 April 1954.

each of the hypotheses thus far offered to account for McCarthy's grass roots support.

The nation-wide questionnaire tapped possible pro-German sentiments among respondents, with the results shown in Table IV. The results, while not extreme, are in the direction indicated by the "atmospheric" hypothesis.

TABLE IV

*Sentiment about Germany of Those Favorable and
Unfavorable to Senator J. McCarthy*

Would you, yourself, like to see Germany again become one of the three or four most powerful countries?

	F (%)	U (%)
Yes..............	29	25
No	56	59
No opinion.....	7	8
Qualified........	8	8
	100	100
	(N = 454)	(N = 690)

Source: Gallup Survey 529 K, April 1954.

Authoritarians, it is said, tend to be politically confused and badly informed.[24] The nation-wide survey asked a series of questions designed to elicit political information of various kinds. McCarthyites and non-McCarthyites were able to identify Far East-

---

[24] See Adorno *et. al.*, *op. cit.*, pp. 658 ff.; Fillmore H. Stanford, *Authoritarianism and Leadership* (Philadelphia: Institute for Research in Human Relations, 1950), p. 159. Low levels of political information have been found to correlate with low personal involvement in politics, and these in turn would lead us to assume that authoritarians participate less in politics than non-authoritarians. See Morris Janowitz and Dwaine Marvick, "Authoritarianism and Political Behavior," *Public Opinion Quarterly*, 17 (Summer 1953), pp. 185–201; Paul F. Lazarsfeld, Bernard Berelson, and Hazel Gaudet, *The Peoples' Choice* (New York: Duell, Sloane and Pearce, 1944); and Morris Rosenberg, "Some Determinants of Political Apathy," *Public Opinion Quaterly*, 18 (Winter 1954), pp. 349–66. The relationship is regrettably not so simple, as Robert E. Lane has demonstrated: "Political Personality and

TABLE V

*Political Information of Those Favorable and
Unfavorable to Senator J. McCarthy*

Will you please tell me which of these men you have heard of? And will you tell me what country he is from?

	Favorable			Unfavorable		
	Chiang (%)	Mao (%)	Nehru (%)	Chiang (%)	Mao (%)	Nehru (%)
Yes, correct country .	89	34	60	88	42	67
Yes, incorrect or don't know country..................	6	19	12	8	20	9
Not heard of, no answer................	5	47	28	4	38	24
	100	100	100	100	100	100
	(N = 458)	(N = 455)	(N = 454)	(N = 700*)	(N = 689)	(N = 690)

Source: Gallup Survey 529 K, April 1954.

* The fact that the Ns here exceed the total unfavorable population of 693 is perhaps on account of double responses in a small number of cases.

ern political leaders correctly to about the same degree, but, once again, the slight differences recorded were all in the expected direction. This is also true of the questions asking about participation in the last election, and in elections generally (see Tables V, VI).

The same thing happens when crude tests of the "status" hy-

Electoral Choice," *American Political Science Review*, 49 (March 1955), pp. 173–90. Apparently, when class is controlled, authoritarians have been found to participate in elections about as much as non-authoritarians, but probably for different reasons. I include figures on participation here, first because they were available, and second because they reinforce both my own conclusion—that McCarthyites differentiate themselves slightly by their lower rates of participation—and Lane's conclusion—that the differences between presumably authoritarian and non-authoritarian populations with respect to their political participation is negligible.

TABLE VI

*Political Participation of Those Favorable and
Unfavorable to Senator J. McCarthy*

Question I.   Have you ever voted in any election, or don't you pay
              any attention to politics?
Question II. In the election in November 1952, did things come up
              which kept you from voting, or did you happen to vote?

	Favorable		Unfavorable	
	I (%)	II (%)	I (%)	II (%)
Yes...............	86	77	89	81
No	3	20	2	14
Never...........	11	—	9	—
No, too young	—	3	—	5
	100 (N = 456)	100 (N = 455)	100 (N = 692)	100 (N = 687)

Source: Gallup Survey 529 K, April 1954.

pothesis are applied, the assumption being that a higher proportion of McCarthyites come from the Catholic, lower class, and
less educated parts of the population. The tables (VII, VIII, and
IX) show, once again, tendencies in the direction of confirmation.

But this relatively meager empirical confirmation is unimpres-
sive when set against comparable figures describing the two populations by their political affiliations (see Table X).

These findings speak for themselves, but do not stand alone.
The distributions of McCarthy's vote in Wisconsin, where, it
should be admitted, "The impact [of McCarthyism] on the political and cultural life of the state was not particularly great," [25] indicate strongly that McCarthy ran best in the most heavily Re-

[25] Leon D. Epstein, *Politics in Wisconsin* (Madison: University of Wisconsin Press,
1958), p. 4.

TABLE VII

Religious Preference of Those Favorable and
Unfavorable to Senator J. McCarthy

Question: What is your religious preference:—
Protestant, Catholic, or Jewish?

	F (%)	U (%)
Protestant.	68	71
Catholic...	28	20
Jewish.....	1	5
Other......	2	3
	99 (N = 452)	99 (N = 685)

Source: Gallup Survey 529 K, April 1954.

TABLE VIII

Social-economic Rating of Those Favorable and
Unfavorable to Senator J. McCarthy (Rating by interviewer)

	F (%)	U (%)
Upper	3	3
Above average.	32	34
Average.........	2	1
Below average.	47	45
Lower	11	14
	95* (N = 433)	97* (N = 675)

Source: Gallup Survey 529 K, April 1954.

* Totals are less than 100 per cent apparently because interviewers failed to rate some respondents.

TABLE IX

*Educational Levels Attained by Those Favorable and
Unfavorable to Senator J. McCarthy*

	F (%)	U (%)
No school	1	1
Up to 8 years school.....	26	21
9–12 years.................	53	51
Over 12 years	17	24
	97 (N = 441)	97 (N = 682)

Source: Gallup Survey 529 K, April 1954.

publican areas, and conversely. James G. March has demonstrated this point conclusively with respect to the 1952 primary election.[26] Samuel Lubell has observed that Senator McCarthy in 1952 ran well ahead of his state average in townships populated heavily by people of German extraction, but this also was true of other Republicans, including Senator Taft in the 1952 primary, and Republican Presidential candidates in 1944, 1948, and 1952.[27] Inspection of election returns bears out the thesis that McCarthy ran best where the Republican party was strongest. McCarthy's strongest showing in 1952, for example, generally took place in those counties giving Walter Kohler, Republican candidate for Governor, their heaviest support. Out of the 71 counties in Wisconsin, 30 gave McCarthy a margin of 2–1 or better, and of these 30, 24 were counties in which Governor Kohler beat his opponent by 3–1 or more. In the 29 counties where he made his strongest race, capturing 75 per cent or more of the two-party vote, Kohler received only 28 per cent. of his statewide vote. But in the 30 counties where McCarthy received 65 per

[26] James G. March, "McCarthy Can Still Be Beaten," *Reporter*, 7 (28 Oct. 1952), pp. 17–19.
[27] Lubell, *Revolt, op. cit.*, p. 269.

TABLE X

Party Sympathies and Voting Records of Those
Favorable and Unfavorable to Senator J. McCarthy

Questions
  I Did you vote for Eisenhower (Republican) or Stevenson (Democratic)?
  II If the elections for Congress were being held today, which party would
    you like to see win in this state—the Republican party or the Democratic
    party?
  III (If undecided)
    As of today, do you lean more to the Republican party or to the Demo-
    cratic party?
  IV In politics, as of today, do you consider yourself a Democrat, Republi-
    can, or Independent?

Question	*Favorable (%)*				*Unfavorable (%)*			
	I	II	III	IV	I	II	III	IV
Republican	76	53	37	46	49	29	28	24
Democratic	21	29	23	30	49	57	38	58
Undecided	—	17	27	—	—	13	26	—
Other	3	1	13	24	2	1	8	24
	100	100	100	100	100	100	100	100
	(N =	(N =	(N =	(N =	(N =	(N =	(N =	(N =
	350)	456)	77)	456)	560)	693)	88)	693)

Source: Gallup Survey 529 K, April 1954.

cent. of the vote or more, fully 35 per cent of McCarthy's state-
wide vote was concentrated.[28]

These figures demonstrate that the McCarthy vote was concentrated in areas of Republican strength, and was neither scattered,
nor distributed in some pattern unique to McCarthy, nor particularly strong.

Deciding where McCarthyites at the grass roots were located is

[28] It should be remembered that we are not talking about Wisconsin's more popu-
lous counties in this analysis, which no doubt explain why a majority of the state-
wide Republican vote is not located in those counties giving Republicans their
heaviest majorities. See also Bean, *op. cit.*

of course not sufficient to explain his success in official Washington. Many cogent reasons for McCarthy's success have been given, and since they are mutually complementary it is unnecessary to choose between them. McCarthy was, at first, the weapon of a desperate Republican party. Senator Taft's famous advice, "If one case doesn't work, then bring up another," [29] is a measure of the lengths to which Republicans were willing to go in those days to embarrass a long-entrenched Democratic administration. Secondly, there was McCarthy's protected position as a member of the Senate.[30] While he was never even remotely a significant member of the Club, attacks on him might have been construed by powerful Senators as attacks on Senatorial prerogatives and practices. McCarthy's place in the Senate also gave him the protection of immunity from libel suits, the services of the staff of a Committee, and the powers to hold hearings and issue subpoenas.

Third, one can scarcely discount his personal effectiveness as an imaginative political entrepreneur who exploited the mass media by accommodating his "exposés" to the exigencies of deadlines, and who employed the bulging briefcase, the non-existent "document," garbled figures, and so on, with stunning effect.[31] A fourth reason for McCarthy's success was no doubt the vulnerability (real or imagined) of the Truman administration on the issue of communists in government, and a fifth reason would certainly be the emasculation of administrative resistance to McCarthy's activities, by order of President Eisenhower.[32]

All of these are "factors" which contribute to an explanation of McCarthy's phenomenal success in demoralizing federal employees, in blackening the name of the United States abroad, and

[29] William S. White, *The Taft Story* (New York: Harper, 1954), p. 85; Jack Anderson and Ronald W. May, *McCarthy: The Man, The Senator, The "Ism"* (Boston: Beacon, 1952), p. 353.
[30] One analysis which covers these points especially well is Aaron B. Wildavsky's "Exploring the Content of McCarthyism," *Australian Outlook*, 9 (June 1955), pp. 88–104. See also John B. Oakes, "Inquiry into McCarthy's Status," *New York Times Magazine*, 12 Apr. 1953.
[31] See Rovere, *op. cit.*, and Cecil Holland, "Short Course on McCarthy Techniques," *Washington Star*, 11 April 1954.
[32] See Martin Merson, *The Private Diary of a Public Servant* (New York: Macmillan, 1955), pp. 72–81.

in dominating the headlines for more than four years. But they do not explain the remarkable fear of McCarthy that seems to have afflicted those somewhat outside his line of fire—newspaper people, professional folk, most academicians, and his colleagues in Congress. This fear can be accounted for, I think, by adding one more factor, a critical assumption made by almost all those for whom McCarthyism was of daily concern. This assumption was that McCarthy was in fact uniquely powerful at the grass roots; that he had a vast following which cross-cut party lines and loyalties, which he could call upon to defeat his enemies. Richard Rovere reports: "After the 1952 elections, it was believed in the Senate that McCarthy was responsible for the presence there of eight men—which meant that he was responsible for the absence of eight others." [33]

A Test for a Critical Assumption

Surely a useful task for policy science would have been to test such beliefs of policy-makers against the available evidence. It is disquieting to wonder how history might have been changed if the evidence had shown a more modest number of scalps on McCarthy's belt—or none at all. After all, the only thoroughly documented victory of this kind for McCarthy was the replacement of Republican Senator Raymond Baldwin by Democratic Senator William Benton of Connecticut—hardly a net gain for the right wing of the Senate. Baldwin has made no secret of the fact that abuse at the hand of McCarthy during the investigation of the Malmedy massacre was the determining factor in his decision to leave Washington. [34]

It does not seem entirely pointless to undertake an analysis of at

[33] Rovere, *op. cit.*, p. 37. Rovere has named only five of the eight casualties in his book, and has never responded to a letter asking him to name the other three. He includes Raymond Baldwin and William Benton of Connecticut, Millard Tydings of Maryland, Ernest McFarland of Arizona, and Scott Lucas of Illinois.

[34] McFarland is generally supposed to have been the victim of the uncommonly vigorous campaigning of his opponent, Barry Goldwater, and Scott Lucas was thought by many observers to have fallen prey to the aftermath of the Kefauver crime investigations. Rovere may be claiming more for McCarthy here than most people ever gave him credit for.

least one of the other seven cases. There are those who still believe that McCarthy was a powerful influence with voters all over the nation and that these voters rose up and smote some of his most distinguished adversaries. It seems important to make at least a token effort to verify this belief. If it is correct, the usual supposition by political scientists that political support is in general not transferable from one figure to another must go by the board. We would have to conclude that American politics is a more dangerous and unstable game than we had suspected, if a demagogue can criss-cross the country and impose his will upon the electorates of states far from his own.

Political observers seem most willing to grant that McCarthy was important in the defeat of Senator Tydings in 1950, and of Senator Benton in 1952. Rovere says: "McCarthy, a nobody in 1949, threw his weight against Tydings in 1950, and, lo, Tydings lost"; [35] and, ". . . he had, in fact, attended to Senator Benton's expulsion by the voters of Connecticut." [36] McCarthy's reputation for grass roots political effectiveness outside his home state rests most heavily on these two cases. The easy availability of appropriate statistical materials prompts me to select the Benton case for further examination here.[37]

William Benton was appointed Senator from Connecticut in 1949 by Governor Chester Bowles, his erstwhile partner in the advertising business, to succeed Raymond Baldwin, who retired to the Connecticut Supreme Court of Errors. There was some question at the time of Benton's appointment as to whether he was a *bona fide* resident of the state of Connecticut, but he was duly qualified, and took his seat. Benton's occupational record was unusually distinguished. He had been an advertising execu-

[35] Rovere, *op. cit.*, p. 37.

[36] *Ibid.*, p. 189.

[37] Those interested in the Tydings case might consult the long, but for our purposes inconclusive, Hearings and Report of the Subcommittee on Privileges and Elections of the U.S. Senate Committee on Rules and Administration, *The Maryland Senatorial Election of 1950.* Hearing, 20 Feb.– 11 Apr. 1951. Senate Report 647 (82 Cong., 1st sess.), or Stanley Kelley, Jr., *Professional Public Relations and Political Power* (Baltimore: Johns Hopkins University Press, 1956), pp. 107–43.

tive, Vice President of the University of Chicago, President of the *Encyclopedia Britannica*, and an Assistant Secretary of State. In 1950 he stood for election to the seat he had held by appointment, and won with 50.06 per cent of the state-wide two-party vote.

Returning to the Senate, Benton went out of his way to tangle repeatedly with Senator McCarthy, urging an investigation of McCarthy's finances, among other harassments. McCarthy struck back with characteristic resourcefulness, and managed to have Benton investigated too. When Benton stood again for election for his full term, in the fall of 1952, McCarthy campaigned briefly in Connecticut against him. Benton lost, polling 45.8 per cent of the vote.

Rovere, and presumably others, concluded that McCarthy "got" Benton. But no reasonable construction of the evidence at hand seems likely to sustain this conclusion. A few elementary facts about Connecticut politics should be noted. First, Connecticut had no primary system, a situation which has since been changed; hence at the time there was little incentive for most voters to reveal their party affiliations to registrars of voters, and only a minority did so. However, Connecticut voters generally vote straight tickets, for all the reasons for which straight tickets are popular in other parts of the country, and also because the voting machines in use in Connecticut make a split ballot difficult. In order to split a ticket, it is necessary first to pull a party lever and then cut individual candidates off the ballot, replacing them with other candidates.[38]

It should surprise no one to learn, then, that just as Benton's vote went down in 1952 as compared with 1950, so Democratic fortunes generally declined in the same period. For each of these years, the Democratic percentage of the two-party vote for the

---

[38] But even without this mechanical aid to straight ticket voting, Connecticut voters seem generally to favor the straight ticket. In 1956, in Wallingford, Connecticut (pop. 11,994), where an overwhelming majority of voters was registered as independent, I conducted a pre-election survey of between 3 and 4 per cent of the population, using paper and pencil ballots, and over 80 per cent of all ballots were straight tickets. The results and methods of this survey are reported in the Wallingford (Conn.) *Post*, 1 Nov. 1956.

Political Promises

"top" of the ticket (excluding the race in which Benton figured)
was calculated, giving Democratic "norms" for each year.[39] For
both years Benton's percentage corresponds exactly with the
Democratic norm, as Table XI demonstrates.

TABLE XI

_Democratic Percentage of Two-party Vote in
1950 and 1952, Connecticut_

	1950 (%)	1952 (%)
Benton	50·06	45·80
Democratic norm.	50·19	45·87

Now, how are we to account for this general depression in the
Democratic vote? It would be too much, I think, to attribute
these results to McCarthy's efforts, since a more parsimonious explanation is readily at hand. Clearly Connecticut Democrats in
1952 were caught in the landslide that elected Dwight D. Eisenhower President.[40]

[39] In 1950 I averaged the Democratic percentage of the two-party vote for the offices of Governor, Lieutenant Governor, Senator (long term), and at large Representative. In 1952 I averaged the Democratic percentage of the two-party vote for
President, Senator (short term), and at large Representative. In 1950 Benton ran for
the short term, and in 1952 for the long-term Senatorial seat. His percentage of
the two-party vote is in both cases excluded from the Democratic norm. For their
painstaking help in collecting and tabulating these statistics, I want to thank Daniel D. Polsby and Linda O. Polsby.
[40] Two plausible alternative explanations might be mentioned. The first is that
1950 Democratic voters changed over to the Republican party in 1952 not because
they were attracted by Eisenhower but because they were repelled by Benton.
This explanation is not testable, given the data available. The second is that Mc-
Carthy and McCarthy-generated issues supplied a substantial part of General
Eisenhower's personal appeal in 1952. This seems highly unlikely on the basis of
much evidence: (1) McCarthy was much less well known than Eisenhower; (2) Ei-
senhower had a tremendous personal appeal to voters, apart from _any_ issues;
(3) Eisenhower ran better in 1956, after McCarthy became passé, than in 1952.
Consult Stouffer, _op. cit._; Angus Campbell, Gerald Gurin, and Warren E. Miller,
The Voter Decides (Evanston: Row Peterson, 1954); and, especially, Herbert H.
Hyman and Paul Sheatsley, "The Political Appeal of President Eisenhower,"
Public Opinion Quaterly, 17 (Winter 1953–4), pp. 443–60.

256

It still might be argued that Senator McCarthy affected the outcome of the Benton race by robbing Benton of support he had in 1950 and which he could not replace elsewhere. This argument would be based on the premise that Benton would have improved his position as compared with the rest of the Democratic ticket if McCarthy had not campaigned against him.

How to test this assertion? Each of Connecticut's 169 towns reports election returns separately, and so it is possible to detect changes in the location of a candidate's political strength within the state. Fig. 1 shows that Benton deviated by more than 3 per cent in 1952 from his 1950 relationship to the norm in only two towns in the entire state. Benton gained on the norm in 71 towns, stayed the same in 51, and fell behind in 47. Nine of ten towns

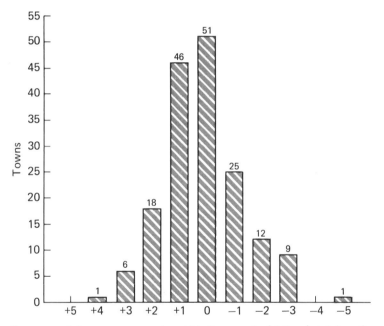

Percentage of the two-party vote by which Benton gained (+) or lost (−) on the Democratic norm.

Fig. 1. Net change, 1952–1950, in Senator Benton's percentage of the two-party vote compared with the Democratic norm, by towns in Connecticut.

where Benton fell behind by 3 per cent or more are located in the home county of the 1952 Democratic ticket leader, Abraham Rib- icoff, who ran for Senator (short term) in that year, and lost by a narrow margin. Thus Benton's comparatively poor showing in these towns can be attributed to Ribicoff's unusual popularity, and not to some disability of his own.

We have in effect judged McCarthy's impact against two base- lines, by comparing Benton's performance in 1952 with his per- formance in 1950, when McCarthy did not campaign against him, and, secondly, by comparing Benton's performance with that of the rest of the "top" of the statewide Democratic ticket in 1952, against whom McCarthy did not campaign. This evidence shows that Benton's record deviates hardly at all from the record of his party in state-wide elections for both years. In general, it appears that Benton maintained or improved upon his 1950 record in 1952, a fact obscured by the effects of the Eisenhower landslide. In the light of these findings, the granting of credit to McCarthy for Benton's defeat is no doubt unjustified, if not entirely errone- ous.

Policy Science and McCarthyism

It cannot be overemphasized that most of the facts on which this analysis has been based were available while McCarthy was still very much alive, and in the headlines. I think this analysis shows McCarthy to have been more dependent on his party, and per- sonally much less effective at the grass roots, than has been com- monly supposed. The erroneous supposition that McCarthy was a powerful figure with some politically meaningful segment of "the people" no doubt served to make him so in the peculiarly isolated subculture that is official Washington. The consequences of this error are well known to all those who were "tuned in" to news media anywhere in the world over the last decade.

As men of knowledge, policy scientists could profitably turn their attention to making sure that information is readily available which bears on policy questions in order to reduce the incidence of errors of this kind in the future. In the case of McCarthy, com- mercial polling organizations expended huge sums of money taking the public pulse. Yet time and again opportunities to test important hypotheses about the sources and nature of McCarthy supporters were lost. One example of this was a Gallup poll which turned up two small neighboring Pennsylvania communities—one of them 2–1 in favor of McCarthy and the other 5–3 against him. Nothing in the report accompanying this finding disclosed any other basis for differentiating these communities—nor did subsequent inquiry to the Gallup organization.[41] Instead of using successive waves of data collection to refine hypotheses about the locations within the population of McCarthy supporters, to over-sample strategic portions of the population, or otherwise to take advantage of the research opportunity before them, the Gallup survey wastefully repeated the same battery of questions with the same type of sample. Hopefully, policy scientists interested in McCarthy's political potential could have brought their working hypothesis to the attention of pollsters who planned in any event to exploit public interest by conducting polls on the McCarthy question.

The political potential of McCarthy was, of course, a major point of interest throughout his brief period of notoriety. Prompt attention to such data as were available could quickly have scotched widely prevalent notions that McCarthy was a fascist leader, or that he was a serious Presidential contender. The essential aimlessness of McCarthy's appeal could be deduced, for example, from the fact that McCarthy support seems to have been highly diffused and multidimensional, rather than effectively mobilized and focused on concrete political goals.

Consider the following evidence. Pro-McCarthy sentiment has been measured from time to time on different issues. We would assume that McCarthyites according to one measure would be the same people as McCarthyites on another; otherwise, McCarthy's potential political effectiveness must be seen as greatly reduced. Table XII shows the results of such a comparison. Those who express themselves as favorable to McCarthy on particular

[41] Gallup, "Two Pennsylvania Test-tube Towns . . . ," *loc. cit.*, and letter to author from Emery H. Ruby, editor, American Institute of Public Opinion, 22 July 1954.

TABLE XII

*Populations in Common Among Various
Pro-McCarthy Attitudes*

N	I (%)	II (%)	III (%)	IV (%)	V (%)	VI (%)	Total population (%)
I = 309		38	57	84	64	39	22
II = 198	60		64	71	58	32	14
III = 430	41	41		60	42	25	30
IV = 458	57	31	56		57	33	32
V = 306	65	38	59	86		40	22
VI = 178	69	36	60	85	69		13

Source: Gallup Survey 530 K, April 1954.

Responses compared
I. Extreme liking (+ 3 − 5) for McCarthy on 11 point scale.
II. No to "Do you think that McCarthy and Cohn used improper means in trying to get a commission for Schine?"
III. Yes to "Do you think that Stevens and Adams tried to stop McCarthy from investigating the Army at Fort Monmouth?"
IV. Favorable general opinion of Senator McCarthy.
V. "Approve" to "In general, do you approve or disapprove of the methods used by McCarthy?"
VI. McCarthy's support would make respondent more likely to vote for a Congressional candidate.

points tend with some (but by no means unanimous) regularity to be "generally" favorable to McCarthy. Otherwise, populations in common are irregular, and not conspicuously high. Table XIII, on the other hand, indicates a tendency for anti-McCarthy sentiment to be somewhat more cohesive and self-consistent on a variety of issues.[42]

---

[42] Perfect consistency of responses would be scored in these tables as 100 per cent, which would mean that all of those answering in a pro-McCarthy way on one question also answered in a pro-McCarthy way on another. While 100 per cent is a "perfect score," an unknown percentage is undoubtedly lost through failure to respond to questions, misunderstandings, incorrect recordings of answers, and so on. If we assume that such failures in communication and in the mechanics of

I do not mean to argue that evidence such as this would have been influential in the calculations of political decision-makers, had it become known among policy scientists. Politicians have been known to ignore expert advice, even when they were paying for it themselves. On the other hand, the fact that information of this kind was neither known nor sought by policy scientists entirely precluded its diffusion to politicians.

Let me summarize, in conclusion, what policy scientists could have established about McCarthyism during the period when it was still a live issue. First, they could have confronted myths about McCarthy with facts. It would have been especially useful if they had mobilized information about the actual consequences of crossing McCarthy and diffused it to those in a position to withhold from him the freedom he enjoyed for so long to create the political atmosphere in which he thrived. Second, they could have indicated the extent to which pro-McCarthy sentiments were ineffectively mobilized politically, revealing that McCarthy was unusually dependent upon regular Republican support both in the Senate and in his home state. McCarthy was more deeply a political phenomenon, perhaps more vulnerable to a change in the definition of his position by Washington politicians, than these

polling occur with equal probability in both anti-McCarthy and pro-McCarthy questionnaires, it becomes possible to compare Table XII, which shows consistency scores for a pro-McCarthy population, and Table XIII, which shows similar scores for an anti-McCarthy population. Comparing each of the cells of the tables in turn, we find: 15 cases where the anti-McCarthy population is 20 or more per cent above the pro-McCarthy population in self-consistency; 3 cases where the anti-McCarthy population is 5–19 per cent above the pro-McCarthy population; 6 cases in which the pro- and anti-McCarthy populations are within 4 per cent of one another; 1 case in which the pro-McCarthy population exceeds the anti-McCarthy population in self-consistency by 5–19 per cent; 4 cases in which the pro-McCarthy population is 20 or more per cent above the anti-McCarthy population in self-consistency.

These last four cases all fall in the third question. A moment's reflection will no doubt suggest the obvious proposition that the anti-McCarthy population could reasonably be expected to embrace both people who are willing to defend Army Secretary Stevens and people who disapproved of him. But the pro-McCarthy population could scarcely be expected to find virtue in McCarthy's enemy of the moment. I do not want, however, to over-interpret these tables. They are meant only to provide a simple thumbnail example of the kind of thing one might have done with the data available.

TABLE XIII

*Populations in Common Among Various
Anti-McCarthy Attitudes*

N	I %	II %	III %	IV %	V %	VI %	Total population %
I = 527		61	36	86	84	64	37
II = 541	60		38	68	80	55	38
III = 295	65	69		80	81	63	21
IV = 611	74	60	39		88	63	43
V = 721	61	60	33	75		56	51
VI = 466	73	64	40	83	87		33

Source: Gallup Survey 530 K, April 1954.

Responses compared
  I. Extreme dislike ($-3-5$) for McCarthy on 11 point scale.
 II. Yes to "Do you think that McCarthy and Cohn used improper means in trying to get a commission for Schine?"
III. No to "Do you think that Stevens and Adams tried to stop McCarthy from investigating the Army at Fort Monmouth?"
 IV. Unfavorable general opinion of Senator McCarthy.
  V. Disapproval of McCarthy's methods.
 VI. Less likely to vote for a Congressional candidate supported by McCarthy.

politicians themselves realized. Third, policy scientists could have assembled information about current states and locations of pro-McCarthy sentiment. By tracing the ebbs and flows of McCarthy's popularity, inferences could have been made about the kinds of events triggering gains and losses in his popularity, hence about the size and locations of the margins of McCarthy's political appeal.

A latent function of making concerted demands for these kinds of data would no doubt have been a general improvement in the sources of supply for such data—notably the commercial polls. Issues that capture extraordinary public attention are precisely those in which polling organizations are willing to make their greatest investment; hence it is uniquely possible in these cases for policy scientists to help decision-makers to make rational choices, to help data-collection agencies to improve on the relevance of their inquiries, and, finally, to help themselves by cultivating increasingly meaningful and useful sources of information. The brief demonstration I have made in the case of McCarthy is meant to suggest that such developments as these are not only desirable but feasible.

Index

Index

Index